Where Have All the Pop Stars Gone?

Volume 2

Marti Smiley Childs
and Jeff March

Authors of **Echoes of the Sixties** (e-book ISBN: 978-1-937317-02-7), and **Where Have All the Pop Stars Gone? – Volume 1** (paperback ISBN: 978-1-937317-00-3; e-book ISBN: 978-1-937317-01-0)

EDITPROS℠

EditPros LLC, Davis, California, USA • www.editpros.com

Published by EditPros LLC
423 F Street, suite 206
Davis, CA 95616
www.editpros.com

ISBN-10: 1937317064
ISBN-13: 978-1-937317-06-5

Library of Congress Control Number: 2012952918
Printed in the United States of America

CATALOGING INFORMATION:
Childs, Marti Smiley, and March, Jeff
        Where Have All the Pop Stars Gone? – Volume 2
    Filing categories:
        Biography
        Biography, musicians
        Biography, pop music
        Biography, rock music
        Biography, rhythm and blues music
        History, musical
        History, pop culture
        Music, popular
        Pop culture

Cover photo by Amanda Domingues depicts the Fremont Theatre (built in 1940) on Monterey Street in San Luis Obispo, California.

Table of Contents

Acknowledgments

We would not have been able to create this book without the enthusiastic cooperation of the performers about whom we wrote, as well as their family members, producers, managers and musical colleagues, and others with whom we spoke. We offer our gratitude to all of them listed here.

THE BUCKINGHAMS
Nick Fortuna
Carl Giammarese
Marty Grebb
Dennis Tufano
Dale Fahey
Burton Jespersen
Dawn Lee Wakefield

BOBBY GOLDSBORO
Bobby Goldsboro

DONNIE BROOKS
Donnie Brooks
Ron Kurtz

MOODY BLUES
Mike Pinder
Ray Thomas
Tara Pinder
Lee Thomas
Maggie Grayson

SAM & DAVE
Sam Moore
Joyce Moore
Sarah Caruthers-Jackson
Lillie Prater Demps
Rosemary Prater
Dave Booth, Showtime
  Music Archive
Chuck Rubin
Atlantic Records/
  Warner Music Group
  Archives

RAY STEVENS
Ray Stevens
Cyrus "Buddy" Kalb
B.J. Haas

GRASS ROOTS
Creed Bratton
Rick Coonce
Denny Ellis
Warren Entner
Willy Fulton
Rob Grill
Joel Larson
Dennis Provisor
Dave Stensen
Steve Barri
Ron Elliott
Nancy Grill
Ron Meagher
Alec Palao
Bob Sherwood
Barbara Smith
Sal Valentino

PHOTOGRAPHY
Wes Adams
Neil Anderson
Carlo Chiavacci
Amanda Domingues
  (amandadphoto.com/)
Irene Ellis
Lora Evans
Shannon Fontaine

Barbara Giammarese
Debra Hendsch
Andrew Hreha
Sarah La Du
Madona Larson
Jeff March
Mike Preston
David Ramert
Barbara Smith
Maggie Smith
Sara Stensen
Gabe Tolnay
Guy Webster

MUSIC CHART DATA

Joel Whitburn's Record
  Research Inc. (www.
  recordresearch.com),
  Menomonee Falls,
  Wisconsin

Preface

The decade of the '60s dawned inauspiciously. Dwight D. Eisenhower, America's leader through most of the 1950s, remained in office for the final year of his term. Alfred Hitchcock was putting the finishing touches on his motion picture *Psycho,* and Burt Lancaster and Shirley Jones turned in Academy Award-winning performances in *Elmer Gantry.* Family-oriented westerns including *Bonanza* and *Rawhide,* and *Sea Hunt, 77 Sunset Strip* and *Route 66* and other adventure shows captivated prime-time television viewers.

Marty Robbins inaugurated the new year with his chart-topping hit "El Paso," a four-and-a-half-minute ballad that rode the popular "story record" trail ridden in 1959 by Johnny Horton with "The Battle of New Orleans" and the Browns with "The Three Bells." The formula took Johnny Preston's "Running Bear" and Mark Dinning's "Teen Angel" to the top of the Billboard charts in early 1960.

Novelty tunes, epitomized by David Seville's "Witch Doctor" and Sheb Wooley's "Purple People Eater" in 1958, continued to sell in 1960, when the Hollywood Argyles scored with "Alley-Oop" and Brian Hyland's "Itsy Bitsy Teenie Weenie Yellow Polkadot Bikini" squawked from tinny six-transistor radios all summer long.

Yet subtle changes distancing America from the '50s began to occur. The Ford Motor Co. brought to a close production of the Edsel nameplate, which had been introduced only two years before. At Cape Canaveral, a rocket launched Echo 1, America's first experimental communication satellite. In Detroit, Berry Gordy launched a new record label, Motown. And a ruby crystal was used to produce the first burst of laser light.

We look back on the '60s as a convulsive era of civil rights marches and antiwar demonstrations, of fiery riots in our inner cities, draft card burning, assassinations, and the decade during which the generation gap eroded into a chasm. As American astronauts orbited the Earth and ultimately stepped onto the surface of the Moon, the planet convulsed in epochal change. The pill. The Berlin Wall. The Bay of Pigs Invasion. The Cuban missile crisis. *Silent Spring.* **The Feminine Mystique.** "I Have a Dream." The touch-tone phone. The Free Speech Movement. The Tonkin Gulf Incident. The Great Society. The Six-Day War in the Mideast. The "summer of love." Haight-Ashbury. The counterculture. Hippies. Flower children. Grass. LSD. Mescaline. Students for a Democratic Society. Black Panthers. Bloodshed at the 1968 Democratic National Convention. The Tet Offensive. The My Lai Massacre. Woodstock. The Stonewall Riot. Helter-Skelter.

The youth culture was likewise fomenting change, engaging in behaviors and listening to music that puzzled, exasperated and antagonized their parents. In those days before home computers, before the Internet, before smart phones, Facebook, Twitter and YouTube, young people were drawn to the music of their generation – the hit songs that AM "top 40" radio stations played, and later in the decade the rock album tracks that "underground" and "progressive rock" FM radio stations broadcast.

The '60s brought us the twist, the mashed potato, the frug, the Watusi, the hully gully and the limbo. Surf music. Folk hootenannies. Soul music. Discotheques. Go-go dancing. Dylan. The British Invasion. Folk-rock. Protest songs. *Hair.* Jazz-rock. Psychedelia.

The musical performers profiled in *Where Have All the Pop Stars Gone? – Volume 2* were agents of that change. They were among the recording artists whose words and actions influenced a generation of young people. Like the audiences, the performers themselves were young, and many of them had veered from intended career paths when fame came to them. In the span of weeks, many had jumped from anonymity to a new dimension in which they suddenly were household names, with their pictures in teen magazines and plastered on the bedroom walls of kids in every walk of life.

Some of these singers and musicians become firmly entrenched enough to establish lifelong careers in music. The visibility of others, however, declined as their hits became fewer and finally disappeared from the playlists of radio stations. Many of them pursued other interests and found work in other fields in the decades that followed, prompting fans to wonder "Whatever happened to...?"

That question, and our abiding passion for the music and our respect and admiration for the performers, prompted us to write this, our third book about the lives of performers who created the music that escorted us on our journeys from adolescence to adulthood.

All of our books are the product of five guiding principles:

1. We obtained information about all artists we profiled from conversations we had with the performers themselves (and with family members of some of the deceased performers);
2. We collaborated with the performers, who reviewed and authenticated our manuscripts;
3. All performers profiled were soloists or members of vocal groups or bands whose recordings scored on the national pop music singles and/or album charts during the 1960s;
4. We have placed an emphasis on achievement, celebrating the personal and professional triumphs of performers within and outside the music industry following the 1960s;

5. We intentionally selected artists who are representative of the widely
    divergent musical styles that distinguished the 1960s from all the
    other decades of the 20th century – musical diversity encompassing
    and influenced by rockabilly, rhythm and blues, surf music, jazz, folk
    standards, calypso, pop ballads, novelty tunes, folk-rock, art rock,
    psychedelia and country music.

This book does not dwell on the sordid or the sad. Although the text
does acknowledge significant hardships, including financial and personal
problems, our focus was on successful resolution of conflicts and
discovery of what individuals learned about life as a result of confronting
difficulty. Even though its content is entertaining and it has a nostalgia
component, *Where Have All the Pop Stars Gone? – Volume 2* also seeks to
teach and inspire by example.

Each chapter encompasses three segments:

- A historical overview of the highlights of each artist's recording
  career;
- A discography list of prominent hit recordings of each artist; and
- Biographical epilogues chronicling the life experiences of soloists and
  band members.

Where Have All the Pop Stars Gone? – Volume 2 affords many new
insights into the personal lives of these individuals. We look beyond
the music and peel away misperceptions and debunk myths about
21 individuals with the same concerns as ours: establishing a stable
household, the challenges of parenthood, paying the mortgage and the
phone bill, caring for aging parents. We discover that beneath the public
veneer, they are simply people whose jobs have involved creating music
and performing in front of thousands of fans.

We hope you enjoy reading about them, and the others about whom
we will write in future volumes.

With appreciation,
Marti Smiley Childs and Jeff March

The Buckinghams in 1968. From left, Nick Fortuna, Marty Grebb, John Poulos, Carl Giammarese, Dennis Tufano (photo courtesy of Dennis Tufano)

Kind of a Drag

The Buckinghams

The right song, look, and sound are keys to musical fame; however, the right mix of talent, personalities, musical roots, and management results in the continued success and longevity of a group. For many artists of the 1960s, the light shined brilliantly for a very short time. But the sheer love of music and performing has kept the pride of Chicago, the Buckinghams, in front of audiences more than four decades after the five-piece band first broke onto the national charts. Consisting of lead singer Dennis Tufano, drummer-band leader John Poulos, keyboard and saxophone player Marty Grebb, guitarist Carl Giammarese, and bassist Nick Fortuna, the Buckinghams honed their appreciation of jazz, blues, and rock into a dynamic fusion of those genres. The hybrid "pop-rock horn sound" that made them unique would later be embraced by other bands: Blood, Sweat and Tears, Chase, Chicago, Lighthouse, Earth, Wind and Fire, Cold Blood, the Electric Flag, the Ides of March, and Tower of Power through the 1970s and beyond.

In early 1965, the Holiday Ballroom on Milwaukee Avenue on the northwest side of Chicago regularly featured two popular groups with strong followings: The Pulsations and the Centuries. The Pulsations had two lead singers, George LeGros (pronounced lee-GROW) and Dennis Tufano, drummer John Poulos, and keyboardist Dennis Miccolis. Often sharing the bill with the Pulsations were the Centuries, whose lead singer was drummer Gerald Elarde, his cousin, lead guitarist Carl Giammarese (pronounced gee-AM-er-EE-see), rhythm guitarist Nick Fortuna, and bass guitarist Curt Bachman. When personnel changes in the Pulsations found them searching for a new guitarist, they naturally turned to the Centuries first, who had a compatible sound and style. Carl joined the Pulsations, while Nick joined a band called Jimmy V and the Entertainers, for which he switched to bass guitar.

The new lineup of the Pulsations – consisting of Giammarese, Miccolis, Poulos, Bachman, and singers Tufano and LeGros – was first noticed by Holiday Ballroom owner and big band leader Dan Belloc (who had co-written Nat King Cole's 1953 hit "Pretend"), and Carl Bonafede, Chicago radio's Screaming Wildman. "The Holiday Ballroom was a real local thing for all of us, because we all lived maybe a half hour to 40 minutes away from that central location," said Dennis Tufano. "A lot of people used to go there to dance, and after about our third performance, we started to get more people standing and watching us than dancing. And that's when we started to feel that something special was going on."

Bonafede picked up on the excitement and became the band's manager, booking them across the Midwest to bring them to the attention of a regional audience. But the real break came in the autumn of 1965 when a producer from Chicago's popular WGN-TV called Bonafede to ask if he had any musical group in mind who'd like to audition for a new syndicated variety show called *All Time Hits*. With lead singers Dennis Tufano and George LeGros the Pulsations "battled" against three other bands, won the contest and were awarded a 13-week contract to perform as the house band on the show, which had a studio audience and was recorded for later broadcast.

"They loved the group, but they wanted a name that sounded more contemporary and more British, because we were in the middle of the British invasion," said Giammarese. "A WGN security guard named John Opager became friends with us, and he came up with a list of British-sounding names. Of those names we chose the Buckinghams. We just liked the way it sounded." It also appealed to the band because of a subtle connection to a Chicago landmark: Buckingham Fountain in Grant Park.

Dennis Tufano recalls, "On the first show they introduced us as 'the Buckinghams – royalty in rock and roll,' and that became our tag line. We never even thought about the royalty thing, because we were just street kids from Chicago, but it worked."

All Time Hits was a Saturday evening TV program on which recording artists performed the most popular and best-selling songs of the week. "There were regulars on the show like singer Billy Williams – his claim to fame was 'I'm Gonna Sit Right Down and Write Myself a Letter' – but we were the young rock band that was performing the current hits of the week," said Giammarese. "I remember doing 'What's New Pussycat,' and we would do some Beatles songs – I think we did 'Help,' 'A Hard Day's Night,' and 'I Should Have Known Better' – songs like that. The show got us a lot of recognition around Chicago, and between that and playing gigs in the area, we built quite a following."

After about the fourth week of the show's airing, George LeGros was called to serve in the military. "We were playing at the Holiday Ballroom, which is where we built our following. It was kind of our Cavern Club, like the Beatles had," said Giammarese. "I remember that night performing and not expecting George LeGros to be gone, and he was gone – just like that – on a train. We were saying goodbye to him. We had to go on and play, so that's when Dennis became the established lead singer of the band." Curt Bachman replaced George LeGros on bass for a short time, and then Carl Bonafede recruited Nick Fortuna from Jimmy V and the Entertainers to replace Curt.

Bonafede and Belloc co-produced the Buckinghams' first tracks and arranged their first record deal with Chicago-based U.S.A. Records. Chicago's biggest stations, including WLS and WCFL radio, played the Buckinghams' versions of James Brown's "I'll Go Crazy," which U.S.A. released in March 1966; the Beatles' "I Call Your Name," a May 1966 release; and the Hollies' "I've Been Wrong," which U.S.A. released in September 1966. Audiences for their performances grew, but they were a "hometown" group, with little recognition outside the Chicago area. Just as their contract with U.S.A. Records was about to expire, their last scheduled release, "Kind of a Drag," took off in Little Rock, Arkansas. Radio programmers in other markets noticed. Overnight, it started going to the top of every playlist across the country.

Giammarese recalls the band's introduction to "Kind of a Drag," the song that would give the Buckinghams national exposure and become a No. 1 hit. "We needed our own material, so Bonafede approached a guy by the name of Jim Holvay, a musician and songwriter in a Chicago show band called Jimmy Ford & the Executives, which later became The Mob. I remember getting this tape from Jim that sounded like he just got up that morning and he was strumming on his electric guitar. It wasn't even plugged in. And he was singing this catchy little tune with the lyrics 'kind of a drag.' It didn't grab me right away because I think I was too caught up in the way he was singing and playing it," Giammarese said. "We started rehearsing it in my parents' basement. And I remember my mother coming down and saying, 'You know, guys, that's a great song. I really think it's got something. It's very catchy.' So we went into the

5

studio over at 2120 South Michigan, which was Chess Studios. It was a very famous studio for a lot of the blues artists around Chicago – Muddy Waters and Howlin' Wolf and of course, the Stones came in and did tracks for their *12 x 5* album there. And so we went in and Bonafede and Belloc produced it. Belloc was an old-time arranger-producer-songwriter. I think he initially got the idea for putting the horn sound in it because we had done 'I'll Go Crazy,' which was a James Brown song – we were big James Brown fans, and we loved that horn sound."

The horn section, suggested by Belloc and arranged by trombone player Frank Tesinsky, gave "Kind of a Drag" its magic sound. Everyone thought it was a great song, including U.S.A., but it seemed to have gotten lost in the shuffle for a few months before finally being released in late 1966, backed with Chris White's "You Make Me Feel So Good" (the "B" side of the Zombies' 1964 hit "She's Not There"). Just before "Kind of a Drag" took off, the band replaced keyboardist Dennis Miccolis with Larry Nestor, who stayed for only a short time, and was replaced by Marty Grebb. He had been the keyboard player, saxophonist, and singer for the Exceptions, a local band that included Peter Cetera. Grebb added vocal skills to the Buckinghams, along with his exceptional keyboard and saxophone talent. That personnel shuffle solidified the Buckinghams' lineup: lead singer Dennis Tufano, drummer John Poulos, keyboard player Marty Grebb, lead guitarist Carl Giammarese, and bassist Nick Fortuna.

On February 18, 1967, "Kind of a Drag" punched its way to the top by ending the seven-week reign of the Monkees' "I'm a Believer" as the nation's No.1 record. The rise to No.1 was a coup not only for the Buckinghams as a new group, but also for their small independent label, U.S.A. Records. "Kind of a Drag" held on to the No.1 spot for two weeks, but it took the Rolling Stones' "Ruby Tuesday" to unseat it. The giddy success of "Kind of a Drag" prompted U.S.A. to compile an album of the same name from previously recorded tracks, including covers of the Drifters' "Sweets for My Sweet" and the Beatles' "I Call Your Name." While "Kind of a Drag" was still on the charts, U.S.A. released a follow-up single, "Lawdy Miss Clawdy" (which on some pressings the label also spelled "Laudy Miss Claudy"), an energetic horn-driven celebration of Lloyd Price's 1952 R&B hit.

Back in the 1960s the Buckinghams used studio musicians to record the horn sections on their records, but they didn't have a horn section on the road. "Bands just didn't do it back then. It was probably too expensive or maybe too hard to travel," said Giammarese. "We were doing about 300 dates a year – many of them one-nighters. Now we have horns. A good part of the time, we have a three-piece horn section."

Amid their newfound fame in early 1967 the band members were introduced to James William Guercio – bass player for Chad and Jeremy's touring band and composer of their top 30 hit, "Distant Shores" – and they agreed to work together. He signed the Buckinghams to a management contract with Ebbins-Guercio Associates, and the group traveled to New York to record with Columbia Records with national representation by the William Morris Agency, for which Garrick Ebbins' father worked.

"Guercio was really a good producer. When he brought us over to Columbia Records and introduced us to Clive Davis [the label's president], it all happened so quickly," Giammarese told us in 2000. "Guercio took us to the next level, because as good a record as 'Kind of a Drag' was, all of a sudden we were at Columbia studios in New York, recording on 16 tracks instead of eight, and Guercio really knew the sound we were looking for. At that time we were proclaimed the first pop band to establish a sound with horns."

With Guercio as manager and producer, the Buckinghams created four more top-20 hits: "Don't You Care" (co-written by "Mob" members Gary Beisbier and Jim Holvay with Guercio); a remake of Cannonball Adderley's soulful "Mercy, Mercy, Mercy" (composed by jazz pianist Joe Zawinul with lyrics by Johnny "Guitar" Watson); "Hey Baby (They're Playing Our Song)" (another Holvay and Beisbier composition); and "Susan" (a Beisbier-Holvay-Guercio collaboration). Columbia released the band's second album, *Time and Charges,* with "Don't You Care" as the lead-off track. The album's 10 selections included "You Are Gone" (the flip side of "Don't You Care"), "Mercy, Mercy, Mercy" and "Foreign Policy," the B-side of "Susan." At the top of their game, in 1967 the group was honored by *Billboard* magazine as "The most listened-to band in America," and *Cashbox Magazine* named them "The most promising vocal group in America."

The Buckinghams toured extensively in 1967 and 1968, and appeared on several TV shows, including *The Ed Sullivan Show, Smothers Brothers Comedy Hour, The Jerry Lewis Show, The Joey Bishop Show,* and *American Bandstand.* "When we performed on the *Smothers Brothers Comedy Hour,* we arrived to find the set decorated with the Union Jack flag, because the producers actually thought we were from England," chuckled Giammarese. "The TV crew even served us fish and chips to eat during our rehearsal break – we would have preferred pizza."

The band performed in front of capacity crowds in arenas and festivals, sharing the bill with Gene Pitney, the Beach Boys, Sonny and Cher, Neil Diamond, America, Tom Jones, the Hollies, the Kinks, the Yardbirds, and the Who. Dennis Tufano recalls a concert in which the Buckinghams were the opening act for the Who. "It was a college concert in Kansas, and it wasn't a very big hall. We couldn't believe that the Buckinghams and the Who were booked at the same place. They absolutely destroyed the place, though. The microphones went, as the Who was known to do. But it was such a small place, and it was just sad to see these guys tear it up. We were all staying at the Holiday Inn, so we met at the bar at the end of the night, and we were drinking and talking with the Who. We couldn't believe it!"

Two large concerts in Alabama also brought back memories for Tufano. "There were two major radio stations – one in Montgomery and one in Birmingham – that sponsored concerts. We'd play one concert, and then get on a bus and drive across the state to the other one," he said. "We'd be on the bill with Paul Revere and the Raiders, Tommy James and the Shondells, the Cowsills, solo singers like Lou Christie. We would all play in order of where we were on the charts in that city. For example, if your band had a No. 2 record, you went on second to last. We would move four days later to someplace else, and three of the bands would be with us, and another two extra bands would come in – Strawberry Alarm Clock would jump in, or somebody else. At that period in time, there was no such thing as just one headline act. It was like everybody was on these shows. So as the audience, you got a chance to see everybody that was on the charts in one show. It was great!"

Performances at the Hollywood Bowl and the Cow Palace in San Francisco left a big impression with Giammarese because they were such large venues. "We were on the bill with Donovan, which probably wasn't a good fit at the time," he said. "A few artists who opened shows for us turned out to be bigger than us. I remember once playing a theater and having Jose Feliciano open for us. That was right before 'Light My Fire.' Flip Wilson was our opening act for a while on shows, and then right after that his career took off and he had his own TV show."

While Guercio helped to propel the Buckinghams' career in the beginning, band members felt he monopolized their business by being both manager and producer. Marty Grebb recalled, "At the time, Guercio was a road manager and bass player for Chad and Jeremy. So he basically went in and made a really good deal with CBS for himself, because he wanted to be a producer. He wanted to produce Chad and Jeremy, in fact, and they wouldn't let him. So he went to CBS after 'Kind of a Drag' was No. 1 and said, 'I'll tell you what. I'll let you have the Buckinghams. I'm their manager, but you have to let me produce them.' So that's how he became a producer – quite a famous producer."

Severe differences occurred between the Buckinghams and Guercio when he added a psychedelic crescendo to their song "Susan," which sounded very similar to the Beatles' song "A Day in the Life." Several radio stations banned the song from the airwaves, or cut it short of the psychedelic passage.

"'Susan' was a gorgeous, gorgeous song and, after we recorded it, we felt the manager was orchestrating our devastation and that he was trying to phase us out so he could move on. That may not be true, but it certainly seemed like it in retrospect. So he started adding some stuff to the music that was way outside of our realm," said Tufano. "When we started recording the song, Guercio said, 'I've got this really interesting thing that we're going to do, and when you get to this point in the song there's going to be a click-track and then you just count, and when we get up to this bar, just come back in and we'll do the ending.' And, you know, we were trusting. He was our manager, our producer, and we said, 'OK, well, you must know.' But the fact is, he put in that horrible thing. Most radio stations edited it out. And I think we played it a couple of times live, just as a surprise, near the end, when we were playing less-than-desirable jobs and we were pretty down about the whole situation. We'd get to the end of 'Susan' and we would look at each other and say, 'Oh, let's play it,' and we would do this totally psychedelic explosion thing to get rid of our angst."

The Buckinghams in 1968. From left, Dennis Tufano, Marty Grebb, Carl Giammarese, John Poulos, Nick Fortuna (photo courtesy of Dennis Tufano)

The Buckinghams' second Columbia album, *Portraits* – which included "Susan" and "Hey, Baby, They're Playing Our Song" – was an adventurous, progressive 1967 release that was an underappreciated exploration of horn-driven rock. Band members wrote all of the album's tracks with the exception of the two singles. The album's cover photo was a sepia-toned portrait of the band dressed in Civil War uniforms, similar to those for which fellow Columbia recording artists Gary Puckett and the Union Gap would soon become known. As much as the band members infused the album with their hearts and their energy, it bore the unmistakable imprint of James William Guercio – to the growing displeasure of the Buckinghams.

Tufano continued, "We were having a lot of disagreements with Guercio because we finally started to realize that, 'Hey, this guy's getting rich, and we're not. We're not even close.' We were drawing a small salary every week, and so we started to realize how important it is to own your publishing. And Guercio was controlling it all. So the last album we did with him, *Portraits,* we demanded that we get a percentage of the publishing, and verbally he agreed, but then he reneged on it when it came down to actually doing it. And we fought with him to the point where we wound up firing him."

By 1967 the Buckinghams, who had rented a house in Los Angeles, were ready to take their careers into their own hands and hired a new manager. Columbia assigned staff producer Jimmy "The Wiz" Wisner, who produced the group's third Columbia album, *In One Ear and Gone Tomorrow,* a well-rounded but prophetically titled collection of ballads, pop and jazz rock tunes. The album yielded only one chart single, Marty Grebb's composition "Back in Love Again," a brassy, driving rocker with hit potential, but it peaked at only 57 on the charts and was the band's last entry to make the top 100. Wisner produced another Buckinghams song titled "Where Did You Come From?" for the soundtrack of a Twentieth Century Fox comedy film called *The Guru,* starring Rita Tushingham and Michael York. An advertisement that Columbia Records placed in a trade magazine to announce the single smugly declared, "This one will reach the charts, just like every other one of their singles has. And just like their album *In One Ear and Gone Tomorrow* has. Meditate on that." Radio programmers disagreed however, and the single failed to reach the charts.

A sequence of events contributed to the breakup of the Buckinghams. "At the same time our relationship with Columbia was not doing real well, the whole music scene was changing," said Giammarese. "Groups like us, the Beach Boys, the Association, and Gary Puckett and the Union Gap were kind of being forgotten because the heavier under-ground sound was becoming popular. [Columbia Records President] Clive Davis went to Monterey and Woodstock and signed Janis Joplin and Carlos Santana. The album *Portraits* was our answer to a heavier sound, but our audience wasn't buying it. It was kind of the Bucking-hams sound with the horns. I always look at *Portraits* as a continuation of the sound that the group Chicago created on their first album. That was sort of a continuation of that album in a lot of ways, the arrange-ments, and a lot of the same horn licks and horn sound. People ask me, 'Why'd you break up?' It's not one thing; it's a lot of different things. We were all becoming disillusioned because we wanted to experiment more and do more musically, and the label wanted to hear 'Kind of a Drag' over and over again. And Dennis and I were starting to write a lot, and we wanted to do something different."

Tufano recalls *Portraits* as the Buckinghams' last chance to evolve into the group it wanted to be, instead of what they were being told to do. "We were musicians, we were singers, we were entertainers. But our bridge to the next step was pretty much taken down, because we had plans from our *Portraits* album to start changing. We wrote a lot of that album, which really had more of us into it," he said. "It wasn't that big a departure from the hits, it was just a nice, logical step. And we were try-ing to be conscious of that, and not to just all of a sudden change and be somebody else. But that all fell apart." Marty Grebb, disillusioned, left the band in 1968 and moved to Los Angeles to seek a career as a studio musician. Nick Fortuna departed soon after. Keyboardist John Turner replaced Grebb, and former Centuries bassist Curt Bachman replaced Fortuna.

Soon afterward, Columbia Records selected producer John Hill to produce the Buckinghams' tracks that resulted in their final singles, "It's a Beautiful Day (for Lovin')" and "I've Got a Feelin'" – neither of which appeared on the charts. When the remaining Buckinghams mutually decided to disband in early 1970, all of them would remain entertainers except for John Poulos, who shifted into talent management. John's clients included the duo of Tufano and Giammarese in the early '70s. After battling drug and alcohol dependence, Poulos died on March 26, 1980. "John and I were best friends. We were very close at the time it happened," Giammarese said. "He left a wife and a daughter, who was just a little girl, and a stepson."

In the spring of 1980, Chicago's WLS radio program director John Gehron called Carl Giammarese on behalf of then-Mayor Jane Byrne to ask about the possibility of the Buckinghams reuniting and performing for ChicagoFest, a summer music festival held annually at Navy Pier that lasted for roughly two weeks in August. It featured 16 separate stages, each sponsored by a national retail brand and a media sponsor. Giammarese called Nick Fortuna and Dennis Tufano, and they recruited Tom Radtke on drums (in place of John Poulos) and John Cammelot on keyboards. The Buckinghams' reunion drew record crowds to ChicagoFest's Navy Pier rooftop stage.

"We had about 15,000 people at that stage, and it felt so good that we wound up doing a couple of other dates around the city, and then the following year we did the same thing. And it seemed like every year we were doing a few more dates," said Giammarese.

After three years of playing a few select ChicagoFest dates, Dennis Tufano decided to return to working in the film industry in California in 1982 as well as lending his vocal and writing talents to other West Coast projects including working with Olivia Newton-John, Tom Scott, Bernie Taupin, and Chevy Chase.

Original founding member Carl Giammarese (lead vocals and lead guitar), and Nick Fortuna (bass guitar and vocals) continued to perform after the ChicagoFest dates with various other members of their band.

Today's accompanying band members include Bruce Soboroff (keyboards and vocals), Dave Zane (guitar and vocals) and Bruce (Rocky) Penn (drums and vocals), and are frequently joined by Carlo Isabelli (trumpet), Charles Morgan (trombone), Rich Moore (saxophone), and Steve Frost (trumpet). Together, they are keeping the legacy of the pioneering brass-rock band the Buckinghams alive and in top form.

Visit the Buckinghams' official website at **www.thebuckinghams. com** to check their concert schedule.

THE BUCKINGHAMS U.S. HIT SINGLES
ON THE NATIONAL CHARTS

Debut	Peak	Title	Label
12/66	1	Kind of a Drag	U.S.A.
3/67	41	Lawdy Miss Clawdy	U.S.A.
3/67	6	Don't You Care	Columbia
6/67	5	Mercy, Mercy, Mercy	Columbia
9/67	12	Hey Baby (They're Playing Our Song)	Columbia
12/67	11	Susan	Columbia
6/68	57	Back in Love Again	Columbia
4/73	68	Music Everywhere*	Ode

*Tufano & Giammarese
Billboard's pop singles chart data is courtesy of Joel Whitburn's Record Research Inc. (www.recordresearch.com), Menomonee Falls, Wisconsin.

Epilogue: Carl Giammarese

Singer and guitarist

Carl Giammarese loves the windy city in which he was born, grew up and became famous – first as a member of the Buckinghams on WGN-TV's *All Time Hits* syndicated variety show and later as a prominent jingles singer for radio and TV advertising. A major center for music in the Midwest, Chicago is where legendary blues artists Muddy Waters, Junior Wells, Howlin' Wolf and both Sonny Boy Williamsons emerged, along with jazz greats Nat King Cole, Gene Ammons, Benny Goodman, and Bud Freeman. Carl has traveled the world, but still calls Chicago "home."

The oldest of three children, Carl was born on August 21, 1947, to Nick and Jennie Giammarese (pronounced gee-AM-er-EE-see, or, in proper Italian, gee-AM-ar-A-tzee). He and his sister, Rosalie (three years younger), and brother, Victor (seven years younger), grew up on the north side of Chicago. Their father sang professionally before World War II, and during the war he traveled overseas as part of the special service USO with his big band, the Continentals.

"After the war, my dad sang part time and worked as a tailor, and then as a foreman in a factory for most of his life. After the war, things were tough and he was raising a family, so he kind of drifted away from music, but one thing he always liked to tell me was that he got to know Glenn Miller during the war, and Glenn Miller said to him, 'You should come to New York and see me after the war.'" Unfortunately, Carl's father never got the opportunity to visit Miller in New York because while traveling to entertain U.S. troops in France, the aircraft on which Glenn Miller was aboard disappeared on December 15, 1944, in bad weather, apparently over the English Channel. His body was never found.

Before the war, Uptown, the district of Chicago in which Carl grew up, was a

Courtesty of Carl Giammarese
(photo by Lora Evans)

14

popular entertainment destination. Charlie Chaplin, Gloria Swanson, and other early stars produced films at the Essanay Studios on Argyle Street. The Aragon Ballroom, Riviera Theater, Uptown Theatre, and Green Mill Jazz Club are all located within a half block of Lawrence and Broadway. But by the 1950s, the middle class was leaving Uptown for the suburbs, as commuter rail and elevated train lines were extended. Residential hotels that had housed wives of sailors attached to the Great Lakes Naval Station during World War II began filling up with low-income migrants from the South and Appalachia.

Both of Carl's parents, who have passed on, had been very proud and supportive of his musical career. "By the time I was 10, Uptown was becoming home to people struggling to get by. There were gangs and lots of fights going on. It was scary to be out," said Carl. "My parents were happy when I started taking guitar lessons at 13, because they were look-ing for a diversion – something for me to do. My mother was in love with Elvis at the time, so she said, 'Oh, you've gotta play the guitar, and you could sing and play.'"

By high school, Carl became interested in automotive design, and his parents enrolled him at Lane Technical High School, an all-boys school at the time. "It was a dream of mine to work for one of these great Ital-ian design companies, like (Sergio) Pininfarina, and there are a couple of others. It would be great, for example, to see your tail light on a car, or the door panel, or whatever," said Giammarese. "Lane Tech was a great school to prepare you for college and for going on to do that sort of work, but by my junior year, I was totally distracted with music. The Beatles had come to this country and once I heard them, once I saw them, I was just pulled right into it. And all of a sudden I realized that's what I wanted to do my whole life. At the moment, I wanted to be a Beatle, but what I really wanted to do is play, sing, and write tunes, and be in a successful band."

At the age of 15, Carl joined a band called the Centuries that his cousin Jerry Elarde had formed with Nick Fortuna, and Curt Bachman. Their repertoire included Ventures and surf music instrumentals, and some of the current hits for parties and dances around Chicago. When the Centuries broke up, Carl joined the Pulsations, another popular band that played a lot of the same dances and venues.

Carl was the youngest member of the Pulsations, still in his senior year of high school, when the band became the Buckinghams and was starting to take off. "The next youngest after me, John Poulos, had already graduated in '65. I graduated in '66," said Giammarese. "They would come by and get me out of school on Friday and we'd head to a

15

gig in Aberdeen, South Dakota (683 miles away), or somewhere like that. We'd all pile into a van on top of our equipment, and we were about six inches from the roof of the van. And we would drive all the way there, play a gig, and drive all the way back. It was a tough year. I went from being an 'A' student to about a 'C' average in my last year. I just struggled through because of the band, and the distraction of the whole thing."

By the time Carl graduated from high school, the band started playing more and more gigs on weekends and during the week, and they were getting a lot of recognition around the Midwest. They had the look, the talent, and the style, but they were looking for that great song – the one that would put them over the top. They found it with "Kind of a Drag," which sat in the U.S.A. Records vault for a while after recording but when finally released, soared to the top of the charts.

Carl recalls, "When 'Kind of a Drag' was No. 1, we met Marty Grebb, a great, seasoned player, and we pulled him into the group. We had the nucleus of the band, but our record contract with U.S.A. was up, which was kind of crazy on their part that they didn't re-sign us right away before it was a hit," he said. "We had left our booking agent, Willard Alexander, and our manager, Carl Bonafede. Some people in Chicago looked at it like we were a bunch of ungrateful kids, but even though we were just kids at the time, we realized that we got real lucky with 'Kind of a Drag,' and that if we weren't careful and didn't get involved with the right people and the right label, we'd be a one-hit wonder."

Several Chicago bands, notably the Cryan' Shames, the New Colony Six, and the Ides of March, had regional success but they hadn't peaked nationally, so Giammarese was intent on extending the group's repertoire beyond "Kind of a Drag." Carl explained, "When you've got the No. 1 record in the country, every label is after you, and through a friend of ours, we found James William Guercio, who was partners with Gary Ebbins in a management company. I remember certain people in the music establishment said we'd never get another record played in Chicago after 'Kind of a Drag' because of the way things went down and us leaving Chicago. But you know what? 'Don't You Care' was a No. 1 record in the Midwest and Chicago, and it was a top-10 record nationally."

Carl claims that "Mercy" was his favorite Buckinghams song because it brought the band back to its roots. "We were really into that R&B bag, and it was kind of an afterthought," he said. "We took it from Cannonball Adderley's recording; he had a jazz instrumental hit some months before. Guercio brought us the soul version that Johnny 'Guitar' Watson and Larry Williams recorded. They had a minor R&B hit with it. Guercio used to play bass with them years before. In those days it wasn't as common to get more than one hit off an album. So that was kind of a surprise hit for us."

While 1970 closed the first chapter of the Buckinghams' reign, many new changes would help to shape Carl's life. One such life-changing event was his marriage that year to Barbara Williams. Carl reminiscences, "Barbara actually knew me before I knew her. She came up to me one night while I was on a break, and I forget exactly what she said. She had asked somebody what my name was, and they told her my name was Curt, and that was one of the other guys in the band. They thought she was pointing at him. And for about a month she thought my name was Curt. She finally came up to me, and I think she said something like, 'Is your name Curt?' And I said, 'No, it's Carl.' And she just went, 'Oh, OK,' and she just walked away. But all I had to do was to see her, and I was hooked. We dated on and off for years before we were married."

Barbara's career took off after she and Carl were married. She was one of Chicago's top 10 fashion models for more than 20 years. Following her modeling career, Barbara became a concierge at Chicago's Park Hyatt Hotel for a few years, and recently retired as a fragrance buyer for Nordstrom. "She had a great career, did a lot of traveling, and worked a lot with famous Chicago photographer Victor Skrebneski," said Carl.

Well known for his commercial work for the cosmetic company Estée Lauder, Skrebneski also photographed for *Town & Country* and *Fitness* magazines, and for Chanel, Grosvenor Furs, Kohler, Northwestern Mutual Life Insurance, and Saks Fifth Avenue, among many other clients. He has photographed numerous celebrities, including Cindy Crawford, Oprah Winfrey, Audrey Hepburn, Diana Ross, and Diahann Carroll.

While Barbara was in the midst of her modeling career, Carl reunited with Dennis Tufano, who had moved to Los Angeles. They formed Tufano and Giammarese in early 1972, and enlisted former Buckinghams drummer John Poulos to manage them. "John was the most even-tempered, nice guy. He had this personality that just pulled you right in, because he was so likeable," Giammarese said. "Right after [record producer] Lou Adler had won all the Grammy awards that year with Carole King's Tapestry album, he got Lou on the phone and persuaded him to listen to a copy of the demo we recorded. Before you knew it, we were signing a recording contract with Lou Adler." Tufano and Giammarese recorded three albums for Lou Adler's Ode Records, and toured with many acts, including Carole King, Bread, and Cheech & Chong. Carl's composition "Music Everywhere," the duo's first release, reached No. 68 on the *Billboard* chart. "It was probably one of the best experiences I ever had, because I spent a lot of time out in L.A. recording and working with some of the best studio musicians," said Carl. "But I could never call it home."

In late 1976, Carl started singing advertising jingles. Chicago is home to many national ad agencies, and Carl found the work to be very lucrative. He was featured on more than 160 national radio and TV spots for McDonalds, United Airlines, RC Cola, beer commercials, and many other products and companies.

"The very first commercial I ever did that ran nationally was for Lava Soap. There were three guys singing, and everybody was excited," said Carl. "I remember getting paid about $300 for the session and I thought, 'Oh, this is great!' But you know what? Over the next four years, I made about 25 thousand bucks from that same spot. Because you get paid for every time it runs."

Although Carl was well known around Chicago because of his musical history, he credits two people for getting him involved in the jingle business – Bonnie Herman and Tom Radtke. "Bonnie is, in my eyes, the best female singer as far as her voice, her pitch, her ability to read, arrange vocals," said Carl. "I met her in about 1967, when she was married to our road manager, a British guy by the name of Peter Shelton. When I got into the jingle business, she had divorced Peter and was married to Tom Radtke, who was a well-established drummer in the jingle business. The two of them were responsible for getting me in the door, and introducing me to the business and to people in Chicago."

Carl sang jingles from 1977 until 1982, when the Buckinghams began touring again. "I had to make a decision about what I wanted to do more, and I was getting more enjoyment out of going on the road and playing once again. It was a great feeling to have that response from an appreciative audience."

In the late 1970s, while the Buckinghams group was formally retired, Carl found out that Dennis Miccolis, who had been fired from the group, had put together a band called the Buckinghams and advertised it using the names of some of the original members. "The promo packet showed a picture of Dennis Tufano then, and Dennis Tufano now, and it was a whole different person," said Carl. "It was clearly a trademark infringement, because I owned the Buckinghams' name, so we went to court and sued, and won. The case, Giammarese v. Delfino, is in the law books (Delfino was the name of the band member who was calling himself Carl Giammarese). As a matter of fact, one of my best friends, Jim Faught, is dean at Loyola Law School in Chicago, and he said the case is used as an example in a music law class."

After once again experiencing the thrill of grateful audiences beginning with ChicagoFest in 1980, and recognizing a resurgence in the popularity of the '60s music, Carl and Nick convinced Dennis Tufano to come to Chicago to record some demos to resurrect the Buckinghams. Initially Dennis had agreed to the arrangement, but the more he thought about it, the less it appealed to him, and he retracted his decision.

"We decided to go ahead with the band, and Nick suggested that I try singing lead," said Carl. "At first, I was scared to death. It was a scary thing to be out fronting a band. Now it feels real natural. It's been enough years now. But it used to come so naturally to Dennis. He was so good at it, and I tried to learn from a lot of different people that I would watch. The hardest thing to try and figure out is what to do with your hands, because I was used to having this guitar to hold onto. But I think that it's really helped me gain a lot of confidence and establish myself."

After playing several dates in 1984, Nick and Carl were asked to join the 1985 Happy Together tour, which included the Turtles, the Grass Roots, and Gary Lewis. The groups performed in about 170 cities that year. In 2010, the 25th anniversary of that tour, the Buckinghams again joined the Turtles, Grass Roots, Micky Dolenz and Mark Lindsay for another grueling schedule. That tour was such a success, they repeated it in 2011 with the same lineup, plus the Association; and in 2012, the Buckinghams joined the Turtles, Grass Roots, Gary Puckett, and Micky Dolenz, playing 46 dates across the United States in the months of July and August.

Photo taken by Carl's wife, Barbara, in September 2012

Besides music, Carl likes to play tennis and golf, and he loves exotic sports cars. "The first thing most people I haven't seen for a while ask me is, 'What kind of car do you have now?' Years ago, I owned a string of Alfa Romeos that I used to like to work on, but I've kinda passed that now and just like to drive. I had a Porsche Carrera for about 10 years, and now I'm driving a Mercedes-Benz."

What types of music does Carl listen to today? "A lot of people think that just because we come from that classic rock oldies era that's what we listen to. I enjoy that to an extent, but I like to listen to a lot of the new pop music and groups today to hear what's going on. I like the Goo Goo Dolls, John Mayer. I like some country, like Rascal Flatts, Zac Brown Band. I love Joni Mitchell, Crosby, Stills & Nash, Jackson Browne, James Taylor. Thanks to my wife, I listen to a lot of different music because she's really into jazz, including Tony Bennett. I love a lot of the old music, too,

19

because of my dad. I listen to a lot of old Frank Sinatra and so forth."

When asked what he feels are his greatest achievements, Carl took a deep breath and said, "Ummm, well, gosh. Probably one of my proudest achievements is the longevity of being part of a band that had five top records. I guess a real achievement is staying married all these years – being in the music business, that's not always easy. I'd have to say the thing I'm most proud of is what I've accomplished with the Buckinghams. I've enjoyed my experience more in the last 20 years than I did back in the '60s. We still have a strong following, and people come to hear us. Speaking of achievements – there's still an audience that wants to hear us play, which makes me realize that, hey, we did something right. And thank God for oldies radio. It's like having hits all over again."

In 2002, Carl completed his first solo album, called *Trying Not to Fade*, a collection of songs that he describes as reflective of everyday experiences. In 2011, he completed his second solo album titled *My Journey*, which is the companion to his autobiography *Reinventing the Buckinghams: My Journey*, which he wrote with Dawn Lee Wakefield.

For more information, visit his website at **www.carlgiammarese. com.**

Epilogue: Nick Fortuna

Bass guitarist and singer

The middle of three children born to Rose and Anthony Fortuna in the Cabrini-Green neighborhood of Chicago on May 1, 1946, Nicholas "Nick" Fortuna learned to appreciate all styles of music, from his grandfather's Italian opera to the rock and roll that his older brother, Frank, enjoyed. But rhythm and blues became a lifelong favorite.

While Frank was listening to Elvis and other popular performers of the times, Nick paid little attention to music early on because he was involved in baseball, basketball, and track in his Lincoln Park neighborhood. He developed his first interest in the guitar about 1960 as a student at Niles West High School.

"I had a couple of school chums, two brothers, who had guitars at their house. It had to be when I was a freshman in high school. When I would go over to the house, if they were tied up doing

Nick performing with the 2012 Happy Together Tour at Cal Expo in Sacramento, California (photo by Jeff March)

21

chores or eating dinner or whatever, and they had a couple of guitars lying around. I would watch what they were doing and then mess with the guitars. And slowly but surely I developed my own interest."

Nick's first guitar was a gift from his grandfather, who saw him admiring it, saying to him in Italian, "take it, it's yours to keep." That gift opened the door to his future career. His first song on that guitar was the theme song from the 1958–1961 private eye television series *Peter Gunn*, but soon he was playing along to other popular songs of the day.

Nick, whose father owned a neighborhood corner grocery store, attended three high schools, and graduated from Maine East High School in Park Ridge, a northwestern suburb of Chicago. A high school classmate invited him to join a band he was forming, along with his cousin and another friend. At their first practice, leader Jerry Elarde, vocalist and drummer, introduced Nick to bass guitarist Curt Bachman and Jerry's cousin, guitarist Carl Giammarese. Practicing in the basements of their family homes, the assembled group became a band called the Centuries, and their first gig was outside an appliance store in Morton Grove. The band, which performed "cover" versions of pop songs, began playing at private parties, dances, and weddings in 1964, then began earning gigs in clubs, including Like Young, Holiday Ballroom and the Embassy Ballroom.

The Centuries lasted a little more than a year. In early 1965 Carl Giammarese and Curt Bachman left to join the Pulsations, and Nick followed the music out to Chicago's Mannheim Road clubs that featured R&B talent. He auditioned for a white R&B group called Jimmy V and the Entertainers and was invited to join immediately. Nick brought his guitar to the audition and the leader, Jimmy V, shook his head "no," pointed to the bass guitar and said, "if you want the gig, that's what you're playing." After hours of practice, Fortuna adapted to playing the bass, which has been his instrument since then.

Nick had been performing Motown, Memphis, and Chicago R&B tunes with the Entertainers for several months when, across town, the Pulsations needed a bass player. Their manager, Carl Bonafede, called Nick to see if he'd consider joining them. They'd been featured on WGN-TV's *All Time Hits* show for three weeks with another 10 weeks to go on their booking. He accepted. When Columbia Records misspelled his surname as "Fortune" – a typographical error – the group just decided to leave it at that.

Nick explained what he thought distinguished the Buckinghams from other groups at the time. "We were the first white pop group that came out with horns in the band. So that was a distinctive part of the

Buckinghams. Secondly, we had a lot of harmony going on in our music. And third, the band had a real distinctive look – the dress, the haircuts, the body structure. We looked like we could be related. I think Carl and Dennis had more of that type of thing happening, except that Dennis was much shorter than Carl, but once in a while people would ask if they were brothers or cousins."

After five years in the pressure-cooker world of pop music concert touring, Nick returned to Chicago, married Judy Koziol in 1969, and the couple had two sons: Nicholas, born in 1971; and Demetri, born in 1975. The marriage lasted for 11 years. Today, Nicholas is a Chicago fireman, and Demetri is a bartender in Wrigleyville, a popular neighborhood on Chicago's north side.

In 1970, Nick joined a band called Music Power '69, playing soul music six nights a week, with several shows a night, in the Chicago region. Then he formed his own band, Crystal, in which he played bass, along with Billy Corgan Sr. on guitar, Steve Fultz, lead vocals, Tyrone Green on drums, and Steve Ostoyich on Hammond B-3 organ. This funk-R&B style band built a strong local following. After that band underwent some personnel changes, Fortuna decided to create another band, Kinky Kids, featuring Billy Corgan Sr. and Steve Fultz, plus a new drummer named Bobby Mizialko, and John Suchan on keyboards.

"We were doing a lot of real heavy funk – not even R&B, more funk, you know, dance – from Commodores to Harold Melvin and the Blue Notes, all that kind of stuff," said Nick. "I was playing solid, making my living, and then – hello – here comes disco. I was playing disco music before disco came out, but club owners didn't want to hire live bands – they wanted to have record players and deejays, which cut our work down to about a tenth of what we had."

In order to supplement his income, Nick decided to go to school for his hair styling license. He had an interest in cutting hair since high school, and he cut hair for all the guys in the band when they were on tour, but he needed to have a license to work professionally. "So I went to school and became a hairdresser in 1979. I worked about a year for Paul Glick and Associates salon on North Michigan Avenue, whose clients included Chicago politicians and TV personalities. We had 30 hairdressers in that shop. It was three floors, and haircuts were 40 bucks back then. It was good money, but it takes a while to build up a clientele. I have nothing against gay people, but I was the only straight guy in the whole shop. I had to scrimp and scrape, to try to get my own people, so it was little rough."

Nick then joined a smaller shop (with five hairdressers and a

23

shampoo station) called Shampoo on Clark Street and Broadway, in the Newtown area of Chicago. "I never did color because at the time color was a lot of blond on blond stuff, and I have a real slight bit of color blindness, so I was swapping people – I was doing a lot of permanent waving, and switching off and having other people do my color. But the haircutting and the permanent waving was my forte."

While at Shampoo, Nick met his soul mate, Pam Gazda. They would remain partners for more than 20 years, until Pam passed away in 2001.

After the Buckinghams re-formed in 1980, Nick gave up hair styling to go on the road. "Carl, Dennis, and I put this thing together with a couple of other players for ChicagoFest, and they expected probably around 5,000 or 6,000 people. The first night, 13,000 showed. And there were more the second night," said Nick. "Then agents started calling us left and right wanting to re-book the band, and no one was really interested in doing it at that time professionally. So they said, 'Well, just go out and do a certain amount of dates and see how it works for you.' We were playing at the best places in Chicago, like Park West and a lot of other large venues, and we were doing a lot of outdoor shows during the summertime. The money was good, one thing led to another, and we're still playing."

In 1993 Nick bought a two-flat apartment building in a nice little German neighborhood off Lincoln Avenue in the heart of Chicago. He lived on the first floor and had tenants on the second floor. "The problem was that when you live in a nice neighborhood in Chicago, people like to steal stuff," he said. "I had my garage broken into three or four times. I own a Harley, so every time I parked it in my garage, I would have to bolt it down to the ground."

Tired of the long, cold Chicago winters and dealing with break-ins, in 1997 Nick decided to take a look at housing in Las Vegas. The Buckinghams had performed from time to time in Las Vegas for years, and Nick enjoyed the milder weather, where he could enjoy riding his Harley year-round. "After one of our shows, a friend convinced me to take a ride off the Strip and look at neighborhoods," said Nick. "So I did. And I thought I was in Beverly Hills. And then I found out what the prices were, and I couldn't believe it."

He went back home and started packing his furniture to move to Las Vegas, intending to rent out both apartments. But while he was loading furniture, a woman came to his front door and said she'd been looking at his building for years, and wondered if he'd be interested in selling it. Nick replied, "I never really thought about it, because I was just going to rent both of the units out, but I said, 'Throw me a price and we'll see what it is.' She threw me an offer I couldn't refuse."

Nick, who still enjoys living in Las Vegas, says performers who have influenced his life include the Beatles, James Brown, Ike and Tina Turner, Roy Orbison, Elvis Presley, Aretha Franklin, Van Morrison, Stevie Wonder, Larry Graham of Sly and the Family Stone, Graham Central Station, and Eric Clapton. He also admires fusion jazz bass players Jaco Pastorius and Stanley Clarke.

"A lot of great players influenced my musical career," he said. "And, as a hobby, I got into bodybuilding, and I was fortunate enough to work out in a gym with three-time Mr. Olympia and bodybuilding legend Sergio Oliva out of Chicago, a good friend of mine who put me on the right path. I still work out every day."

In 2010, Nick and Carl were featured in the 25th Anniversary Happy Together Tour, joining Mark Volman, "Flo" (aka Phlorescent Leech), and Howard Kaylan, "Eddie" of the Turtles, the Grass Roots, Micky Dolenz, and Mark Lindsay in a tour of more than 20 cities from California to New York, celebrating the silver anniversary of the original Happy Together Tour in 1985. In July 2011, concerts began for the second Happy Together Reunion Tour that included the Buckinghams, the Turtles, the Grass Roots, Mark Lindsay, and the Association. Later in 2011, Nick and Carl learned that they would join the 2012 Happy Together Tour, alongside the Turtles, Micky Dolenz, the Grass Roots, and Gary Puckett. The 2012 tour, which grew to a grueling touring schedule of 46 shows across the United States from the end of June to August 31, was a resounding success.

Nick explains, "The way the tour works is that each act plays separately with the same backup band. For example, when Carl and I do our set, it's just the two of us – Carl sings and I play bass, and we sing our hits with the backup band. All the other acts do the same thing, and at the end of the show, we all go on stage together and do the encore song – 'Happy Together.'"

While reflecting on the 1960s, Nick says, "I think that was probably one of the most fun parts of my life. Of course, I miss my youth back then. There's an old saying: youth is wasted on the young. Well, hello. Of course, everybody wants to be 20 forever. But fortunately enough, I've held up pretty good."

Epilogue: Dennis Tufano
Singer, composer, actor

Dennis Tufano has been engaged in a live musical documentary of the life of Bobby Darin for the past six years, starring in the brilliant production of his tribute stage show featuring music of the singer, songwriter, multi-instrumentalist, and actor who died at the age of 37 in 1973. Tufano's show, titled *I Remember Darin,* is a chronological timeline following Darin's career from his late-'50s pop tunes "Splish Splash" and "Dream Lover" to country-flavored "18 Yellow Roses" (1963), and folk-inspired "If I Were A Carpenter" (1966).

Tufano credits his sister, Cheryl, for encouraging him to pay tribute to the late singer. "When I visited her in Chicago, she heard me singing along to her Bobby Darin CD, and she said, 'Do you know that your voice has the same tonal range as Bobby Darin's?' I guess I never thought about it, but I always felt comfortable singing his songs." When Dennis returned home to L.A., he bought Darin's box set and started making a list of songs that could potentially become a show. He hired Grammy Award-winning arranger and performer Michael Acosta as his musical director, and returned to the stage.

"My mother liked to tell the story about my stage fright when she'd get a good group of people around her. She'd say, 'You know, it's amazing that Dennis became a singer because when he was in kindergarten at 5 years old, he was cast in the kindergarten play as Prince Charming,

Dennis Tufano

Photo by Maggie Smith
© 2011

but he had stage fright so bad he couldn't say his lines.' My teacher kept calling my mom, saying, 'You know, he's only got a few things to say but when it comes to his time to say them, he won't say anything.' So I was actually then un-cast, and I got a non-speaking role in the kindergarten play as a raindrop," he chuckled. "I think the universe gave me that one last chance in kindergarten: 'Do you want to be a raindrop for the rest of your life?'"

Dennis Stanley Joseph Tufano was born on September 11, 1946, in Chicago, Illinois, to Joseph and Bernice. He attended St. Sylvester grammar school and Gordon Technical

High School in Chicago. He inherited his musical talents from his father, who was also a singer, and played the violin, saxophone, and harmonica.

"My dad had a band called Tuffy and the Red Birds. His nickname had been 'Tuffy,' short for Tufano, since high school. But he was kind of phasing out of his band days when we were growing up because he had to go out and make a living. I was always kind of around music and pretty much discovered things on my own. My parents never said, 'Why don't you learn how to play something?' They just let me discover music on my own. Like I wanted to play accordion when I was about 6, and they said, 'OK, we'll get you a little accordion and get you lessons.'"

About the time he was in junior high, Dennis became interested in drums when he discovered an old set of drums in his uncle's basement. "My first public appearance as an amateur was in Wisconsin. One of my cousins, Ronnie Prazuch, was a drummer in a polka band. And he was 13 or 14 and played in a band called the Flying Dutchmen. We were at a big dance and I was standing in the wings, pretty fascinated by my little cousin doing this, and all these people dancing, and in between songs he said, 'I want to go to the bathroom. Why don't you play the drums on the next song?' And I didn't really have a set of drums that I played, but he said, 'It's simple. Just sit down and play the next song.' And I did. And the guys in the band turned around and looked at me, and they were all kids, and he said, 'OK, here we go.' They counted it off, and I started playing. And I thought, 'Hey, this isn't bad.'"

But when Tufano heard Elvis Presley's "Teddy Bear" and other top songs of the day playing through a jukebox while on a weekend trip with his family at a lake in northern Illinois, he knew music would be a big part of his life. "I remember that was a big deal, and that's what made me start to buy 45 rpm records," said Tufano. "Then I started going to sock hops and stuff in school. We used to have these Friday dances – I guess the last Friday of every month. And we would be in the little cafeteria area. They had a jukebox, and they'd play and we'd dance, and that was when I started to get into the whole thing about how much music there was out there."

He started listening to the radio, which played a mix of R&B, Bobby Darin, Jimmy Clanton, Bobby Rydell, Frankie Avalon, Buddy Holly, the Righteous Brothers, and the Everly Brothers. "But just before that was all the standard kind of things. There was the Frank Sinatra stuff and there was Rosemary Clooney," said Dennis. "Around the house, I used to hear all those big old 78s on the Victrola that my parents would play, because they liked music a lot. So I heard the best of singers just being in the house, and then whenever I could get in the car and listen to the radio,

I would hear the pop stuff. That was a great time because it was really about the purity of the act, and the singing, and the style. It was kind of light and fun and entertaining. It was easy to get involved in."

Bobby Darin was always a favorite of Tufano's. "Something about the tone of his voice always got me," he said. "A friend of mine is a big music fiend. He was always sending me little compilations, tapes of things, and he sent me a thing once that was songs that I had sung, and in between every one of them was a Bobby Darin song. He called me and said, "I'm sending you this tape because there's a similarity between you and Bobby Darin that's really cool."

In 1963, Dennis tried out for the choir at Gordon Tech, which was a Catholic, all-boys high school in the Irving Park section of Chicago. He recalls, "They said that my voice wasn't strong enough. And so I was a little disappointed because my family was musical and we used to sing and I thought I could sing. And then I tried out again the last year, because the last year I started getting involved with an a cappella group. And that's when I started getting into singing more. But I still didn't make it. They said that my voice wasn't strong enough. And so I said, 'OK, fine,' and then pretty much about three or four months later a group of us would go to restaurants at night and sit in the parking lot in our '57 Chevy, pound on the dashboard, and sing to the radio. We thought we sounded good together, so we started getting together in a friend's basement and arranging songs that we liked."

That first group was called the Darsals, the name of which was a combination of the Dovells and Marcels – popular groups at the time. "We used to mostly sing in the basement or at parties, and then after we got pretty confident at parties, we would go to dances. We would have our song list with the keys that we sang the songs in, and we'd go up to the band when they took a break and ask, 'Do you guys know any of these songs in this key?' And if they did, we'd ask them to play, and we would sing because nobody wanted an a cappella group at a dance – there was no beat. So we had to find some music behind us in order to do that. So that was my 'singing college.'"

Dennis's favorite class in high school was architectural drawing, and he was considering a career in commercial art. He came by his artistic talents naturally as, by day, his father was a machinist at a factory to support his family, but he was also a musician as well as an artist. "As a kid, I used to wake up from taking a nap and sometimes there would be a piece of paper on my chest, and I'd lift it up and it would be a nice pencil drawing of me sleeping," he said. "My father never really displayed any of his work. He went to the Art Institute in Chicago for a couple of years when he was a younger guy, but back in the early '40s, most of those people had to pretty much make it their hobby as opposed to their job."

In high school, Dennis started his first business enterprise as an artist. "Every guy had a favorite car in school, and they'd say to me, 'Hey, how much would you charge to draw my favorite car on the cover of my folder here?' And I would be making like 75 cents a cover. So I got into that commercial thing right away. Of course, I used to get caught by the teachers sometimes. History class was not a good art class," he chuckled.

Following graduation in 1964, Dennis got a job as an apprentice commercial artist in downtown Chicago at the Emmet J. Newman Studio on Wabash and Lake. He worked there for almost two years, until John Poulos heard him and George LeGros singing at a party. "John came up to us and said, 'You know, you guys sing really well, and I have a band that can't sing at all. And maybe you guys would like to be the singers.' The band was the early Pulsations, and it wasn't that good. It was a bunch of kids who could hardly play, and we could hardly do anything but sing. But we actually started getting some gigs here and there, and we played a lot at drag races, and we'd just set up in the pits and try to get people to hear us. That band just kind of fell apart, as bands do when they're just kids."

In their quest to find talented musicians and form a working band, Tufano and Poulos heard Carl Giammarese playing guitar in a band called the Centuries. "He used to bend the strings, where most guitar players were still doing that kind of surfer sound. It adds a little soul to them," said Dennis. "So we took him to a place called Bon-Bon's, a drive-in restaurant kind of place where all the kids hung out. It was a real lively spot, and we bought him an ice cream sundae, or something. A little payola," he laughed.

Tufano's parents were cautiously supportive of his musical interests. "I came to them after about a year of working downtown in my art apprentice job and just playing on the weekends, and I said, 'I want to talk to you because I have an important decision to make. I know I've been working for almost two years now in a regular job and bringing home a paycheck. But I'm making more money on the weekends now just playing in the band. It's been going on now for a while, and I think it could be steady, so I would like your blessing to leave my day job and really push on this.' So we had some negotiations, but they said, 'If that's really what you want to do, you can. The only thing is, you can't come back and moan to us when it all falls apart. Don't come back and say, 'Why did you let me do that?' So I said, 'Fine. If that's the deal, let's do it.' And I was blessed that it worked out OK." Dennis's parents gained

29

confidence as the following of the Pulsations strengthened, as the band began recording, got its break on local television, and became the Buckinghams.

Because the Buckinghams performed a lot in the Chicago area, Tufano's parents attended many of the concert dates. "They were always supportive. It was like they were in the band. They got off on all the autograph stuff, and I had to autograph pictures and leave them at the house because people would come by and say, 'Is Dennis home?' And they used to say, 'No, but here's a picture for you.' They got excited about the whole process."

Tufano says a few things distinguished the Buckinghams from other groups of the time. "There's a certain kind of clarity to our music. It was pretty simple and straight-ahead. It wasn't cluttered at all. And the horn sound, of course, gave us a little bit of a good solid foundation. Now I'm saying this as the singer, but I think that there was kind of a sincerity in the delivery of our songs. I always felt like I had songs that I could actually just really sing, but I didn't have to do any kind of selling, or any kind of gimmicky stuff. We had the reputation of looking clean and being clean. We were just regular guys."

Tufano describes his struggles just prior to the breakup of the Buckinghams. "After about year and a half of us trying to make money again doing smaller gigs, trying to regain the consciousness of the band, just because we had so many lawyers' fees that we had to pay off, I just said, 'You know guys, I can't do this anymore.' John and I were best friends. He started the band and we were roommates and friends throughout the whole time. And so I just came to him and said, 'John, I don't know what else we could do. We can't go on like this. It's just not a good way to do music anymore.' And he realized that too, and so we all sat down and talked and decided, 'OK, let's just stop.' So, unfortunately, when that happened, there were a lot of loose ends out there. I've been trying to find bits and pieces of those days that were left dangling, because the carpet was pulled out from under us."

Tufano got a job in a Chicago clothing store for about a year, and then spent several months trying to figure out what he wanted to do for the rest of his life. "I let my hair grow, and I just tried to get away from who I was. Not consciously, but it just became this evolution that I went through, because I wasn't that anymore, so I just became this other guy, and I just kind of let myself 'be.' I ended up having hair down my back, and a beard, and I pretty much turned into John Lennon, who was my big idol," he said. "I had my little Teac recorder, my little two-track, and I was sitting there writing songs, and recording them, doing overdubs, just sitting there doing my own thing at home. We all just pretty much scattered. I saw John Poulos a lot because he lived very close to me, about two blocks away, near the lake in Chicago."

In 1971, Dennis and Carl hooked up again, and the two of them wrote some songs together and formed the duo Dennis and Carl, and later became Tufano and Giammarese. "We were two ex-rock and roll guys who were playing acoustic guitars and auditioning at folk clubs, trying to play our music that we were writing – not even telling anybody that we were Buckinghams, and we finally started to get some work."

In the beginning, they did their own promotion and John Poulos acted as their interim manager, arranging some work for them in clubs. He was also instrumental in getting them a record deal with Lou Adler. "We were rejected by every record label – even Columbia. In early 1972, John was going through the trades and said, 'You know, there's this guy, Lou Adler. He's got Carole King, he's a custom label. He's really different. I'm going to give his office a call and send the demo out to him, just as a last resort, because he's a small label [Ode Records, distributed by A&M Records]. Let's go after him.' A week later, Adler called back and said, 'I really like the demo. I want to fly you guys out for a live audition.' We played live for about 40 minutes, did our whole repertoire, and the next morning, he said, 'I want to sign you to the company, but I also want to produce the record.'"

Adler produced the debut Tufano and Giammarese album: *Tufano–Giammarese 33$\frac{1}{3}$* (Ode, 1973); *The Tufano & Giammarese Band* (Ode, 1974) was produced by Jack Richardson (the Guess Who producer); and *The Other Side* (Epic/Ode, 1977) was produced by Tom Scott and Hank Cicalo. They toured to promote their albums, including a four-month stint with Cheech and Chong. "I don't think anyone has ever experienced anything like an acoustic act opening for Cheech and Chong," said Tufano. "It was an interesting venue."

While their first album did fairly well with "Music Everywhere" reaching No. 68 on Billboard's pop singles chart in the spring of 1973, the duo began to experience some problems. "Carl got a little frustrated because the first album was good but didn't really do much for us. Lou was still hot on us even though we weren't selling records because he liked what we were doing. So he was supporting us and said, 'Let's make another record,' but about three weeks into making our second record Carl kind of burned out a bit, and went home to Chicago to be with his wife. He called me the next day and said, 'I can't do it anymore, I quit.' I said we have a contract you can't just quit! He sounded serious, so I said, 'OK, fine. We've been through all kinds of stuff. No need to make yourself crazier.' Our contract was sitting there but we couldn't do anything. Carl walked away leaving me to explain to Lou Adler what had happened. Lou asked to have Carl call him personally but Carl refused. This was an insult to Mr. Adler and he chose not to be our producer any longer. But later down the road, through a lot of negotiations and talks between Jon Poulos, myself, and Lou, I went back to Chicago for about six months and we put the band back together and did two more albums over the next two years. This action fulfilled our contractual obligations. But nothing really came of it, and Carl and I just both decided that we might as well try to go out and do something else."

Following the split, Dennis started a transition into theatrical performing and resumed taking acting classes, which he had begun in 1974–75 while in Chicago. "I started to meet actors and go to plays, and I was really starting to get the bug to want to go up on the stage and act. It wasn't so much of being in the movies or anything, it was just really neat to be a live performer. I had gotten some good basics in Chicago, but some friends told me about a couple of interesting classes in L.A., two of which were taught by this woman director named Joan Darling. I studied with her for about two years, and then also from Samantha Harper, a protégé of Joan's. So it was an ongoing thing with about 25 actors in that class that really worked well together. We learned from each other, and it was a good combination of people. Jon Voight was in the class for about seven or eight months. I did a lot of live theater, and I got a few little bit parts on television here and there, but never really hit it big, obviously. But I always enjoyed the process of it. And being an entertainer. I did live radio dramas at the Gene Autry Museum here. And I did about 14 of those live in front of an audience, plus live broadcasts on the radio. And then through that organization, I directed three of those radio dramas. And I really enjoyed working with all the people that way. It was kind of like being in a band again, in a sense. Everybody's involved to make the show happen."

Tufano remained friends with Lou Adler, who owned the Roxy on Sunset Strip and ran a private club upstairs called On the Rox, which he established for celebrities who wanted to be on the Strip or see a show at the Roxy without having to be inundated by fans. One night Dennis happened to be at On the Rox when he ran into Bernie Taupin, whom he had met a year prior through a friend from Chicago. The two of them were sitting at the bar having a beer and engaging in some chitchat when Bernie asked Dennis what he was doing professionally. Dennis told him he had been doing some acting and that he was also working on some music demos with Tom Scott. Bernie happened to be working on a new album of his own, had lyrics and was looking for a music writer. The two of them got together and released *He Who Rides the Tiger* (Electra/Asylum) in 1980. Dennis co-wrote with Taupin, played rhythm guitar and sang backgrounds. Elton John also contributed background vocals on the song "Love (the Barren Desert)." The album was released on CD by American Beat Records on March 10, 2009.

Tufano had become good friends with Tom Scott through their session work together at Adler's Ode Records. In 1982 Scott told Tufano he was scheduled to go on tour with Olivia Newton-John and asked Tufano to join the tour as Newton-John's duet partner. "Tom Scott worked with me on my demos that Bernie heard, so we had become friends. He said to me 'She has two duets and I know you're a lead singer, so if you get the gig, you get the two duets. But you have to sing backgrounds too.' I said, 'Well, I could use the work.' So I sang 'Suddenly' from the film *Xanadu* with her for the audition, and I got the job. It was a lot of fun." The duets "Suddenly" and "You're the One That I Want," from the movie *Grease,* with Tufano were also featured on Newton-John's HBO special *Olivia in Concert,* which aired in January 1983.

In 2000 Tufano produced, directed and filmed a documentary in Chicago, called *Major Hall: Therapy Tuesday.* "It's a little piece from the heart about my mother and her gang that run around in Chicago," he said. "They have this little tavern that they go to on Tuesday mornings in a banquet hall, and they have a live band and they do polka dances. I should mention that I'm Polish on my mother's side. So there's a live band, and about 150 people between the ages of 75 and 90 go to this every Tuesday. So I decided to go to Chicago and see what it was about. They're the elders of the tribe, and they've all been through horrendous things – wars, family deaths, divorce, whatever, but here they all are at this dance. The polka dance is not an easy dance. It's pretty aerobic. These people do this four or five hours a day and they actually call it 'therapy Tuesday,' so I decided to bring this information to more people. It's nice to know that there's another path that some people are taking. To me, this place is like *Cocoon* without the aliens. Outside, it's just a regular neighborhood tavern. There's nothing special about this block. But when you walk inside the place, something happens, and it's just amazing."

Not even contemplating retirement, Dennis still has aspirations. "I would hope that I would be able to achieve everything I set my heart to, which has kept me going for a long time. I try to take the down time as just down time, and not the end of the world – not that I haven't had my moments. But I try to keep that going as part of what my family instilled in me, I guess. But I would hope that I could do things that are meaningful. I want to do things that have some substance to them, that inform people, that give people a chance to see what people are about. When I was singing with the Buckinghams I couldn't wait to get together with the guys and do one of our songs, and go on tour. This part of my life now has the same kind of feeling and drive behind it. So I would hope that would be what I want to accomplish."

Tufano taped a performance for the PBS music series *My Music: My Generation – The '60s*, which first aired in March 2008, and was a part of the award-winning PBS DVD series. An expanded version of the show aired on PBS in September 2008.

He performed a classic Chicago rock concert with the Cryan' Shames in the summer of 2008, and appeared with Marty Grebb and Bruce Conte outside Manila in the Philippines in late fall 2008.

Tufano continues to perform with his tribute to Bobby Darin, the Live CD *I Remember Darin* is available on CDBaby.com, and he also makes appearances with his classic rock show.

Visit his official websites at www.dtsings.com and **www.tufanofans. com** for more information and concert dates.

Epilogue: Marty Grebb

Saxophone and piano player, and singer

"I knew I was going to be a professional musician when I was still in grade school. It was definitely my aspiration. I was totally focused on that," said Marty Grebb, who continues to record his own albums and has performed on numerous albums by hit-making artists in the music business.

The middle of three kids, Marty was born on September 2, 1945, to Mel (Kucik) and Harry Grebb, in Chicago, Illinois. His father was a professional musician – a singer and multiple instrumentalist – and his mother plays piano. "My mom and dad met in high school. He played in a 20-piece band with a leader named Bill Bishop, and she came to one of the performances, and they ended up going on the road together. My dad sang and my mom played piano. He also played with various jump blues bands under names that featured him, like 'Big Daddy and the Sounders.'"

When Marty's brother Bob – two years older – started school, their parents decided they needed to settle down, so they, the boys and Marty's sister, April, moved to a house at 51st and Ashland on the south side of Chicago. His dad started a music school called Bridgeport Conservatory of Music at 31st and Morgan Street, which Bob took over in 1983. "My brother writes music books. He has written with a lot of jazz greats – guitarists. He's probably the most analytical mind when it comes to guitars and guitar playing, and what people are doing when they play them," said Grebb.

Photo courtesy of
Marty Grebb

An accomplished saxophone and piano player, Grebb took his first formal music lessons from a nun at the Catholic school he attended. "My parents decided it would be good for me to have a regular weekly lesson from her, because my father was really busy teaching everybody else," he said. "That didn't last very long, and then I started taking lessons from my dad."

Rock and roll invaded Marty's consciousness at a young age. He says two of his early favorites were Little Richard and Chuck Berry. "I liked Little Richard's singing and piano playing, and I admired his tenor saxophone player named Lee Allen, who played on a lot of music that came out of New Orleans. Chuck Berry's first piano player was a guy named Johnnie Johnson, who played on his early recordings."

Another great saxophone player, named Clifford Scott, who played for R&B great Bill Doggett on his 1956 hit "Honky Tonk," influenced Grebb's musical taste. "Where I grew up, if you couldn't play that song, you couldn't be in the good bands," he said. "I still have an autograph from Bill Doggett from when I was 16. He took music in a certain direction from where it was and he filled a gap; he crossed over from sort of a swing-jazz thing into an R&B thing that created a certain step toward rock and roll."

Marty's first band, a five-man outfit appropriately called the Quintones, played for parties and school dances during his years at Mendel Catholic Prep High School on E. 111th Street. In 1962 when Quintones' bass player decided to go on the road, Grebb and drummer Denny Ebert joined vocalist and guitarist Kal David (born David Raskin), and bass player and vocalist Peter Cetera – a high school classmate a year ahead of Grebb – in forming a group called Kal David and the Exceptions.

"We did some recording for Vee-Jay Records because we backed up a group called the Dells (famous for "Oh, What a Night"), who were on that label. We performed with them at a few different clubs, some concert performances, and we played at what I would call the chitlins' circuit. One of the clubs was the Tri-State Inn in Indiana. Now it's a famous place that's written up in blues history books. At the time, it had a dirt floor, and we were the only white people there – just the four of us – and a lot of people there were wearing sunglasses. It was quite an eye-opener for me."

The Exceptions also played at a Rush Street nightclub called the Happy Medium, where Grebb became acquainted with the Missing Links. The members of the Missing Links included guitarist and bass player Terry Kath, saxophone player Walt Parazaider and drummer Danny Seraphine – all of whom subsequently became members of the band Chicago. Grebb and Kath established a friendship and were roommates for a while.

While Grebb wanted to write original music for the Exceptions, he said it was really frowned upon at the time. "Every once in a while I give Peter Cetera a little nudge when one of his new records comes out. I say to him, 'You know, we're not supposed to write our own songs,' because that's what he used to say to me back when we were kids. He thought that there were people to do that, and we weren't those people. But I had been obsessed with wanting to write since I was about 13."

In 1965, David left to join the Rovin' Kind, later to become Illinois Speed Press. Jim Dondelinger (aka Jim Vincent) replaced David, and the band became known as simply the Exceptions. By 1966, Grebb was unhappy with the direction the Exceptions were heading, and Peter Cetera had joined the Big Thing, which soon changed its name to Chicago Transit Authority – a name that eventually was shortened to Chicago. The timing couldn't have been better when the Buckinghams brought Grebb on as their new keyboard player.

The Buckinghams traveled to Los Angeles for the first time in 1967. Marty recalls, "After years of watching all the television that came from Hollywood, as a little kid watching the *Mickey Mouse Club* and all the scenery that you always see around L.A., it was just so exciting to see it, and to see it in such a nice, comfortable, warm way in the middle of winter. That's when I decided I was going to move out here. So we worked it out with our manager to get a house and live here for about six or eight months while we worked on an album. Then after that was over, we all went back to Chicago."

Grebb explains the sequence of events that contributed to the break-up of the Buckinghams. "We didn't agree with the direction Guercio was trying to take us. We were trying to become more in step with the times in our own way. We had a song after 'Back in Love Again,' called 'What Is Love.' That song could have taken us into the realm of Chicago and Blood, Sweat and Tears – which was another group that Guercio ended up producing on the heels of our success," Grebb told us in February 2000. "We were a horn band, and we didn't even take horns on the road, which was another mistake. I quit because through all those dealings with CBS, Guercio went in there and kind of stabbed me in the back as the person that was making it difficult for him to deal with the band. And in a certain way, that was very true, but he was killing the band. And so I felt that after our meetings with CBS, the only real way the band would be able to try to have a career with CBS Records, was for me to leave. So I left."

In 1969, Grebb put all of his belongings in a trailer and drove to California. With his connections from recording and touring with the Buckinghams, he began to establish a new direction for himself as a studio musician and side man for Lou Adler, who had managed Jan and Dean and produced Sam Cooke, the Mamas and the Papas, Johnny Rivers, Barry McGuire, Scott McKenzie, the Grass Roots, Spirit, Carole King, and Cheech and Chong. "I had set aside some money and for the first six months, I just really sort of tried to re-form myself after going through the trauma of being in a No. 1 band in 1967 – over the Beatles, over the Monkees, over Jimi Hendrix, over all the people that were out that year," said Grebb. "Coming from that and feeling sort of trashed, it took me a while to really be motivated. But then once I was, I started to make more hookups and tried to figure out what I was going to do. I just kept plugging away, and more doors kept opening."

Through his connections, Marty joined the psychedelic rock band H.P. Lovecraft, which was formed in Chicago in 1967 and named after the horror and science fiction author of the same name. The band had relocated to San Francisco and was being managed by concert promoter Bill Graham. Marty performed with the group for a lot of San Francisco Bay Area venues, including the Fillmore and the Winterland Ballroom, and produced an album with Warner Bros. "In the midst of all that, I met Harvey Brooks, who was bass player for the Electric Flag and was doing a lot of other work as a side man. He played keyboards on a record called *Super Session* with Steve Stills, Mike Bloomfield, and Al Kooper from the first group of Blood, Sweat and Tears," said Grebb. "Harvey was starting a new band in Woodstock, New York, called the Fabulous Rhinestones."

By late 1969, the psychedelic era was beginning to wind down and H.P. Lovecraft decided to disband, so Marty joined the Fabulous Rhinestones and moved to Woodstock in the winter of 1970. "That's when my career really opened up, because there were so many bands in Woodstock. It was a boomtown right then."

Woodstock has a long history as a community of artists and painters. After Bob Dylan and Dylan's manager, Albert Grossman, moved to the area as a retreat, and Grossman started buying real estate and building his recording studio and Bearsville Records label there, many musical performers followed. The Band, Janis Joplin, Jimi Hendrix, Paul Butterfield Blues Band, and Maria and Geoffrey Muldaur had homes there, and a lot of artists came through to perform there.

"In 1972, while I was there playing with the Fabulous Rhinestones, which was sort of a pop rhythm and blues band, we'd play with Sly and the Family Stone, and our opening acts would be groups like the Eagles, the Doobie Brothers. We were the headliner. It was at a time when we were well-known there in that little pocket." The Fabulous Rhinestones, which included Grebb, Harvey Brooks, guitarist Kal David, drummer Greg Thomas, and percussionist Reinol "Dino" Andino, recorded three albums on a label called Just Sunshine, owned by Michael Lang, one of the promoters of the Woodstock festival.

When Bonnie Raitt came through Woodstock in 1972 to make her second album, *Give It Up*, for Warner Bros., she asked Marty to play on it after seeing his band at a club called Cafe Expresso. "That was a place where you could see early pictures of Bob Dylan sitting there play-ing chess," said Grebb. That began a 25-year working relationship with Bonnie Raitt, and through that association, Grebb left Woodstock in late 1973, moved back to Los Angeles, and started working with Etta James, Rick Danko, Gregg Allman, and Bonnie Bramlett, of Delaney and Bonnie. He went on tour with Bonnie Raitt, and worked with Leon Russell and Willie Nelson, and performed with Peter Cetera in the band Chicago for a couple of years.

"It was probably 1979 and 1980 that Peter brought me in as the pivot guy in the band Chicago, because I could play horn parts with the horn section and I was the second keyboard player, and the second gui-tar player. But it was in a down time for them. It was the lowest period in their career. And actually Peter was going through a lot of changes about his own identity and wanting to do his own thing, so not long after I left, he left."

Following the stint with Chicago, Grebb was able to coordinate a schedule of performing on the road with Rick Danko, Bonnie Raitt, and Leon Russell. "Rick Danko was just putting out a solo album and going on the road to promote it, so he asked me to go help him do that. I was able to go between one person and the other, and the scheduling worked out. It hasn't ever been like that before or since." He continued his ses-sion work through succeeding decades, working with numerous distin-guished artists, including Maria Muldaur, Eric Clapton, Joe Walsh, David Sanborn, Rosanne Cash, Levon Helm, Willie Nelson, Stevie Nicks, and Otis Rush.

Grebb, a long-time admirer of Bob Dylan's songwriting genius, has numerous writing and co-writing credits of his own, including compo-sitions for the Fabulous Rhinestones and H.P. Lovecraft albums, and a song called "What a Wonderful Thing We Have" with Harvey Brooks. His admiration of the canon of Bob Dylan is unrestrained. "I think Bob Dylan is the most amazing living songwriter America has. He has changed the direction of music more than once because of that talent, and pointed the way for a lot of other artists to change their lyric writing."

Marty has two daughters and two stepdaughters from his 1983 marriage to Lyvonne (Lolli) Nadeau, a schoolteacher. His stepdaughters are Lee (born in 1970) and Bridget (born in 1972), and daughters with Lolli are Nikka (born in 1984) and Anna (born in 1986). The couple divorced in 2003.

Grebb's daughter Anna and his father, Harry, both performed on his 1999 album *Smooth Sailin'* on the Telarc label out of Cleveland. Anna sang with a choir on the album and his father played saxophone. Marty sings, plays piano, Hammond B-3 organ, saxophone, and guitar, accompanied by friends Bonnie Raitt, guitarists Taj Mahal, Steve Cropper and Amos Garrett, trumpet player Rick Braun and many other high-profile musicians. The 13 R&B-style tunes are all originals written or co-written by Grebb.

"My daughter Anna is pursuing a singing career and can be heard on YouTube under the name Anna Natasha Grebb. She was on tour a couple of years ago with a group called Chicago's Finest, which included ex-Chicago band members with her as the opening act," Grebb told us in 2012. She sang all of the high harmonies with Peter's brother Kenny Cetera, Chris Pinnick, myself, and a bass player that was with Tower of Power. We did the Chicago set list," said Grebb. "Anna always says to me, 'I wish I was born when you were,' because the music business is a lot tougher than it was when I started out."

From 2006 to 2009, Marty wrote and performed music for Fox TV. "They would tell me how many songs they wanted, and I would compose them and perform them. They would use the music in a lot of contexts, for example, Chicago Bears' games and some of the playoff games. They would also use my music for some of their TV shows. It was fun, but when the economy started getting bad, they cut my position and about 20 others in Fox Sports, the division I was in."

Marty Grebb's newest album, *High Steppin'*, produced by Grebb and released on Nashville's Luna Chica Records in 2011, is his "homage to American blues and R&B music." *High Steppin'* incorporates influences of searing "big city blues," Delta, and combo styles blues, along with a mix of New Orleans music to which he was exposed along the way. Grebb not only produced the project and wrote most of the songs on *High Steppin'*, but he also played all the instruments on the album. "*High Steppin'* started out as a challenge by my friend Leon Russell, who knows I'm a multi-instrumentalist because he used me as one in his band for a bunch of years. He said, 'Why don't you do your own record and play all the real instruments live – not the computer thing.' So I did, and I'm my own little big band," chuckled Grebb, who continues writing songs with Leon Russell and other artists he's producing. On the album, Grebb adroitly channels the soul of Ray Charles, Buddy Guy, Charles Brown, Eric Clapton, the Allman Brothers Band, Bobby "Blue" Bland, B.B. King and other blues luminaries.

Bonnie Raitt said this about Grebb and *High Steppin'*: "Marty has always been one of the most talented, soulful, and versatile artists I know. From our years playing together in my band, to his broad history playing on his own and with many of the greats, Marty is one of the very few musicians who can nail singing, keyboards, saxophone, guitar, bass, drums, songwriting and arranging with equal passion and authenticity. He's made another great, funky record in *High Steppin'*... terrific all the way around!"

Despite his musical legacy, Grebb humbly admits, "I hope to maintain gratitude for being able to play music. I feel at this point in my life the way I did when I originally started playing music, performing it live when I was 13 years old. Throughout the '70s and '80s that focus was lost because of the drug culture. I would call it the party aspect. The business for me became more multi-unfocused instead of multi-focused," he said. "If I could pass on anything that I've learned to up-and-coming kids that want to play music, it would be to impress upon them how important it is to stay as far away from drugs as they can, because that's not what it's about. I've seen it destroy so many careers and lives. And alcohol, too, for that matter, but primarily the drugs. I mean, how many have we lost?"

Check out Marty Grebb's website at **www.martygrebb.com** to learn more about his recordings.

Epilogue: John Poulos

Drummer, artist management

March 31, 1947 – March 26, 1980

"John grew up the youngest child in a family of proud Greek heritage. His olive complexion and bright eyes set him apart on stage," wrote Carl Giammarese in his forthcoming book, *Reinventing the Buckinghams: My Journey*. "He was insistent in wanting the Buckinghams to have 'a look' just as importantly as 'the sound' as dual components of who we were as a band. When John was around, we truly were a band of brothers, though none of us were related. His wild sense of humor made the long days on the road bearable, and his indefatigable spirit reminded us that optimism is a more powerful attitude than cynicism."

John Peter Poulos Jr. was born in Chicago on March 31, 1947, to Ann and John Poulos. When John was in the seventh grade, he and his family moved into an apartment building, where he met his lifelong friend Burton Jespersen, who told us, "John was the leader of the Buckinghams. It was John's vision. When we were kids, that's what he wanted to do – he wanted to be in rock 'n' roll. I remember one day he grabbed me around the neck and stuck an Elvis Presley album in my face, and said, 'That's where I'm going.'"

John Poulos in 1979 (photo courtesy of Dale Fahey)

John and Burton attended Grover Cleveland School on the northwest side of Chicago through the eighth grade, and then Albert G. Lane Technical College Preparatory High School (Lane Tech), where they shared the same music class – Burton played the clarinet and John played on practice pads in preparation for his drumming career. While John transferred and went on to graduate from Roosevelt High School in the Albany Park neighborhood of Chicago, Burton's family moved to Glendale, California, when he was

42

15. Jespersen recalled, "Women loved John. He was mister charisma. I'll never forget when he moved into our neighborhood, the local girls from our school were marching up the stairs to John's apartment on the third floor to introduce themselves to him. I was standing in the alley looking over the fence saying, 'What's this? Why doesn't this happen to me?'" he laughed. "John was a star before he was a star."

Dennis Tufano has fond memories of John. He told us, "John and I were best of friends from the very beginning. His energy and honesty bonded us together. We got together almost everyday to plan the evolution of the band. During some of those visits to his apartment his father, a vibrant Greek man with a strong connection to the practical as well as the spiritual, would sit me down and randomly choose a page from *Aesop's Fables*. From the aluminum foil homemade cover, to the ground-shaking information he would offer to me in a matter of minutes, he changed the scope of my future. I believe John had the same gift of love and insight."

Jespersen said that John got his nickname, Jon-Jon, from his high school sweetheart named Pet. Her death when she was no more than 18 years of age devastated John. "Pet was a real meaningful part of John's life. His mom had told me she was very important to him."

Jespersen's cousin "Jimmy" Guercio was bass player for Chad and Jeremy and subsequently became their manager. Guercio recruited Jespersen as road manager for Chad and Jeremy. When the Buckinghams decided they wanted to branch out and take a look at the L.A. music scene, John flew to California with Dennis Tufano and stayed with Burton's family in Glendale. "At the time, my cousin Jimmy had a partner named Garrick Ebbins, whose father was an agent for the William Morris office, and Jimmy and Gary had a little office space there. 'Kind of a Drag' had just been released by U.S.A. Records, and Dennis and John brought it with them. First I introduced them to Gary and he listened to their record. Jimmy was recording a friend with Chad at Whitney Recording Studio in Glendale, so we went over there and I introduced them to Jimmy. Later, we went to Sunset Strip and saw the Turtles at the Whisky. In those days it was like a $2 cover. I took them to Fred Segal to buy clothes, and Cher was in there getting fitted for some clothes. All the entertainers shopped there because they had the best mod clothes."

John took great pride in his drumming, and two of his musical influences were Hollies' drummer Bobby Elliott, and Ringo Starr. However, he had a distinctive style of his own. "John was a real powerful drummer, and his drumming was on all of the singles. They wanted that unique, signature Buckinghams' sound that John's style brought to their music."

43

After the Buckinghams disbanded in 1970, Jespersen went to work with John at John Poulos Management Company in Chicago. Their office was in a building owned by Chicago attorney Barry Fox. "He gave us office space and use of the telephones for John's advice," said Jespersen. Although Barry Fox was managing several bands, he depended on John because he didn't know as much about the music business as John did.

"John was brilliant. He was grass-roots, hands-on brilliant," said Jespersen. "I remember Barry coming in and saying, 'My band Kracker just came off the road and they have a bunch of original material, and I think it's time to get them a record deal. John, what do I do?' John reached over, picked up *Billboard* magazine, looked up who produced the top 10 albums, and he said, 'Here's *Sticky Fingers*. Rolling Stones' Jimmy Miller would be a great producer for Kracker.' We found out that Jimmy Miller had a production deal with Dunhill Records, and he was being represented by George Greif [New Christy Minstrels co-manager]. Barry called George Greif and, of course, Greif refused his call. So John said, 'Just keep calling. Find out his secretary's name. Send her flowers.' Barry kept calling, and finally George Greif got on the phone and said, 'Okay, Barry Fox from Chicago, what's on your mind? You've got 30 seconds.' Barry explained about Kracker as quick as he could, and Greif said, 'Okay. I want three first-class, round-trip tickets to Chicago. We'll come in Wednesday night and see your band.' So I picked up Jimmy Miller, George Greif and Bobby Whitlock [keyboardist for Derek and the Dominos]. We went to the club, saw the band, had dinner afterwards, and they signed and did two albums with Dunhill Records. Kracker ended up doing a European tour with the Rolling Stones. It was Barry's band, but John was responsible for all of that." As a result of all the time John spent on Kracker, he eventually became their manager.

Jespersen had been staying in Chicago with John, his wife, Dale, and their two children – she had a son from a previous marriage, and he and Dale had a daughter together. But after about five months in the artists management business, which wasn't turning a good profit for him, Burton returned to L.A. – just about the time John was negotiating to manage Dennis and Carl as a duo.

In 1971, John took Dennis and Carl's demo to L.A. and managed to get an appointment at Ode Records with Lou Adler, who had won Grammy awards that year with Carole King's *Tapestry* album and was managing Cheech and Chong.

"Everybody wanted to get in to see Lou Adler," said Jespersen, "and John had the knack and charisma to get in there. John said to Lou, 'Before we talk, let me play you a record.' So he put the record on and

Adler got up from his desk after about a minute of listening, he took the needle off the record and said to John, 'What do you want?' John said, 'First of all, I'd like you to fly Dennis and Carl out here and listen to all their material.' Lou flew them out, gave them a house in Hollywood Hills to stay in, got them in the studio, and they played their whole repertoire. Lou Adler was the one to change their name to Tufano and Giammarese. He thought he could market the name better."

John continued living in Chicago and managing bands until his shocking death on March 26, 1980 – five days shy of turning 33. One of the bands he managed and promoted was The Boyzz from Illinoizz, which is still performing in concert, reunited by original member Michael Tafoya.

"John had a heart murmur, and he shouldn't have been doing all the things he did, like smoking and drinking," said Jespersen, "and he was always going 100 miles per hour. No one could keep up with him. He always had a pack of cigarettes in his pocket and one in his hand, and he was always playing with his lighter."

Tufano recalls, "Finishing a show out in the suburbs of Chicago, John and I would scramble to tear down our equipment and jump into his Chevy and race back to the city. We would get back to his apartment and run all his drums up three flights of stairs and change our clothes, blow dry our hair and head downtown to Rush Street to hear some local music and, hopefully, meet some girls. I miss John and the friendship we had, but every once in awhile when I'm performing I could swear that Jon-Jon Poulos was back there playing right along with me, shooting me that big Jon-Jon smile, just like the old days." He concluded, "Thank you, John. We made it, thanks to you!"

Carl Giammarese wrote in his memorial to Poulos, "John's greatest dream, unfulfilled from 1970, when we broke up, until August 1980, when Dennis, Nick, and I reunited for ChicagoFest, was to get the band back together at least one more time. John died only five months before his dream for us came true."

Photo courtesy of Bobby Goldsboro

ON AIR

CHAPTER
2

Autumn of My Life
Bobby Goldsboro

In an era when many performers relied on the cadre of prolific songwriters in New York's Brill Building to compose material, some singers began defying convention by writing their own songs to record. At the vanguard of that singer-songwriter movement in the late 1950s and early 1960s were Carl Perkins, Buddy Holly, Paul Anka, Roy Orbison, and Bob Dylan. Their ranks also included Sam Cooke, Jackie DeShannon, Neil Sedaka, and Bobby Goldsboro.

"I've always been fortunate to be at the right place at the right time," says Goldsboro, whose 26 *Billboard* Hot 100 hits span from 1961 to 1973. His first lucky break came in 1961, when he and his fellow musicians in a band called the Webs were invited to finish a tour with the legendary Roy Orbison, who had fired his band for drinking on the job. Bobby Goldsboro would go on to spend three years traveling the world with Orbison, and accompanied him in Europe on a performance tour with a "new group" called the Beatles.

Goldsboro recalls, "At the time, Orbison was allowed to bring only one American musician to Europe, because the Americans were over-running the musicians over there and a lot of them were out of work. So he took me with him. By the time we got there for the concert tour, the Beatles had become the biggest thing in the world," he said.

Orbison originally was supposed to close the European shows as the headliner, but the Beatles had become so popular that promoters didn't know who would close the show. They finally decided that Roy would close the first half preceding intermission, and the Beatles would close the second half of the show. "Roy had never been to England," said Bobby, "and he was second only to Elvis Presley at the time. It was just pandemonium every night, because you couldn't hear anything over the screaming. They wouldn't let Roy off the stage. He would do two or three encores before the Beatles came out."

Bobby first joined the Webs as he entered his senior year of high school in Dothan, Alabama, in the autumn of 1958. The Webs performed rock and rhythm and blues music at sorority and fraternity parties in the area, and clubs and beer joints in Panama City Beach, Florida. The band consisted of lead guitarist and lead singer John Rainey Adkins, bass player Amos Tyndall, drummer Dave Robinson (later replaced by Paul Garrison), and Bobby, who sang and played guitar. They dressed in suits and ties with spider stickpins, and all except Tyndall wore eyeglasses similar to Buddy Holly's specs. Bobby remained with the band even after he entered Auburn University in 1959. The Webs were good – talented enough to land a deal with Heart Records, a small Birmingham label. The band recorded a couple of tunes, which the label released in 1961 as singles – "Dizzy Boy," which Bobby wrote, and "Lost (Cricket in My Ear")," with Adkins mimicking cricket sounds and Bobby performing his later-famous tree frog imitation. During the summer of 1961, a local concert promoter booked an appearance by Roy Orbison, who had just fired his touring band and needed another one. By that time Orbison had been recording for five years, and was touring on the strength of several hits, including the No. 2 hit "Only the Lonely (Know How I Feel)," "Blue Angel," "I'm Hurtin'" and the No. 1 hit "Running Scared," as his next hit, "Crying," was climbing the charts. Buddy Buie, a high school friend of Bobby's, told Orbison he knew of a good replacement backup band.

"He called and wanted to know if the Webs would like to work with Orbison," said Bobby, "and I'm thinking, 'Are you kidding me?' It wasn't that we were that good, it was just that we were the only band around." The band members bought a stack of Roy Orbison records and studied them. "We learned his songs the best we could, and we played four nights with him in Ozark, Alabama; Pensacola, Florida; Montgomery, Alabama; and Panama City, Florida. We really hit it off with him, so after the four dates, he asked us if we'd like to go on the road as his band. We happened to be in the right place at the right time." (Buie became Orbison's tour manager, subsequently established himself as a songwriter, then as a producer worked with B.J. Thomas, Tommy Roe, Billy Joe Royal and the Classics IV before forming the Atlanta Rhythm Section.)

Many stories have been told about why Roy Orbison wore his signature dark glasses, and Bobby happened to be with Roy when the transformation began. "We were playing in Duluth, Minnesota, and had been out on the road for about 10 days. My band was in a 1955 Chevy, pulling all of the equipment in a U-Haul trailer, and Roy would fly to the dates. We became really good friends, so Roy had me travel with him on the plane so he'd have someone to travel with. We flew from Washington, D.C., to Duluth, Minnesota, and Roy took off his regular glasses and put them in the seat pouch in front of him and put his sunglasses on. When we got to the concert and started rehearsing, Roy started looking around for his glasses, and I remembered he had never taken them out of the seat pocket of the plane. It was too late by then, so he had to wear those sunglasses day and night. After the first night, he came back and said, 'You know, I like wearing these sunglasses, because people can't see where I'm looking.' So he started wearing them and it became a thing with him. People would ask me, 'I know you were with Orbison, when did he start going blind?' Roy could see better than I could at the time."

Bobby's first studio recording was made in Birmingham, Alabama, while he was attending Auburn University, majoring in business administration. "The tapes were sent to a New York producer named Jack Gold, who heard the songs and signed me to a recording contract [with Laurie Records]. However, I didn't hear back from him for a year, so I figured he forgot about it," said Bobby. "He finally called and said he found a song for me called 'Molly,' which was about a soldier who came back from the war blind, and he could no longer see his son. So Jack brought me to New York, and I recorded the song just before going on tour with Orbison. In 1962, we were playing Houston, Texas, with Orbison and after every song the audience was chanting, and I couldn't make it out. Finally, Roy figured out they were saying *Molly*. 'Molly' had become No. 1 in Houston at the time. So he asked me, 'You want to sing it?' I said, 'Are you kidding me?' I didn't even know the lyrics to it. After the show, we went backstage and a disc jockey said, 'We didn't realize that you're with Orbison, and you've got the No. 1 hit in Houston.' I babbled my way out of it to keep from having to get up and sing it, because I never sang it live." Molly appeared on the *Billboard* Hot 100 at No. 96 on December 22, 1962, when the instrumental "Telstar" by the Tornadoes was No 1.

The success of the gently rocking ballad "Molly" opened doors for Goldsboro's solo career. After producer Jack Gold mailed three song suggestions for him to record in New York, Bobby decided he could write his own that would be better suited to his style and voice. "I wrote 'See the Funny Little Clown' out of necessity," Goldsboro told us in December 2011. Upon arriving in New York, Bobby played it for Gold, who said he could record it if they had time. "We had a three-hour recording session in the studio, and we tried to get three to four songs done. We had 15 minutes left when we finished the third song, and I asked, 'Can we do "Funny Little Clown"?' Jack said okay. We cut it twice and the second take was the one that became my first big record." Even though the release of "See the Funny Little Clown" coincided with the first shock wave of Beatlemania, it broke onto the charts on January 11, 1964, rose to No. 9, and impressively remained on the *Billboard* Hot 100 for 13 weeks.

Jack Gold had started as an independent producer for Laurie Records but by the time "See the Funny Little Clown" had taken off, he had been named head of A&R for United Artists Records, which he persuaded to buy Bobby's contract. United Artists would go on to release the rest of Bobby's hits.

Bobby describes his early recording sessions at Bell Sound Studios on W. 54th Street in New York. "We did the first three singles and the first album in New York, and I was never comfortable up there because most musicians came in with a coat and tie, and they were smoking pipes and reading the *Wall Street Journal*. When it came time to record, they would put down the *Wall Street Journal* and open up their music and start play-ing. I had been to some sessions in Nashville with Orbison, and it was totally different. Everybody was laid back and throwing ideas around. Here I was from Alabama and Florida, and these New York guys played with Sinatra and people like that, and I'm afraid to speak," he said. "I'll never forget we were doing this little rhythm thing that I had written, called 'If You Got a Heart,' and the guy was playing the notes that were written, but it sounded really stiff. I said, 'Can you bend it a little bit and make it sound like this?' He looked up and said, 'Why don't you play it then?' He might as well have slapped me, because I said, 'Oh, no. What you're doing is great,' and I walked over and got in my corner and didn't say anything else. After that, I convinced Jack Gold to go to Nashville to record, and I started playing on all my own songs. That's where we cut from then on."

While Bobby's 1964 hits "See the Funny Little Clown" and the fol-low-up release, "Whenever He Holds You," were both tender ballads, in 1965 he broke out of that mold with two strong rockers that he wrote: "Little Things" and "Voodoo Woman," both of which were arranged and conducted by Bill Justis. Bobby explained, "Most of my albums had more up-tempo things than ballads, but because of the fact that I had a hit with 'See the Funny Little Clown,' my producer, Jack Gold, said we've got to come up with another ballad. He didn't want to record 'Little Things' or 'Voodoo Woman,' or 'It's Too Late' [another foot-tapping tune]. He wanted ballads. Jack could hear a great song and say, 'That can be a hit.' But if it was a rhythm song that had a lot of things going on in it, he didn't hear it. So, I had to convince him to cut the uptempo things."

Goldsboro admits that the drumming and beat in "Little Things" were reminiscent of Roy Orbison's 1964 hit "Pretty Woman." Bobby originally had written a 2/4 drum beat for "Little Things," but when he heard Orbison's "Pretty Woman" on the radio he asked him if he could use the 4/4 beat, and Orbison gave him thumbs up. "The timing has been so important in my life in everything I've done," said Bobby. "Just like had Roy not come up with that record when he did, 'Little Things' may not have happened. All these things work together, and I've just been fortunate to be at the right place at the right time."

In the autumn of 1965, as U.S. involvement in the Vietnam War sharply escalated, United Artists released a Bobby Goldsboro ballad with a message that made some radio programmers uncomfortable and hesitant to play it. The broadcasters had misinterpreted Bobby's intentions, however. Sung from the perspective of a father watching his young son romping with a broomstick toy horse, the lullaby-like song prophesied the boy's maturation into a man who would be enlisted by his country to go to war and to learn to kill. Radio programmers thought Bobby had joined the emerging chorus of singers, including Barry McGuire, Tom Paxton, Phil Ochs, and Bob Dylan, who were raising their voices in protest of the war in Vietnam. "I wrote 'Broomstick Cowboy' as a poem," Bobby told us in December 2011. "I walked in and looked at my 6-month-old son lying there and I was thinking about what a 6-month-old baby might be dreaming about. Every parent probably goes through this – you hope your son doesn't have to grow up and go to war. So, basically, that's what I said in the song. When the record came out, though, radio station programmers thought it was a protest song and wouldn't play it. It was actually just the opposite, saying you've got to go to war and fight for your country."

By 1967 Goldsboro had 13 *Billboard* Hot 100 hits to his credit when his friend Larry Henley from the Newbeats stopped by his apartment and asked him to walk across the street to the Acuff-Rose Music publishing company to listen to a new song called "Honey" that Bobby Russell had written. While Goldsboro liked the song, he felt that the demo version was overproduced in that the drums drowned out the vocals. A few weeks later when Goldsboro was contemplating songs to record for a new album, he remembered Russell's song and asked him to play it for him again. This time Russell sang it like a ballad, and Bobby liked it and wanted to record it.

"We recorded it and after the first take, the musicians came into the control room to listen to the playback. I'd never seen them do that. They're standing there looking like 'I don't believe this.' I said, 'Man, I think we just cut a monster here.' We called Bobby Russell from the studio and said, 'I think we just cut a No. 1 record with this thing.' He said, 'Well, [Kingston Trio member] Bob Shane's record just came out. Can you give us two weeks, and if it doesn't really take off, you can come out with yours.' We could have released it at the same time, but we called the record company in New York the next day and asked Jack Gold if they could have it ready to release in two weeks. So two weeks to the day, they released my version of 'Honey' and, fortunately, I had the hit with it. I really believe if Bob Shane had sung my version, and I sang his, he would have had the hit. My version had a great arrangement that Don Tweedy wrote. He was as much responsible for it as I was." The record also benefited from its production by Bob Montgomery, who co-wrote Buddy Holly's tunes "Heartbeat" and "Love's Made a Fool of You," and wrote Patsy Cline's "Back in Baby's Arms." Goldsboro's version of "Honey" burst not only onto the pop charts in late March 1968, but also established him as a country music performer. On April 13, "Honey" knocked Otis Redding's "(Sittin' on) the Dock of the Bay" from the No. 1 position on the Hot 100, remained in the top spot for five consecutive weeks, and was on the pop chart for nearly four months. It also topped the country and adult contemporary charts, was No. 1 in Canada, and hit No. 2 in the United Kingdom. The Recording Industry Association of America (RIAA) awarded a gold record for the single "Honey" in April 1968, and certified Bobby's *Honey* album as gold that November.

In 1970, Goldsboro's timing again couldn't have been more perfect. While in a clothing store in L.A., Bobby ran into his friend Jerry Fuller, a singer, songwriter, and record producer, who wrote hits for Ricky Nelson, Gary Puckett and the Union Gap, Reba McEntire, John Conlee, Al Wilson, Tom Jones, and many other popular performers. Fuller told Bobby that Mac Davis had written a song called "Watching Scotty Grow" about his own son. Davis had asked Fuller to pitch the song to Andy Williams, whose recordings he had been producing at the time. Fuller didn't think the song was right for Williams, but thought Bobby might like the song and gave him Mac's telephone number.

"I went back to my hotel and called Mac, and he came over and we sat there and played songs for four hours," said Bobby. "I asked him to play the song that Jerry told me about, 'Watching Scotty Grow.' When he finished playing it, I jokingly asked, 'Can I cut it and name it 'Watching Danny Grow' after my own son? Mac laughed and said, 'I'd love for you to cut it, but if you don't say "Scotty," I can't go home.' On stage, Mac still says today that Scotty thinks *I'm* his father. I've been blessed with timing my whole career."

After scoring hit after major hit throughout the '60s, Bobby moved to TV in 1973 to host the nationally syndicated *Bobby Goldsboro Show,* which ran for three successful seasons and became the highest rated variety show in syndication in the 1970s. His quick wit made him a much sought-after guest on the TV talk show circuit, as well. He made guest appearances on the *Ed Sullivan Show,* the *Dean Martin Comedy Hour,* the *Tonight Show Starring Johnny Carson,* the *David Frost Show,* the *Hollywood Palace,* the *Johnny Cash Show,* the *Jim Nabors Hour, Donahue, Hee Haw,* the *Hollywood Squares* and the *Mike Douglas Show.*

Bobby's last major musical hit came in the summer of 1973. "Summer (the First Time)" is a beautifully orchestrated song that tells a story about a young man's "coming of age," somewhat reminiscent of a 1971 movie called *Summer of '42.* Recalls Bobby, "I started writing that song when I was doing some promotion for my TV show. I had flown to San Francisco with a 12-string guitar because they wanted me to do all these promos for their new fall lineup. I was riding in a limo with the windows up, so I took out the 12-string, and I just automatically started playing the opening of the guitar part. The song just started coming to me, and I got into it. I had it about half written when we got to the TV studio. I couldn't wait to get through with the promo so I could get back to the hotel and write the song," he said.

"This was the only time in my entire recording career that everything that I heard in my head, I've got on the record. I got every string line, every bass line, except for the piano part – that was my piano player, Tim Tappan. The next night I was standing backstage right before they're about to announce me as a guest on the *Tonight Show,* and I said to Tim, 'I've got to play you this song when we get through with the show.' I hummed a few lines for him, he played a few notes, and I said, 'Don't forget that!' So after the show, I asked him if he remembered the lick, and he played it for me." The recurring piano cadence indelibly imbued the song in a wistful mood. "During the next commercial, we went over it, and I said, 'That's the clincher, that's the killer.' Once we had it recorded, I thought, 'This is the best record I may ever make in my life.' I flew out to L.A. with it and played it for the head of the record company. When it was over, he said, 'I love it. First thing we'll do is to take out that intro, take out the instrumental in the middle, and we'll cut it down to under three minutes.' I said, 'No! Wait!' He said, 'It's too long, it's four minutes long, and nobody will play it.' I said, 'If I gave you a novel, and you said it's the greatest book you ever read, would you take out chapter 1 and chapter 11 to make the book shorter? The same thing with this song; you've got to set it up with the ocean and the seagulls to get the mood set, and the instrumental is the release of the whole song.' I finally convinced him to keep it like it was," said Goldsboro, who shared arrangement credits with Tappan and production credits with Bob Montgomery. "When I look back on my recordings now, 'Honey' was the most successful song I ever recorded, but I think the best recording I ever made was 'Summer (the First Time).'"

After his TV series completed its run, Bobby formed House of Gold Music, which became one of the most successful music publishing companies in Nashville, with a catalog that includes "Wind Beneath My Wings" (which Bobby's friend Larry Henley co-wrote) and "Behind Closed Doors." Bobby Goldsboro, the songwriter, has received 27 BMI (Broadcast Music Inc.) awards, and his compositions have been recorded by Aretha Franklin, John Denver, Paul Anka, Dolly Parton, Johnny Cash, Dr. John, Conway Twitty, and Bette Midler. Two of Bobby's compositions, "Autumn of My Life" and "With Pen in Hand" (which Vikki Carr, Della Reese, Aretha Franklin, Conway Twitty, Dinah Shore and more than 60 other singers recorded) qualified for the BMI music licensing organization's Million-Air Award, which distinguishes songs that have been played on the air more than one million times. Bobby's classic composition "Summer (the First Time)," which was more popular in England and Australia than in America, was recently voted the greatest summer song ever by the U.K. public. Over the course of his career he recorded 25 albums, not counting "greatest hits" compilations.

In the mid-'80s Bobby began to devote more time to writing and producing children's entertainment, including a number of audiobooks and television specials. His first effort, *Easter Egg Mornin'*, premiered as an animated Easter special in 1991 on the Disney Channel. The special quickly reached "gold" status in sales and has been the Disney Channel's top Easter special for more than a decade. Concurrently, he scored the music for the CBS TV series *Evening Shade*, and in 1995 launched the children's series *The Swamp Critters of Lost Lagoon*, for which he has written and performed (in assorted voices) more than 100 new songs. He was inducted into the Alabama Music Hall of Fame in 1999, along with the Temptations, Wilson Pickett and keyboard player, songwriter and producer David Briggs.

In 2006 at the age of 65, Bobby began a new career as a nature artist, painting in oils. He continues to perform several concerts a year and often includes gallery showings of his exquisite works of art.

Visit **www.bobbygoldsboro.com** for more information.

U.S. HIT SINGLES BY BOBBY GOLDSBORO

Debut	Peak	Gold	Title	Label
12/62	70		Molly	Laurie
1/64	9		See the Funny Little Clown	United Artists
4/64	39		Whenever He Holds You	United Artists
8/64	74		Me Japanese Boy, I Love You	United Artists
1/65	13		Little Things	United Artists
5/65	27		Voodoo Woman	United Artists
8/65	75		If You Wait for Love	United Artists
9/65	60		If You've Got a Heart	United Artists
12/65	53		Broomstick Cowboy	United Artists
2/66	23		It's Too Late	United Artists
5/66	56		I Know You Better Than That	United Artists
9/66	70		It Hurts Me	United Artists
12/66	35		Blue Autumn	United Artists
3/68	1	Δ	Honey	United Artists
6/68	19		Autumn of My Life	United Artists
10/68	36		The Straight Life	United Artists
2/69	61		Glad She's a Woman	United Artists
4/69	46		I'm a Drifter	United Artists
8/69	53		Muddy Mississippi Line	United Artists
1/70	78		Mornin' Mornin'	United Artists
4/70	75		Can You Feel It	United Artists
12/70	11		Watching Scotty Grow	United Artists
5/71	83		And I Love You So	United Artists
7/71	69		Come Back Home	United Artists
/72	94		With Pen in Hand	United Artists
8/73	21		Summer (the First Time)	United Artists

Δ symbol: RIAA certified gold record (Recording Industry Association of America)

Billboard's pop singles chart data is courtesy of Joel Whitburn's Record Research Inc. (www.recordresearch.com), Menomonee Falls, Wisconsin

EPILOGUE: BOBBY GOLDSBORO
Singer, songwriter, guitarist, publisher, fine artist

Fans of Bobby Goldsboro know about his impression of a Southern tree frog. "I started doing it back in the seventh grade. I would spook all the teachers and everybody would laugh," said Bobby. "I did it on the *Tonight Show Starring Johnny Carson* when he was still in New York. He'd be asking me questions, and I'd do the frog sound and then I would answer the question. He would be looking around. Finally, after two or three times, Johnny said, 'I hate to interrupt you but there's a cricket or frog or something in here,' and the audience just starts laughing. Then I told him it was me."

Bobby and his wife, Diane (photo courtesy of Bobby Goldsboro)

Bobby Goldsboro

Born on January 18, 1941, to Charles and Nell Goldsborough in the small town of Marianna, Florida, Bobby spent his elementary and junior high school years in Marianna. He and his brother, Jimmy (a year and a half older), decided to drop the "ugh" ending from Goldsborough because their teachers kept mispronouncing it.

Marianna, Florida, in the Panhandle near the borders of Georgia and Alabama, is a small town with a current population of 6,200. "It was a great place to grow up. You read about how it used to be when nobody had to lock their doors and kids could go out and play until after dark and you never had to worry," said Bobby. "Everybody knew everybody and it was like one big family. For the first four years of school, I sat in the front row and had no problem," said Bobby, who hadn't realized he was nearsighted. "In the fifth year, somebody moved to town and I was moved to the back row. I thought everybody could see the same way I could. I remember taking a test after that and the teacher said that during recess, if you wanted to keep working on the test you could stay in. Everybody went out to recess except me, and I moved up to the front row and started answering all of the questions. The teacher came over and asked, 'How did you all of the sudden get so smart?' I said, 'Well, you can't see the blackboard from back there.' So she called my parents and they took me to the eye doctor, and he said there were people on blind pensions who could see better than me. So I ended up getting glasses." Bobby began wearing hard plastic contact lenses while touring with Roy Orbison, and in 2004 he underwent LASIK corrective surgery. "It's been a godsend because up until then, I'd wake up in the middle of the night and look at the clock, and I couldn't see what time it was."

Bobby's introduction to playing music occurred when he was about 9 years old. "I remember my best friend had gotten a plastic ukulele for Christmas, and it had an Arthur Godfrey uke player on it. It was a little plastic thing that had about five chords. You would push a button for C and something underneath would mash the strings. So while my friend was eating breakfast, I picked up the ukulele and there was a little songbook with it. The first song was 'Are You From Dixie,' and it said G, so I pushed the thing and strummed. Then it said, go to C. So I was getting into the rhythm of it and I sang the song. When I looked up, the four of them were standing in the doorway, and my friend's mother said, 'Bobby, I didn't know you could play one of those.' And I said, 'I didn't either.' So over the next few weeks I tried to show him how to play it, but he didn't have any rhythm and got frustrated. He said, 'Why don't you take that thing home with you? I can't play it.' So I took it home and looked to see what strings the little device was mashing, and I took it off and didn't need the little uke player anymore."

Bobby's aunt Wilhelmina ("Willie") had helped his father open a flower shop in Marianna, and when she died in 1955, she left her florist business 35 miles north in Dothan, Alabama, to Bobby's parents. Bobby recalls, "I was in the ninth grade when we moved to the big city of Dothan. I hated it at first because I didn't know anybody, and we were already six weeks into the school year. In Marianna, you didn't take algebra until the 10th grade, but in Dothan, you took algebra in the 9th grade, so I was six weeks behind everybody. They were all working problems like a foot long, and I didn't even know what 'X' was. A friend of mine would let me copy his paper because I was so lost. So I said, "Next year, I'm really going to study – I'm going to learn this," but they put me in second-year algebra, and I still didn't know first year. Luckily, my friend was in the same class and helped me out again."

Bobby continued playing the ukulele for a hobby until the summer before his senior year of high school in Dothan. "That's when my parents got me a guitar. For the first six months, I only played the last four strings – like you'd play a ukulele. I got a guitar book and the first page said everyplace you see a black dot, you mash the strings there. I saw seven dots, and I thought, I only have five fingers. I realized you could mash all six strings with one finger as a bar chord. So I threw away the book and just learned them myself," Bobby said. He got a job and earned enough money to buy a tape recorder so he could listen to his own playing and thereby improve his rhythm guitar technique.

Bobby also was passionate about baseball, which he played throughout his youth in Little League, PONY League and on school teams. An ardent Cleveland Indians fan, he had dreamed of a career not as a musician but as an infielder or pitcher in the major leagues. At Dothan High School, he gained greater recognition for his talent on the frets more quickly than for his skills on the baseball diamond.

"In the school cafeteria one day, this guy walked up to the guys in the Webs and said, 'Bobby Goldsboro can play better than any of y'all on the guitar,' and he walked off. So that afternoon, the guitar player for the band called me and asked if I wanted to come over and play guitar," Bobby recalled. "So I went over there and they were working on 'Poor Little Fool' by Rick Nelson, and they couldn't find the chords. So I showed them, and they said 'how did you know that?' I said, 'Well you can hear it on the radio.' They were all really good musicians, but they couldn't play by ear." Impressed, Webs guitarist and lead singer John Rainey Adkins asked Goldsboro to sit in with the band at a gig. "They were playing a little dive dance place out on the outskirts of town, and I sat in with them and made $10. After that, I started working with them more and more, and during rehearsal one day, John couldn't remember the words to 'Poor Little Fool,' so I started singing it and he said, 'You sound kind of like Rick Nelson, so why don't you sing it?' I didn't want to sing – I just wanted to play guitar. But they talked me into singing about three dates later, and I finally got used to singing. The Webs were all really good guys."

Bobby graduated from Dothan High School in 1959 and reluctantly enrolled in Auburn University, 120 miles north, with a business major, only because that's what his older brother had done. "I didn't really like it up there, but the Webs started playing all of the college fraternity and sorority parties and we were making really good money. I remember one weekend, we played an afternoon at a sorority, that evening at a fraternity, and the next day, Saturday, we did an afternoon and then another show that night, and the same thing on Sunday. We did six shows and we were making $100 apiece per night, and my tuition was paid. I was living it up," Bobby laughed. He left Auburn after two years to pursue a full-time musical career with Roy Orbison. Goldsboro recalls, "My father was not at all pleased about it, but I said, 'Listen, this is a chance to go on the road with one of the greatest artists out there. Let me just stay out for a year and do this, and if nothing happens, I'll go back to Auburn.' So he finally said okay. We had made some tapes [at a recording studio] up in Birmingham, Alabama, while I was still going to Auburn, and some of the tapes were sent to New York. A guy named Jack Gold heard the songs and had come down and actually signed me to a recording contract – probably two or three weeks before Orbison came through. He said he was going to find a hit song and bring it to New York and record me. I couldn't believe it. I'd never been to New York. Then I didn't hear from him for a year, and I figured he forgot all about it. But then he sent me a song called 'Molly' that he wanted me to record. When I first looked at the lyrics, it said, 'The war began and Henry left his farm,' and I'm thinking 'Henry, that's not a very poetic name.' But the song was about a soldier coming back from the war and he was blind and he couldn't see his son, and it had a recitation in it. My voice is deeper than it was back then. I sounded like I was about 9 years old, and I hated the song, but I couldn't tell him because he was a New York record producer and he knows his songs. So he brought me to New York, and I recorded it and it actually got into the 'bubbling under' section of the Hot 100 when I was with Orbison."

While touring with Orbison, Bobby became a married man at 21 years of age. In Panama City Beach, Florida, at a performance with the Webs in 1960, Bobby met Mary Alice Watson, whom he dated for two years. Bobby and Mary Alice married in Dothan on November 11, 1962, a few months after her graduation from high school. Bobby had an apartment in Nashville, so the family traveled back and forth between there and Dothan as they began raising their family of three children: Danny, Terri and Brandy. After "Honey" became a hit, the couple bought a ranch home outside of Nashville.

Bobby's determination to write his own music led to his succession of hits. He describes the inspiration for the songs he writes. "The guitar lick for 'See the Funny Little Clown' just came to me. I don't think any songwriter can explain where a song comes from. I may be driving in the car and get an idea for a song. By the time I finish the song, I have the whole arrangement done. A lot of times I'll phrase a certain line in a song around a violin line, and that violin line to me is part of the song, not just part of the arrangement."

While Bobby's TV exposure initially was limited to teen-oriented music shows – including *Shindig, Hullaballoo* and the British program *Ready, Steady, Go* – the success of "Honey" propelled him to the guest lists of numerous family-oriented variety shows. Bobby's ease in front of the camera encouraged Mike Douglas to enlist him as co-host for a week-long run of his daily variety show. Those and other television appearances prompted a Nashville production company to sign Bobby in 1973 to host his own syndicated TV variety series at CBS studios in Hollywood, with the same sound stage and crew that were used for the *Sonny and Cher Comedy Hour.* "Right away I was intrigued about it, but I said, 'As long as I don't become a young Ed Sullivan and bring out four or five acts a show.' I wanted to have one guest who would do a couple of songs, I would get to do a couple of things, and in the end I would get to sing with the guest," said Bobby. "It took a while to line up the guests because, at the time, most musical acts wouldn't do a television show unless it was lip-synced because they'd spend weeks in the studio to get a 'sound' and you only had about 10 minutes to do a sound check and you were on the air. As a result, a lot of them wouldn't perform live on TV. I decided, if we're going to do this we'll cut the tracks using the same arrangement, same musicianship, everything that they have on the record, and we'll cut all the tracks in Nashville with all the best pickers around and do them exactly like the record. They would sing live to those pre-recorded tracks on the show. We spent as much time during the year in the studio recording Seals and Crofts tracks, Mac Davis, and Kenny Rogers, whoever was on the show, and all of the sudden we were getting performers on our show who hadn't been doing TV because they knew we were taking pains to get the music right. Sonny and Cher would film Monday,

Wednesday and Friday, and we filmed Tuesday, Thursday, and Saturday."
The 30-minute *Bobby Goldsboro Show,* which also included comedy segments, ran for three successful seasons, and became the highest-rated
variety show in syndication during the seventies.

By the time the TV show left the air, Bobby wanted to devote more
attention to another interest: music publishing. He had formed House
of Gold Music with singer, songwriter and music producer Bob Montgomery, who had co-written some of Buddy Holly's songs and produced
many of Goldsboro's hits, including "Summer (the First Time)."

"I was playing in Las Vegas and a guy came backstage and said,
'There's a Kenny O'Dell outside who wants to know if he can come
backstage.'" O'Dell had recorded a top-40 hit called "Beautiful People"
in late 1967, and wrote "Next Plane to London," a 1967 hit for the Rose
Garden. "We hit it off right away and Kenny told me that he and his family were thinking about moving to Nashville and he was looking for a
publishing company. I said, 'We'd love to have you write for us.' So we
helped him find a place in Nashville and probably within three months,
he wrote 'Behind Closed Doors' for us. Another hit that we published
was 'Wind Beneath My Wings' (written in 1982 by Jeff Silbar and Larry
Henley). We had some very successful songs with the publishing company, before we sold it to Warner Bros."

By the early '80s, Bobby's 20-year marriage was foundering. He
and Mary Alice had gradually grown apart as they matured. The couple
divorced in 1982. Bobby moved to Central Florida near the Ocala
National Forest, where he bought 120 acres of land along the shore of a
lake and built a home. He took up bass fishing and lived in quiet reflection as he continued writing songs. Single life didn't suit Bobby, who
admits that he's not a good cook. "I was eating out of a can or eating out
all of the time," he told us in December 2011. Bobby's bass fishing inad-
vertently led to a chance meeting with Diane Roberts, the woman who
would become the love of his life.

"I met Diane when she was working with her mother at a camp-
ground at the Ocala National Forest. My place was about 10 minutes
from where she was. I went down to this little store to look around and
see what kind of lures they were using, and when I walked out and saw
her sitting on the front steps, I thought, 'Wow.' She was looking at the
Bible, and I found out later that she was looking at the pictures because
she couldn't read. She left school in the ninth grade because she has dys-
lexia, and nobody knew what that was when she was in school." They
began dating, and the connection between them grew. They married in
1984. "I taught her to drive a car at 23. She's probably one of the smart-

est people I've met in my life. If you dropped a watch and it busted into 50 pieces, she could put it back together."

Diane was born in Lawrence, Massachusetts, with spina bifida, a condition in which incomplete closure of the backbone leaves part of the spinal cord exposed. It can result in paralysis, brain disorders, and other neurological problems. She was known as the "miracle baby," because the doctors had pretty much given up and sent her home to die. A representative from Easter Seals had heard about Diane and asked her mother if they could try an experimental operation on her. While her mom couldn't afford the surgery, Easter Seals paid for everything and saved her life.

"There were about 19 babies born in that area with spina bifida and they tried all these operations on them, and my wife is the only one it worked on," said Bobby. "To this day, when she gets an X-ray of her back, the base of her spine, which is supposed to be closed off, is open. I remember the doctor looking at it and saying, 'And you walked in here?' She's the most amazing person I've ever met in my life."

During the 1990s, Bobby decided to try his hand at children's television production. He had written his first children's book in 1969 – a story called *Snuffy the Elf Who Saved Christmas* that he had made up for his children on a road trip between Alabama and Nashville. He wrote it down and thought one day he might produce it as a TV show. "I found a great cartoonist in Texas. I could start talking about a character and he'd already be drawing him. He could get into my head like nobody else ever could. So we came up with all these characters, and I decided the first show I wanted to do was *Easter Egg Morning*. I started sending out the script, character drawings and music to video companies. They knew my reputation as a singer and musician, but they were skeptical about my ability to produce a children's show. So I decided to put my own money into it, and I produced *Easter Egg Morning*. When I finished, I took it to the Disney Channel. They loved it, and it ran for 11 years. A video company bought all the rights to that one and three more, and after I finished the fourth one, I said, 'The only problem with these things is you have to send it off to animators in China or Taiwan and you don't see anything for six weeks and when it comes back, you hope it's like you pictured in your head, and it's not because you're on a time schedule. So I decided I wanted to do a show that I can do live, and I can see exactly what I'm getting, so I came up with the concept for the *Swamp Critters of Lost Lagoon*."

PBS, The Learning Channel, America One Network, Dish Network, and Sky Angel broadcast *The Swamp Critters of Lost Lagoon*, which touches on important issues such as pollution, cooperation, and prejudice. The show features animal characters with computer-controlled mouth movements produced to a variety of music styles, including blues, rock and roll, country, Dixieland, Cajun, and even a bit of classical. The characters include "Ribbit E. Lee," Bobby's tree frog. "He's a Southern frog," Bobby chuckles. Each episode teaches value-centered lessons in self-esteem and decision-making. Bobby wrote the scripts, wrote and arranged all of the music, played all of the instruments, and performed all of the character voices. "I ended up writing 52 half-hour episodes, and four or five original songs for every show," said Bobby, who also produced a live *Swamp Critters* show that played extended engagements at Jazzland theme park in New Orleans, Silver Springs theme park in Florida, and the South Florida Fair. "It took me seven years to complete the whole series."

While in Tampa editing one of his animated shows, Bobby ran into his old friend Burt Reynolds, who was filming a movie there. Burt asked Bobby if he would write a theme song for the show *Evening Shade*, which was in its third year of production. "I wrote the *Evening Shade* theme song, and Burt and the show's producers Harry Thomason and Linda Bloodworth-Thomason asked me if I would to do all of the music for *Evening Shade* – the backgrounds, the play-offs, the play-ons. I said, 'I've never done anything like that,' and Burt said, 'I know you can do it.' So Burt and I formed a production company, and Diane and I moved to L.A., and I did all the music for *Evening Shade* for the next two years. It got to be where I could do a show in about 30 minutes, and I'd have a whole show done and the rest of the week I could do what I wanted to do. I would write *Swamp Critters* shows the rest of the week."

While working on *Evening Shade,* Burt asked Bobby to produce music for an autobiographical audio book that he was writing. He did, and when author William Peter Blatty heard it, he asked Goldsboro to write the music for his *Exorcist* audio book. Bobby said, "That's a big leap from *Evening Shade*," but he wrote a couple of pieces, sent them to Blatty, who proceeded to contract with him to do all of the music for the audio book, which was published in 1999.

Children's books were a natural follow-up to Goldsboro's TV shows. After seeing *Easter Egg Morning,* the San Francisco publisher of Yes! Interactive Books called Bobby and asked if he would write something new for its "Comes to Life" books series. Bobby wrote a story and music for a book called *The Boy Who Became a Frog.* "The publisher called me one day and said, 'I thought you'd like to know that the top seller at Toys R Us this year is *The Boy Who Became a Frog.* I can't wait for the second book – you've got one for me, don't ya?' I said, 'Yeah,' but I didn't have another book. As I looked out the window of my studio, a bobcat walked by. He asked, 'What is the book about?' I said, 'It's about a bobcat.' He asked, 'What's the name of it?' I said, '*A Cat Named Bob.*' He said, 'I love it!' He asked, 'Can you tell me the story?' I said, 'Give me the weekend,' so that weekend I wrote the story and a song to go with it and sent it to him overnight mail on Monday. He called me on Tuesday, and said, 'I just read *A Cat Named Bob,* and I like this better than *The Boy Who Became a Frog.*' So you see, if the shades had been closed, I wouldn't have seen the bobcat. It's all about timing," Bobby chuckled.

Diane has accompanied Bobby all over the country for concerts, and the two of them would often go to art galleries and museums. Bobby recalls looking at the paintings and saying to Diane, "One day I'm going to give this a shot." This went on for years until Diane finally said, "You've been telling me this for years. When are you going to do it?" Bobby said, "When I turn 65, I'll start painting," and he did. On his 65th birthday, January 18, 2006, Bobby bought canvases, an easel, brushes and paints, and started painting. Five years later, he had sold 60 original paintings and 300 prints, and had produced more than 90 oil paintings.

Bobby and some of his beautiful oil paintings (photo courtesy of Bobby Goldsboro)

"It was trial and error to find out what to paint first. If you're going to paint a tree against the sky, you've got to paint the sky and let it dry, and then you paint the tree. Every time I finish a painting and I start on a new one, I don't remember painting it. Just like when I hear a song on the radio that I've written, I don't even remember writing it. The process is that you're into it and you move on to the next part," said Bobby. "I get up every day and I can't wait to get out to my studio and paint. I waited 35 years to start painting, so I've got 35 years of paintings stored up in my head."

Bobby often combines a musical concert with a gallery exhibition, where he mingles with music fans and art fans alike. A realist painter, Bobby works with oils, and renders his compositions in richly saturated hues with dramatic angular lighting. His subjects include Florida scenery, still lifes, wildlife, horses and other animals, Native American artifacts and, yes, beautifully detailed floral studies that pay homage to his aunt Willie's florist shop in Dothan. Titles for his works include *Magnolia, Venice Morning, Prairie Marsh in Fall, Tangerine Sky, Berries and Cream,* and *Hammock Beach Sunrise.* One of his sold paintings is a still life depicting fresh oranges, lemons and jars of honey. The painting is titled, of course, *Honey.*

The Moody Blues at a 1968 press conference in New York City. Seated, from left, Graeme Edge, Justin Hayward, Ray Thomas, John Lodge, and Mike Pinder (photo from the private collection of Ray and Lee Thomas)

ON AIR

CHAPTER

3

Dawn Is a Feeling

The Moody Blues
founders Mike Pinder and Ray Thomas

Rock music has worn many labels since its emergence in the early 1950s. A hybrid that melded the blue-collar twang of country music and honky-tonk, the anguished cries of the blues, the improvisational plucking of bluegrass, and the infectious rhythms of jazz and swing, rock music in its formative years was rough-edged and rowdy. As much as postwar teenagers embraced it as an outlet of expression, older generations demonized it and the dancing it inspired as primal, crude, immoral, and rebellious. The disdain of older generations probably contributed to its popularity among young people. Parents who were relieved by the 1958 military induction of rock's biggest star, Elvis Presley, soon learned that the genre would survive his departure. Rock and roll was only 10 years old when the Beatles ushered in a phenomenon that eclipsed even Elvis' rapid rise to fame. The "British Invasion" bands and singers who transfixed American kids in 1964 and '65 included the Moody Blues. Even though pop music by then had largely shed its coarse skin, and rock tunes were routinely sweetened with harmonic vocal backgrounds and strings, hit songs remained structurally simple, with a catchy melody, repeated verses and choruses, and perhaps a bridge. As such, pop music was seen as fun but frivolous, a superficial, ephemeral diversion. The

Moody Blues changed that perception in dramatic fashion.

With one avant-garde, ingenious album – which some critics and the band's record label initially underappreciated – the Moody Blues gave rock music legitimacy as an art form. The brilliant 1967 recording, titled *Days of Future Passed,* emerged from the band's vision of a fusion of rock and symphonic music. A pioneering "concept album" with one defining theme, *Days of Future Passed* inaugurated a series of LPs that the band's legions of fans would affectionately dub the "classic seven" – recordings characterized by musical and lyrical sophistication. The Moody Blues are perhaps the most conspicuously deserving band that the Rock and Roll Hall of Fame has overlooked. The Moodys brought intellect to rock music with evocative lyrics that enabled their fans to see with sound. Their vivid musical imagery has transported their devoted followers to mystical places. Some fans have ascribed therapeutic properties to the Moodys' music, saying the band's melodies and messages helped alleviate physical pain they were experiencing. All of those stellar accomplishments might never have happened, however, were it not for the tenacity and support of the production team members who went out on a limb and defied the expectations of the band's record label, Decca. Until *Days of Future Passed* caught fire, Decca executives were growing impatient and threatening to let the Moody Blues' recording contract expire. Accustomed to overcoming obstacles, the band members held firm to their principles. It was in their upbringing. This chapter focuses on Moody Blues founding members Mike Pinder and Ray Thomas, and about why they chose to leave the band as it continued touring and performing in sold-out concerts decades after its formation.

The Moody Blues were a product of Birmingham, England, a manufacturing city that had sustained heavy damage during four years of Nazi blitz bombings during World War II. As children, the band members had endured repeated bombing raids that reduced entire neighborhoods to rubble. Brummies, as Birmingham residents are known, found postwar recovery arduous. Unlike the prosperity that many Americans experienced in the '50s, Britons became accustomed to austerity. During that period, many British teenagers discovered and developed an affinity for American blues. Among them were Brummies Mike Pinder, who played piano and keyboards, and Ray Thomas, who began playing bass before taking up the harmonica. They had become acquainted with each other in 1961 while performing in separate bands at a Birmingham music hall. Mike was the guitar player in a rockabilly band called the Rocking Tuxedos, while Ray was the singer in a band called El Riot and the Rebels, for which John Lodge played bass.

In early 1963 Mike and Ray united in another band called the Krew Kats – an experience that left them destitute and prompted them to go their separate ways by the close of that year. They had embarked on other careers – Mike as a quality control technician at the electronics firm that produced the Mellotron keyboard instrument, and Ray as a manu-facturing toolmaker – before deciding over lunch one day in the spring of 1964 to take one more run at music by forming a new rhythm and blues band that they initially decided to call the M&B 5. In May 1964 they recruited three other Brummie lads: singer and guitarist Denny Laine (real name: Brian Hines) from a group named the Diplomats, and drum-mer Graeme Edge and bassist Clint Warwick from a band called the R&B Preachers that was dissolving. "Clint was his stage name. His real name was Albert Eccles, but he liked Clint Eastwood's rugged image," Mike said. He had met Denny, Graeme, and Clint in a musical instruments shop called Jones Music. Bass player John Lodge, who was a member of Ray's band El Riot and the Rebels, had declined to join the M&B 5 in order to finish an apprenticeship.

Pinder and Thomas chose the name M&B 5 because Mike's mother was the head bartender for Mitchells & Butlers (M&B), a large brewing company that operated numerous pubs. Mike and Ray had hoped that M&B might financially sponsor them. "They owned all of the biggest hotels, pubs, and dance halls, so we thought if we named the band with the same initials, we could get a couple of thousand pounds out of M&B to buy some equipment and some outfits," Pinder told us. Beginning in early May, the band established a name for themselves locally with repeat engagements at the Carlton Ballroom at Erdington in West Midlands. "We were rehearsing and playing at the Carlton, where the promoter was bringing in current stars," Pinder said. "We played on the same bill with Peter and Gordon, who had been touring with their first hit. One afternoon we were at the club rehearsing and Peter and Gordon wanted to know where they could get a bite to eat. I said, 'Why don't you come around and I'll make you an egg and bacon sandwich at my house?' So we all went to my mom's house, had bacon and egg sandwiches and tea, and had a wonderful time."

Although no Mitchells & Butlers endorsement materialized, the musicians persevered, and by July adopted a modified name: the Moody Blues 5, inspired by the name of Duke Ellington's "Mood Indigo" jazz com-position. "I didn't find the tune memorable, but the name stuck with me," Pinder said. "I chose 'Blues' because we were playing blues and 'Moody' because of my interest in the mood-changing power of music." By mid-August, the band dropped the "5" and became simply the Moody Blues.

The Moody Blues soon were booked at the Marquee Club in London, the Crawdaddy Club in Richmond, the Black Cat in Bradford, and other clubs throughout England, backing Sonny Boy Williamson and other blues performers. On November 2, the band appeared on television for the first time, on BBC2's *Beat Room* program, followed by a December 4 appearance on ITV's *Ready, Steady, Go!* With Denny Laine as lead singer belting out the blues, the band took the bold step of renting the Richmond Athletic Association's clubhouse in London on Thursday nights and hosted their own dances. "On Tuesday nights the Rolling Stones did the same thing," said Pinder. "Another club, called the Bag O' Nails, was considered a rock musicians' social club because everyone would meet there after recording sessions – the Beatles, the Stones, Jimi Hendrix. So there was a lot of camaraderie and interaction among the groups," Pinder said.

The connections the Moodys made with a new management company, Ridgepride Limited, led to a recording contract with the British Decca label. Less than six months after their formation, the Moody Blues recorded their first single, "Steal Your Heart Away." It was a pleading blues song that nearly replicated the version that the song's composer, American blues singer and guitarist Bobby Parker, had recorded in 1961. The Moody Blues' version, released in September 1964, unfortunately didn't reach the charts. For their follow-up, they recorded a song that writers Milton Bennett and Larry Banks had composed for Banks' ex-wife, blues singer Bessie Banks. "We released it later that year – Friday, November 13, 1964, it was," Pinder recalled. The song was "Go Now," with Denny singing lead and Mike playing a prominent piano solo. The record not only reached the British charts, but climbed to the top. The last week in January 1965 it reached No. 1 in England, displacing Georgie Fame's "Yeh Yeh" from the top spot. Released in the United States on the London label, it premiered on the American charts in February and reached No. 10. Decca sent the Moodys into the label's West Hampstead studio in London to record additional tracks for an album titled *The Magnificent Moodys*. Released only in monaural (single-channel sound), the album included "Go Now" and other blues tracks, including the band's interpretation of two James Brown songs ("I'll Go Crazy" and "I Don't Mind"), Chris Kenner's "Something You Got" and Sonny Boy Williamson and Willie Dixon's "Bye Bye, Bird." Also included were George and Ira Gershwin's "It Ain't Necessarily So," and three compositions by Denny Laine and Mike Pinder: "Let Me Go," "Stop!" and "True Story."

Promoter Robert Stigwood booked the Moody Blues on a U.K. concert tour that began January 8 with headliner Chuck Berry, along with

Long John Baldry, the Graham Bond Organization, Winston G, the Five Dimensions, and Doc Spencer. On February 17, American kids saw the Moodys on ABC television's *Shindig!* pop music program. By March, the Moodys were themselves headliners, given top billing in a stage show with Brian Poole and the Tremeloes, and several other performers at the Golders Green Hippodrome music hall in North London. They shared the bill in other gigs with the Rolling Stones, the Hollies, and Marianne Faithfull. Although the band's follow-up single, a cover of the Drifters' "I Don't Want to Go on Without You," did not chart in the United States, it hit No. 33 in the early spring of '65 in Great Britain. The band's next single release, "From the Bottom of My Heart (I Love You)" composed by Pinder and Laine, barely made the *Billboard* Hot 100, at No. 93, but peaked at No. 22 in the U.K., giving the Moody Blues their third consecutive top 40 British hit. Another single, "Everyday," reached No. 44 on the British charts that autumn, as the Moodys signed with Beatles manager Brian Epstein. The band had a busy December, with appearances on ABC's *Shindig!* and BBC-1's *Top of the Pops*. The Moodys also made their U.S. concert debut in "Murray the K's Christmas Show," appearing on stage for nine consecutive days beginning December 25 with Peter and Gordon, the Fortunes, Wilson Pickett, the O'Jays, the Spinners and other performers. But throughout 1966 and most of 1967, the band endured a drought. Its 1966 releases "Stop!" (which went no higher than No. 98 on the *Billboard* Hot 100), "This Is My House (but Nobody Calls)," and "Boulevard de la Madeleine" failed to reach the British charts, and the band's concert appearances and income concurrently declined.

Disappointed by the band's loss of momentum, Warwick – who already was married and a father – left the band in July 1966 to pursue his originally intended field of carpentry. His replacement, bass player Rod Clark, remained for only three months. Clark, Laine, and manager Brian Epstein parted company with the band in October, by which time the Moodys were in serious financial trouble. Compounding their decline in income was indebtedness totaling several thousand pounds that Decca had paid them in advances against future earnings. Pinder, Thomas, and Edge decided to persevere. "When the split came, Ray and I looked at each other and said, 'We can do this again,'" Mike told us in April 2012. To replace Rod Clark, they recruited bass player John Lodge, who had completed his tool-making apprenticeship, and had been playing with the Carpetbaggers, the John Bull Breed, and the Question. A tip from Eric Burdon led the band to Justin Hayward (previously of All Things Bright, the Wilde Three, and Justin Hayward & the Shots), who replaced Denny Laine as lead guitarist and lead singer. "I was sitting in a club, having a drink with Eric Burdon when he was forming the new Animals," Ray Thomas told us in March 2012. "He had put an ad in *Melody Maker* that said 'pop recording band, guitarist-singer.' He had already found the guy he wanted. I told him we were looking for a guitarist-singer, and he said, 'tomorrow, come down to the office and you can pick up all the replies to the ad, and go through them yourself.' And that's how we found Justin. He didn't know who he was applying to." Recognizing that their blues repertoire had run its course, the reconfigured Moody Blues decided to develop their own style, and began rehearsing in Belgium. The band's first release of 1967, "Life's Not Life," the last of the band's singles with Laine on lead vocal, failed to chart. The subsequent releases with Lodge and Hayward, "Fly Me High" and "Love and Beauty," performed no better.

In the spring of 1967, the band members conceived a new approach: a stage show – a musical about the passage of a single day. "At the time, we could not get money for enough studio time," Thomas said. "We used to get three hours to do the A and the B side, and everything had to be three minutes or less, with a catchy hook, which was crap." On their own, the band members began writing songs for the musical, and Mike obtained a Mellotron to orchestrate the musical on stage. On BBC's *Saturday Club* program that aired on May 13, 1967, the band premiered one of those songs that Justin Hayward had written. It was "Nights in White Satin." Mike Pinder recalls, "As we started writing more, we knew there was something to it. Once we had 'Tuesday Afternoon' and 'Nights in White Satin' we thought 'oh – we need something for the morning, something for the evening, dawn, and sunset,' and that's how the whole thing came about."

Decca, meanwhile, had developed a recording technique to improve stereo imaging. Following commercial introduction in 1958, stereophonic albums typically were recorded with exaggerated separation between the two channels. On such recordings, the lead guitar, vocal, and drums might have been recorded on the left channel, while rhythm guitar, piano, strings, and background vocals might have been on the right. Produced using two-track, three-track, or four-track tape machines, the results were primitive because they did not accurately replicate the spatial relationships of instruments and singers in a musical performance. Decca engineers devised an improvement in stereophonic imaging by recording on a four-track tape deck, mixing and copying some tracks onto a second four-track recorder, and then mixing all of those tracks onto a stereo master tape. Mingling the audio proportionately to left and right channels yielded a stereo field with more natural aural imaging.

Stereo had been much more prevalent in the United States than it was in the U.K. Decca established a subsidiary label, Deram Records (pronounced DEE-ram) on which to release recordings made with this "Deramic Stereo Sound" technique. The label recorded a few demo albums of orchestral music, but Decca executives wanted to create a more dramatic demonstration of the applicability of the technique for pop music product, and thought of the Moody Blues. Decca assigned A&R executive Hugh Mendl as the executive producer for the "sampler" project, and assembled a team consisting of staff producer Tony Clarke, engineer Derek Varnals, and conductor-arranger Peter Knight. In the 1950s Mendl had produced Lonnie Donegan's early recordings, which sent the popularity of skiffle music soaring in Britain. Mendl, Clarke, Knight, and Varnals met with the band to discuss the project, which had been conceived as a rock-inspired interpretation of Antonin Dvorak's New World Symphony. Uninspired by that idea, the Moody Blues thought about the stage show material they had written. "We talked to Peter Knight and told him we had this idea, and he went along with it. He could have gotten into a lot of trouble for it," Thomas said. The Moodys' cohesive thematic concept – a chronicle of the progression of an archetypical day, from morning into night – appealed to Knight. In defiance of Decca executives and at their own risk, Mendl, Clark, Knight, and Varnals agreed to let the band record their material in secret.

On October 8 at Decca's West Hampstead studio complex, the band began recording the album's tracks: "The Day Begins," Mike Pinder's peaceful composition "Dawn Is a Feeling," Ray Thomas' "Another Morning," John Lodge's frenetic "Peak Hour," Justin Hayward's "Forever Afternoon (Tuesday?)," Lodge's "(Evening) Time to Get Away," Pinder's "The Sun Set," Thomas' "Twilight Time," and Hayward's haunting conclusion, "Nights In White Satin" – the emotional climax of which is Mike's goose bump-inducing recitation of Graeme Edge's poem "Late Lament." Arranger Peter Knight composed orchestral introductions and bridges that framed the songs on the album, titled Days of Future Passed. "When we were in the studio, we were locked down. We'd go in the late afternoon or early evening and work through, and some mornings we'd walk out and the sun was coming up," Pinder recalled. "We would do the tracks, and Peter would take home a copy. He had this little greenhouse in his back garden, and he would work out all the parts for the orchestration." Mike and the other Moodys found their own refuges to refine their melodies and lyrics. "We'd go to Decca's rec room, and one of our spots was Decca's broom closet." The back cover of the vinyl album had a photo of the band and the production team members in a meeting. "That photo was not staged. It was taken during a discussion in the control room," Pinder told us. Knight did not let the Moodys hear the orchestral music until the end of the recording process. "We walked in during the last session they did. It was a 49-piece orchestra, composed of moonlighting members of the London Philharmonic," Pinder said. "We got a standing ovation from the musicians when we walked in the door."

But the Moodys were not home free. The next step was convincing the label to release the record. "Every Tuesday, record producers took all their wares and went before the record company executives to play what they had done that week, to determine what they thought was worth backing," Thomas explained. "They were very strict, but we were lucky because a guy called Walt McGuire, who was head of London Records, which was American Decca, was at the meeting. Tony Clarke went in and he put *Days of Future Passed* on and the Decca executives sat through it and they said, 'What the hell is that? We wanted a demonstration disk that wasn't meant to be released. You spent a whole week –a whole week, mind you – in the studio." Walt McGuire said, 'I think it's fantastic! If you're not going to release it over here, give it to me, because I am.' The Decca people said, 'Well, we spent all that studio time, we might as well release it.' At first, they put 'Nights' out in the states and it didn't do anything, so they pulled it and put out 'Tuesday Afternoon,' which did make an impact."

Deram released the *Days of Future Passed* album on November 10, 1967. All but two of the tracks were more than five minutes long. "Nights In White Satin" was 7:41. American AM "top 40" radio stations, accustomed to playing records under three minutes long, weren't sure what to do with it. But it was perfect for newly emerging "progressive rock" FM radio stations, many of which let the entire album play without interruption. *Days of Future Passed* became a must-have album for the hip listeners of FM rock stations. "Nights In White Satin" gave the band a long-awaited singles hit, reaching No. 19 on the British charts in January 1968. A shortened version of "Tuesday Afternoon (Forever Afternoon)" released as a single premiered on U.S. pop charts in July 1968 and reached No. 24 on the *Billboard* Hot 100. *Days of Future Passed* spent two years on the *Billboard* album chart, and ultimately earned platinum certification from both the Recording Industry Association of America (recognizing sales of 1 million copies) and Music Canada (for 100,000 albums sold).

The Mellotron keyboard instrument was responsible for the orchestral sound that would elevate the Moody Blues to unprecedented heights of creativity and musical imagery, distinguishing *Days of Future Passed* and subsequent work. "The Mellotron is actually a mechanical device, a playback tape recorder with 70 heads and 70 pieces of tape on a giant pinch roller. When you press down a key, you're literally playing a tape recorder," said Pinder. Mike had mastered the idiosyncratic instrument when he worked as quality control inspector at Streetly Electronics, observing production of the recording heads, the electronics, and the mechanical parts. "My job was to play the Mellotron to make sure that each machine worked perfectly and that all the tapes were timed correctly.

Days of Future Passed was the first of what Moody Blues fans call the "classic seven" albums, in which the band contemplated life, love, loneliness, human evolution, and the future of humankind. In January 1968 the Moodys began recording their next album, *In Search of the Lost Chord,* the title of which was inspired by a childhood memory of Mike's. "As a child I listened to the radio a lot. When I was about 5 years old, I heard a song by Jimmy Durante called 'I'm the Guy Who Found the Lost Chord.' I remembered that song 23 years later, and I coaxed the band into calling the next album *In Search of the Lost Chord.* So you can see that what happened to me as a child had a big effect on my entire life." While symphonic musicians performed on *Days of Future Passed,* the Moodys themselves performed all their own musical backing for all subsequent albums, beginning with *In Search of the Lost Chord.* That album explored philosophical themes of spiritualism, meditation, consciousness expansion, the astral realm, and the struggles of life. *In Search of the Lost Chord,* released July 26, 1968, contained John Lodge's "Ride My See-Saw," Justin Hayward's "Voices in the Sky," and Ray Thomas' "Dr. Livingstone, I Presume" and his "Legend of a Mind," a tribute to Timothy Leary on which Thomas performed a powerful, stirring flute solo. The album went gold in the United States (for 500,000 copies sold) and platinum in Canada.

The Moody Blues began recording *On the Threshold of a Dream,* the third in their series of concept albums, on January 12, 1969. The 13 tracks of the LP, which was released on April 25 in the U.K. and May 30 in the United States, included Justin Hayward's "Lovely to See You," Ray Thomas' "Dear Diary," Mike Pinder's "The Voyage," and Hayward's "Never Comes the Day" – the album's only song to be released as a single. *On the Threshold of a Dream* was certified platinum in the United States and in Canada. The album inspired the name of the Moody Blues' own label, Threshold, which they established as a means to gain complete creative control over their recordings and their elaborate album cover designs. As shareholders in Threshold Music, the Moody Blues contracted with Decca to distribute Threshold recordings, and built a state-of-the-art studio that they owned and operated within the Decca complex.

The world's first manned lunar landing, which American astronauts achieved in July 1969, sparked the concept for the band's next album, *To Our Children's Children's Children*. Released on November 21 of that year on the Threshold Records label, the album consisted of 13 songs that contemplated childhood in the context of space travel, the universe, and eternity. Standout tracks on the album included Graeme Edge's "Higher and Higher," John Lodge's "Eyes of a Child," Ray Thomas' "Floating," and the Hayward-Thomas composition "Watching and Waiting." RIAA awarded gold record certification to the album, as did Music Canada (signifying 50,000 copies sold). Artist Philip Travers, who painted the cover artwork for six of the "classic seven" albums – illustrated the gatefold cover of *To Our Children's Children's Children* by depicting a regression of civilization, with primitive cave drawings that commingled images of tribal hunters brandishing bows and arrows along with a biplane and a figure with a rifle. The inner spread of the album portrayed the Moody Blues in an otherworldly landscape, huddled with their instruments in a cave around a campfire, with a case of books and a few other vestiges of 20th-century surroundings they apparently left behind.

Upon the arrival of 1970, the band returned to Decca's West Hampstead studio to record the album *A Question of Balance*, the fifth of their "classic seven" albums. In addition to taking a swipes at the Vietnam War and the futility of combat in general with Justin Hayward's "Question," the album also probed existential themes with Pinder's "How Is it (We Are Here)" and "Melancholy Man," Hayward's "It's Up to You," the Thomas-Edge composition "The Balance," and the Edge-Lodge composition "Don't You Feel Small?" Released as a single, "Question" premiered on the charts in May and peaked at No. 21 in the United States, No. 8 in Canada and No. 2 in the U.K. The album *A Question of Balance* earned platinum certification in the U.S. and in Canada.

The band began work on their next album *Every Good Boy Deserves Favour* in November 1970 at the Wessex Studios in London. The title of the album, released in July 1971, is a reference to the mnemonic slogan that helps music students remember the treble clef progression of notes E-G-B-D-F. Justin Hayward's potent hard-rocking track "The Story in Your Eyes," released as a single, didn't make the charts in Great Britain, but was a substantial hit in North America, reaching No. 23 in the United States and No. 7 in Canada. *Every Good Boy Deserves Favour,* which went gold in the United States and platinum in Canada, rose to No. 2 on the American and Canadian album charts, and hit No. 1 on the British charts in mid-August. By that time former Moody Blues member Denny Laine had joined Paul McCartney's band Wings.

In January 1972 at Decca's Tollington Park studio in London, the Moody Blues began recording the seventh of their "classic" albums: *Seventh Sojourn*. The first single it spawned was John Lodge's "Isn't Life Strange," which after its debut in April reached No. 29 in the United States and No. 13 in Britain. In *Seventh Sojourn,* the band continued to explore abstract and philosophical themes, while declaring in John Lodge's "I'm Just a Singer (in a Rock and Roll Band)" that they had more questions than definitive answers about the mysteries of life. That song, released as a single, hit No. 12 on the *Billboard* Hot 100 in the spring of '73. Edge's and Hayward's rockin' "You and Me" also received significant radio airplay. At the close of 1972, *Seventh Sojourn* on the Threshold label reigned for five weeks as the No. 1 album in the United States. It earned RIAA and Music Canada gold record certifications.

The band, however, was beginning to buckle under the heavy load of the creative process, and the nine-month concert tour that the Moody Blues undertook to promote *Seventh Sojourn* was exhausting. After nearly 10 years of maintaining a dizzying schedule of recording, club dates and worldwide concert tours, the band members decided to separate – with no specific plans to regroup. Following a concert at the Cow Palace in San Francisco on February 4, 1974, Mike, Ray, Justin, John, and Graeme each went on sojourns of their own, to relax and develop solo projects at their own pace. They were able to afford the break because song-publishing royalties were sufficient to support them. Pinder moved to California, bought a deconsecrated vacant Lutheran church on property overlooking Zuma Beach, west of Malibu, and a 90-acre ranch in the hills of Malibu (where he built a recording studio), renamed it Indigo Ranch, and settled in.

All five Moody Blues members recorded and released solo albums on Threshold, and Hayward and Lodge recorded as a duo. In the autumn of '74 Threshold released a double album called *This Is the Moody Blues,* an anthology of 26 songs from the "classic seven" albums, along with Mike Pinder's "A Simple Game," which had not been included on any previous albums. *This Is the Moody Blues* reached No. 11 on the U.S. album charts, No. 2 in Canada, and No. 14 in the U.K. The British Phonographic Industry (BPI) awarded it a gold record (indicating 100,000 copies sold), and it also earned RIAA gold. In the spring of 1977 Threshold issued *Caught Live +5,* a double album that consisted of recordings from the band's December 1969 stage performance at Royal Albert Hall in Westminster, London, along with five previously unreleased studio tracks. Although it did not make the album charts in the U.K., it reached No. 26 in the United States.

In 1977 Decca made the band an offer to record a new album, but the odds initially were against it, as Ray Thomas explained. "I got a phone call from Tony Clarke. He said 'I'm over at Justin's, and we spoke with Mike, who is up for another album.' Justin and John weren't speaking to each other at the time, though," Thomas said. "So John and I went to our local pub and sat in the back room and discussed it. The government in those days was taking 85 percent off us in tax. We said we can't make an album if we owe the treasury 85 percent before we've started." Ultimately, a workable plan emerged. In January 1978, the Moody Blues reunited and with producer Tony Clarke converged at the Record Plant recording studio on West Third Street near La Cienega Boulevard in Los Angeles to record the *Octave* album, as Clarke was enduring the stress of the dissolution of his marriage. On January 10, after the band had laid down a few tracks, a fire gutted the studio and destroyed the tapes they had recorded. They shifted operations to Mike Pinder's home studio at his Indigo Ranch. Festering tension and disagreements that arose during the recording of *Octave,* however, prompted Clarke and Pinder to end their association with the band before the completion of the project. "I had done what I set out to do," Mike told us in July 1997. "The group was really successful and by the time we were halfway through the *Octave* album, I realized this wasn't meant to be anymore. I caught a vision of a new life, which was to be happily married and have children and 'return to the tribe' as I call it. And that's exactly what I've done."

Mike Pinder, Tony Clarke, and Ray Thomas at Ray and Lee's wedding reception in July 2009 (photo by Gabe Tolnay)

Keyboard player Patrick Moraz of Switzerland, formerly of the band Yes, joined the Moody Blues in place of Pinder for the tour to support the album, which was released June 9, 1978. *Octave* yielded three singles – John Lodge's "Steppin' in a Slide Zone," and Justin Hayward's "Driftwood" and "Had to Fall in Love," the latter of which failed to reach the charts in the United States. None of the three singles reached the British singles charts. *Octave,* on the Decca label in the U.K. and on London in the U.S., reached No. 13 on the U.S. albums chart and No. 6 in the U.K. It earned a gold record from BPI and platinum certification in Canada and in the United States.

Pinder, under the impression that Moraz was hired only for touring with the band, had planned to continue recording with the Moodys. The remaining band members, however, disagreed, and prevailed in legal action. With Moraz on keyboards, the Moodys went into their own Threshold studio with producer Philip "Pip" Williams in February 1980 and spent more a year recording *Long Distance Voyager,* the band's 10th album. The album's name is a reference to NASA's Voyager spacecraft missions past Saturn. A faint image of the satellite appears in the sky on the album's cover illustration of a 19th-century village scene with children watching a Punch and Judy puppet show. Singles extracted from the album were the Hayward-Lodge composition "Gemini Dream" (a No. 12 hit in the United States), Hayward's "The Voice" (which peaked at No. 15), and Lodge's "Talking Out of Turn" (which reached No. 65). The album closed with Thomas' wryly self-effacing "Veteran Cosmic Rocker." *Long Distance Voyager* soared to No. 7 on the British album charts, and hit No. 1 on the U.S. and Canadian charts. It earned a BPI silver record award (indicating 60,000 copies sold), platinum certification in the United States, and went triple platinum (for 300,000 albums sold) in Canada. The band's follow-up album, *The Present,* released in August 1983, yielded two modest hit singles: Lodge's "Sitting at the Wheel" and Hayward's "Blue World." Music Canada recognized it with a gold record (indicating sales of 50,000 albums), and it was among the first albums released in both vinyl and in the recently introduced Compact Disc format.

The Moodys stormed back with their 12th album, *The Other Side of Life,* which Polydor released April 9, 1986. Produced by Tony Visconti at his Good Earth studio in Soho in the West End of London, the album relied primarily on the strength of the opening track, Justin Hayward's "Your Wildest Dreams." That song became the third single by the band to crack the U.S. top 10, perching at No. 9 on the *Billboard* Hot 100. The album also included Hayward's "The Other Side of Life," which entered the singles charts in August '86 and peaked at No. 58. The contributions of Ray Thomas, though, were limited on the album to background singing. *The Other Side of Life,* which reached No. 24 on the U.K. album charts and No. 46 in Canada, reached as high as No. 9 in the United States, and earned platinum record certification in the U.S. and Canada.

Sur la Mer, released in June 1988, brought the Moody Blues their last album and single success in the United States. "I Know You're Out There Somewhere," Justin Hayward's superb song about a man's enduring hope for the return of a former lover, premiered in June 1988 and rose to No. 30. Although Ray Thomas continued performing with the Moody Blues on stage, he did not participate in the recording of *Sur la Mer* (the name of which means "on the sea"). The album earned a gold record in Canada.

The band's triumphant concert with the Colorado Symphony Orchestra at the Red Rocks Amphitheatre near Denver on September 9, 1992, was recorded in audio and video and released as a music CD titled *A Night at Red Rocks.* It remains one of the most vibrant concert recordings ever made, and earned RIAA gold record certification. The video was broadcast on PBS as a fund-raising program, and distributed in DVD form.

After *Sur la Mer,* the Moodys recorded only three more studio albums: *Keys of the Kingdom* (1991), on which Ray Thomas sang and played flute, while Moraz departed the band without being replaced; *Strange Times* (1999), which was recorded at Studio Mulinetti in Recco, Italy, and was the last Moody Blues album for Ray Thomas; and the Christmas album *December* in 2003. The Moodys maintained an unremitting concert schedule, performing in indoor sports arenas, auditoriums, gymnasiums, concert halls, stadiums, theme parks, amphitheaters and casino showrooms. Ray Thomas reluctantly retired from the band at the close of 2002 not only to fulfill his longtime determination to retire from touring at age 60, but also due to cerebellar ataxia, a worsening chronic, incurable brain disorder that causes loss of muscular coordination affecting walking and balance. He and Mike Pinder, who hadn't spoken to each other for 20 years, are once again the best of friends, and with their wives enjoy spending time together as often as possible.

Arranger, conductor, and composer Peter Knight, who created the lush orchestration for *Days of Future Passed,* died at age 68 on July 30, 1985. Former Moody Blues bass player Albert Eccles ("Clint Warwick") died of liver disease at age 63 on May 15, 2004. Record producer Hugh Mendl died at 88 years of age on July 7, 2008. Tony Clarke, who had produced the "classic seven" Moody Blues albums, died at 68 years of age on January 4, 2010.

John Lodge, Justin Hayward, and Graeme Edge have continued to tour with supporting musicians. Worldwide sales of Moody Blues albums reportedly have surpassed 55 million copies. Their song "Nights In White Satin" was inducted in 1999 into the Grammy Hall of Fame, the Recording Academy's means of honoring recordings "of lasting qualitative or historical significance." The Vocal Group Hall of Fame inducted the band in 2006. The Moody Blues have created a majestic musical legacy, characterized by thoughtful, sophisticated lyrics, impeccably crafted arrangements, shimmering production, and brilliant musicianship.

U.S. HIT SINGLES BY THE MOODY BLUES

Debut	Peak	Gold	Title	Label
2/65	10		Go Now	London
6/65	93		From the Bottom of My Heart (I Love You)	London
4/66	98		Stop!	London
7/68	24		Tuesday Afternoon (Forever Afternoon)	Deram
10/68	61		Ride My See-Saw	Deram
6/69	91		Never Comes the Day	Deram
5/70	21		Question	Threshold
8/71	23		The Story in Your Eyes	Threshold
4/72	29		Isn't Life Strange	Threshold
8/72	2	Δ	Nights in White Satin	Deram
2/73	12		I'm Just a Singer (in a Rock and Roll Band)	Threshold
7/78	39		Steppin' in a Slide Zone	London
11/78	59		Driftwood	London
6/81	12		Gemini Dream	Threshold
8/81	15		The Voice	Threshold
11/81	65		Talking out of Turn	Threshold
9/83	27		Sitting at the Wheel	Threshold
11/83	62		Blue World	Threshold
4/86	9		Your Wildest Dreams	Polydor
8/86	58		The Other Side of Life	Polydor
6/88	30		I Know You're out There Somewhere	Polydor

Δ symbol: RIAA certified gold record (Recording Industry Association of America)

Billboard's pop singles chart data is courtesy of Joel Whitburn's Record Research Inc. (www.recordresearch.com), Menomonee Falls, Wisconsin.

Epilogue: Mike Pinder

Mellotron and keyboard player, singer, and composer

Mike Pinder was only 4 years old when he discovered, as he says, that "music has magical properties." His mother trusted him to open the bottom of his father's upright Steinway piano so he could observe the inner workings while pushing down the keys. "I would sit for hours under the piano and feel the strings as I played a note and wondered about the vibrations and how the tone changed with every key I played. I could touch and feel the strings when I played the notes on the top," Mike recalls. "That way I could find out what they were – lower, higher, thicker, thinner."

Ray and Mike (foreground) in 1964 at the Carlton Ballroom, Erdington, Birmingham (photo from the private collection of Ray and Lee Thomas)

Although Mike, who played piano as well as ukulele as a child, took about a dozen piano lessons, he plays "by ear" and doesn't read music. "People who don't read music wish they could, and people who do read music sometimes wish they didn't, because it narrows your creative focus," he explained. "Taking that course forced me to develop a style of my own, which I may not have done had I taken the academic approach. So I'm rather grateful for that. Even though I can't read wonderful scales, I've developed something that was perfect for me. The music that I create is like a landscape painting – it is visual music."

Mike and many other British teenagers of the 1950s grew up under decidedly different circumstances than those of American kids. "The blues from the American south was instantly recognized and embraced by the musicians of my generation in Britain. Young British musicians understood and related to the soul of the blues. We understood the hardships of World War II and of the working-class people. The blues was a catalyst for us to build on. *We got the message!* Combine that with the Elvis and Buddy Holly rockabilly music of the 1950s and you get the British Invasion," Mike wrote in his "Pinderings" blog on www.mikepinder.com. His musical influences in the 1950s also included the music of Mantovani, whose lush orchestral arrangements interpreted popular songs of the day with sweeping waves of violins. "We had some Mantovani records in the house. I loved the strings and how they brought emotion out," Mike said. "Mantovani made the most soothing music that I've ever heard."

Michael Thomas Pinder was born on December 27, 1941, delivered by a midwife in the front upper bedroom of his parents' home in Kingstanding, a middle-class housing area on the outskirts of Birmingham, England. During the first three years of Mike's life, World War II was being fought, and his father was in the British Army serving much of that time in India. Mike says he met his father for the first time in 1945. He recalls his mother saying, "Come in, I want you to meet someone. This is your dad."

While Mike was too young to remember the bombs going off, he does recall seeing the destruction of homes the day after an air raid. "The house my mom grew up in was bombed," he said. "We had black-out curtains on our windows, and we used to move around the neighborhood at night. All of the kids would go into a neighbor family's house and stay the night, and then they would all come to our house the next night. We would move around to try and beat the odds of getting bombed."

He fondly recalls May 8, 1945 – Victory in Europe Day. When the war was over, all of the neighbors brought tables, draped with white sheets, into the middle of the street, as well as all the food and drink that they had been saving during wartime. Mike's parents, Bert and Gladys, also rolled out their piano. His father played, and everyone danced and celebrated in the streets all night long. "I was only about 3½, recalls Mike, "but I can see it right now as I speak to you. It made such an impression on me. And then they cleared away all of the tables, all of the neighbors went into their houses and never partied with each other again."

By the age of 12, Mike was playing piano in pubs. "My dad played piano down at a seven-bar pub called Mitchells & Butlers (M&B) that my mother was managing. When he wanted a break, he'd sneak me in, but everybody knew about it. I would play for about 20 minutes, and then he'd take over. I'd invariably end up with a big pint glass full of coins, and I'd come home with a tidy jug of money," Mike said. At about 14, he became interested in the honky-tonk sound. "I remember getting push pins and putting them on the ends of the hammers, and that's how you get the honky-tonk clanky sound. My dad let me do it," he laughed.

In addition to working at an electronics factory during the week and performing at M&B, Mike's father also drove a tour bus on so-called "magical mystery tours" on weekends and evenings, escorting tourists to events, such as dog races and football matches. On Sundays, he would take groups to pubs located in remote towns in the scenic English countryside. "The kids would come along and they would have their lemonade and crisps while their parents enjoyed pub specialties," said Mike. "Consequently, there was always a piano there, and my dad and I would play."

After Mike completed the required general education in England at 15 years of age, his first job was delivering milk by horse and cart. "I did that for about nine months," he said. "I would get up at 5:30 a.m. I was only 10 minutes away from the dairy, and I had to get the horse out of the stable, rig him up and hook him to the delivery vehicle, then back him into the ramp and load up all the crates of milk. So I'd deliver milk to peoples' doorstep and be home by 11 a.m. I could carry seven bottles of milk in one hand, and I never dropped one."

The youngest of four children, Mike has a brother, Reginald (Reg), who is retired and living outside of Sydney, Australia, and two sisters, Maisie and Monica, who live in England. He and Reg, who Mike says "plays a pretty darned good trumpet," performed together in a short-lived skiffle group called the Checkers. "All the guys in that band were quite a bit older than I was at 15, but they needed a piano player and

I was available," said Pinder. "I remember a guy had a Triumph motor-cycle, and he'd come from the other side of town and pick me up on his motorcycle and take me downtown to where we were playing in pubs. That didn't last too long, though."

When the Checkers broke up in 1958, Mike formed the Rocking Tuxedos, whose members achieved considerable local renown based, in part, on their immaculate attire: white dinner jackets with black satin lapels. The band played mainly Buddy Holly music, which Mike claims had the greatest influence on him. "I liked Elvis in the 'All Shook Up' days, but I weaned myself from him as soon as he started doing country music," Mike said.

Mike's grandfather served and was killed in World War I, and Mike's father told great stories about serving in the second World War. Honoring that heritage, Mike joined the Royal Army Service Corps in 1961, in which he served for 342 days, initially as a rocket carrier driver before becoming an acting corporal. While in the camp in Bielefeld, Germany, Mike was asked to play the organ for the commandant, the colonel of the base. "He was very religious, and he wanted someone to play the organ in church on Sunday mornings," said Pinder. "I'd been playing the piano in the mess for the men, and he got word that there was a guy who plays the piano, and he called me up and said, 'Pinder, would you mind playing a little organ for me on Sunday mornings at 10?' I said, 'Yes sir! No problem!' So I started doing that for him, and I put a little band together, and we didn't have to wear combat boots, we could wear shoes, and we could go anywhere we wanted to. We didn't have to do any duties." Pinder's attentive service for the colonel also led to his early discharge. After hearing the Beatles, Mike's fervor for performing rock music was stoked. He told his superiors he wanted to return to civilian life. "They said, 'Pinder you've been a good man,' and they let me out." An understanding military physician diagnosed him with hallux valgus, a malformation of the large toe on his right foot resulting from improperly fitted shoes. "I had been wearing tight shoes because they were all hand-me-downs," Mike explained.

While performing with the Rocking Tuxedos before beginning his military service, Mike had met Ray Thomas and John Lodge, when they were playing at the same dance hall with their group called El Riot and the Rebels. They had established a friendship, and after Mike was dis-charged from the Army, he and Ray formed a short-lived band called the Krew Kats, which toured Germany for a couple of months. The Beatles had played in Hamburg, and Mike had become familiar with Germany through his army service, so they thought the tour might be a good break for them. Instead, it turned out to be a disaster.

Penniless at the end of the poorly paid tour at the close of 1963, Pinder and Thomas struggled to return to England. "We walked from Hamburg to Oostende, Belgium. I remember as we were going through a town in Belgium, we were downtown somewhere close to the red-light area. We went into this place to buy a beer, and we walked down these stairs to the bar and it was full of homosexuals in all their gear and rig – guys dressed up as women – really, really strange. So we walk up to the bar to get a beer and a guy asks, 'Want a blow job?' We ran out of there so fast. We thought, 'You want to stay and be comfortable with all these guys, or do you want to walk home?' We decided to walk home. We'd never been accosted before."

When Mike returned home, he was searching the newspaper classified ads to find a job when he noticed an ad that read, "Wanted: someone with musical and electronic experience." Intrigued by the prospect, Mike interviewed with a company called Streetly Electronics and got the job. His father's hobby had been electronics. "I grew up with the smell of what Americans call 'sah-der' and the British call 'sol-der,' said Mike, with proper British enunciation. "At Streetly Electronics I was introduced to this machine – the Mellotron – and the moment I saw it, I thought, 'This is destiny to me.' It was almost like I knew it was there for me to discover and to use." Mike spent a few days in each department at Streetly Electronics, learning all he could about this magnificent new instrument – observing production of the recording heads, the electronics and the mechanical parts. Soon he was named quality control inspector. "My job was to play the Mellotron to make sure that each machine worked perfectly and that all the tapes were timed correctly." For Mike, landing this job was much like someone who loves ice cream getting a job as an ice cream taster.

The experience solidified a philosophy that he recommends to all of the children and adults with whom he comes into contact. "Follow your bliss," he said, pointing to a T-shirt inscribed with his favorite saying by mythologist and author Joseph Campbell. "When you're on the path you're supposed to be on, then all things will come to you. Being who you're supposed to be and not somebody else. That's something that I've always followed," he philosophized. The Mellotron for Mike was a portal to new musical vistas that enabled his creativity to flourish in blissful ways that he previously had not imagined. Mike remained at Streetly Electronics for a little less than a year, until the rising arc of the Moody Blues demanded all of his attention. The Mellotron meant so much to him that he encouraged the Beatles to buy one; they did, and used it prominently when they recorded "Strawberry Fields."

After seven years of working as a collaborative member of the Moody Blues, Mike got his first taste of individual acclaim in 1971, when the Four Tops recorded his composition "A Simple Game." The song became a hit on both sides of the Atlantic. "Motown's box set calls the song 'Maybe the most adult music ever to grace the pop chart,'" said Pinder. "The song was my way of trying to say, 'be cool' – that life is a simple game and there's nothing, as John Lennon said, 'to get hung about.' Beyond daily reality there's still the thought process and ideas. You think about all the things that have been good for the world as well as the bad things that have happened. For me, it goes back to listening to the BBC as a kid – listening to the lyrics and noticing how what they were saying affected people. It gave me an insight to think of the power of music and lyrics." Mike received the Ivor Novello Award for Social Comment for "A Simple Game," and proudly displays the bronze plaque on his desk. He also takes deserving pride in his compositions "Dawn Is a Feeling" and "The Sun Set," and particularly in "Melancholy Man," a track from the 1970 Moody Blues album *A Question of Balance*. "Melancholy Man" is a portrait of the humanity that a reflective man sees as he contemplates the fate of people whose anger and misery prevent them from recognizing the astounding wonders of our world. In response to demand, the song was released as a single in France, where it became a top hit. "'Melancholy Man' is close to me because it's about me," Pinder said.

In 1970, Mike married Donna Arkoff, the daughter of Samuel Z. Arkoff, an American entertainment lawyer and producer of low-budget action, horror, and teen beach party movies in the 1950s and '60s. The couple celebrated the birth of their son, Daniel, in 1971 in Surrey, England. Mike, unfortunately, was on the road for the Moodys' nearly incessant touring throughout much of Daniel's early childhood. The demands of touring abraded and weakened Mike and Donna's marriage. After moving to the United States, the couple divorced in 1973, but have remained friends.

When the Moody Blues collectively agreed to suspend recording and touring together in 1974, Mike began to reassess his life. He bought a piece of property in 1975 overlooking Zuma Beach on the Pacific Coast, west of Malibu. A vacant octagonal Lutheran church sat on the property. He also bought Malibu acreage that he dubbed Indigo Ranch, another reflection of Duke Ellington's "Mood Indigo" that had given rise to the Moody Blues' name. He converted the old church into his home, and eventually installed recording equipment at the ranch.

Mike began work on a solo album, *The Promise*, an album of introspective and mystic songs with spiritual overtones. Billing himself as Michael Pinder, he composed all nine of the album's songs, including the title track. Portions of the album had a jazzy feel with the contributions of tenor saxophonists Bobby Keyes and Tom Peterson, and trumpet player Steve Madaio. In addition to playing the Mellotron and a synthesizer, Pinder also played piano and guitar on the album. *The Promise,* released through Threshold Records in 1976, registered on the *Billboard* album chart at No. 133.

Mike's bachelor days at Indigo Ranch didn't last long. They ended shortly after he met Tara Grant in the summer of 1977. Tara, who was born in the Los Angeles area community of Glendale and raised in North Hollywood, was attending graduate school at Annenberg School for Communication and Journalism at USC when a girlfriend introduced her to Mike. He recalls, "I was on a date with a girl who turned out to be Tara's friend. We had a nice winter dinner and a nice evening, and she said, 'You know, I've got a friend and I think you'd really like her,'" he said. "Tara drove up to Malibu in her little red Volkswagen Beetle, and we've been together ever since."

Mike and Tara were married in 1978, moved to Hawaii, and had two sons: Michael (born in 1979 in Kahuku, which is on the north shore of Oahu) and Matthew (born in 1980 in Kona, Hawaii). "I became Mr. Mom," said Mike. "We were in Hawaii for four years, but as much as we liked it there, we weren't making friends, and in a year or two the children would be going into kindergarten. It was very strange being in the minority on the islands. Also, the humidity there was warping all of my guitars. So we came to Northern California to visit Tara's father in the Sierra foothills. It was November and cold, and the leaves had fallen off the trees. It was the Englishman in me that liked it, so we moved there."

Tara decided to pursue a career in real estate, becoming one of the two top agents in Nevada County. "She took a hiatus for a couple of years in 1994 to help me form my record company, One Step Records, of which she's the CEO," said Pinder. Following Michael's graduation from high school in 1997, Tara resumed her career in real estate. "She's really good at it, and she really takes pride in what she does. She's one of the few people who has the integrity to be able to do that kind of job well," said Pinder proudly. "Some of her clients have become our friends."

In 1994, Mike produced *Among the Stars,* his first solo album since *The Promise* and his departure from the Moody Blues. In *Among the Stars,* Pinder captured the elegance of the Moody Blues' "classic" period of the early '70s. "I hope to make the music, lyrics, and the songs I write make people think. They're not your typical 'let's get down, let's have fun, shake your booty' sort of thing. Everybody was doing that, and I wanted to do something different. *Among the Stars* is very much in the Moody vein. In the title track is a poem that I wrote." Mike remastered and re-released *Among the Stars* in 2008.

The name of Mike's production company, One Step Records, was derived from the last song he wrote and performed with the Moody Blues on the *Octave* album. "It's called 'One Step Into the Light,' which was very apt because it was all about humanity taking a step further in our destiny," said Pinder. "It's all based on higher consciousness, good principals and good values, without involving the dogma of religion."

Inspired by children's storybooks promoting universal ideas of peace, love, and tolerance, in 1995 Mike released his first CD of multicultural children's stories accompanied by music and sound effects. The collection of whimsical tales, called *A Planet With One Mind*, was followed in 1996 by *A People With One Heart*. Each CD contains seven stories – one for each night of the week. "They're all mythological, cosmic stories with wonderful morals," explained Mike. "All of the stories are spiritually uplifting and for everyone, aged 4 to 104."

In 2009, Mike and Tara started "Songwars," a contest for songwriters. "It was from watching our own children trying to get their songs heard and knowing that there are so many great musicians out there who are

Mike and Tara Pinder in 2012 (photo by Jeff March)

so talented," said Tara. "We thought it was going to be something simple and fun, but we had to listen to hundreds and hundreds of songs to do it justice."

Mike continued, "The idea was to help the writers, too, so we did critiques. But it just became so much work because we were getting thousands of entries. We ran it for about two years, but going through all of the entries was time consuming, and sometimes we'd have to listen to something two or three times. There were entry fees and prizes, but it wasn't a money-making venture." Mike continues to judge once a year for the John Lennon Songwriting Contest, an international songwriting competition that began in 1997 and has numerous sponsors contributing studio equipment, gift certificates, cash, and other generous prizes to different levels of winners in various genres of music.

In 2011, Mike and Tara's sons, Michael and Matthew, opened Imagine Music Instruction studios in Roseville, California. They teach guitar and keyboards, and son Michael teaches voice. Calling themselves The Pinder Brothers, the two have recorded some catchy contemporary pop tunes for their upcoming CD *The Pinder Brothers: Speeding Cars*. Visit their website http://www.pinderbrothers.com/ to hear a preview. Matthew also is the bass player with an Eric Clapton tribute band called the Cream of Clapton, starring Kevin Russell, who Mike says "is a phenomenal guitar player."

Mike's eldest son, Daniel, edits music for movies in L.A. He works with Hans Zimmer, a German film composer and music producer who has composed music for more than 100 films, including *The Lion King* (1994), *Crimson Tide* (1995), *Gladiator* (2000), *The Da Vinci Code* (2006), *The Dark Knight* (2008), *Inception* (2010), and *The Dark Knight Rises* (2012). Mike says proudly, "We're always the last ones in the theater watching the credits for Daniel Pinder." Tara adds, "I tell Danny that, and he says, 'You are?' And I say, 'Hey, we're not in L.A., we're in Sacramento, and no one waits for the credits here.'"

Mike and his lifelong friend Ray Thomas turned 70 years old in December 2011, and they celebrated together in grand style with their families and friends at Ray's home in England seven months later. Mike posted on July 13, "The sun was shining for the belated celebration of our birthdays. 'Seventy orbits around the sun' as I have always referred to the yearly cycle of our life on the planet. It was a lovely evening of friends, music, and memories."

Visit **www.mikepinder.com** for more information.

Epilogue: Ray Thomas

Flute and harmonica player, singer, and composer

Timeless music from the heart can be created only by a passionate soul. Compositions such as Ray Thomas' "For My Lady" speak to our hearts and often leave a lump in our throat. His hauntingly beautiful flute solo in "Legend of a Mind," as in many other Moody Blues' signature songs, sounds as if it could have been written by late 19th-century Romantic Era composer, yet it transcends generations. For a man who claims he doesn't read music, and that musical notes are just "tadpoles on clotheslines" to him,
the creative juices flow copiously. His career with the Moody Blues spans more than 38 years, and he can proudly say it's been a successful run.

Raymond Thomas was born on December 29, 1941, "two years and 119 days after the start of World War II," to Elsie and Marlais Thomas, in Lickhill Manor, Stourport-on-Severn. Lickhill Manor was a country estate that was established as a birthing place for pregnant women, about 20 miles from the Birmingham war zone that the Nazis repeatedly bombed. Ray and his sister, Yvonne (five years younger),

Ray Thomas in 1975 (photo from the private collection of Ray and Lee Thomas)

grew up in England's second largest city, Birmingham – which in the local dialect is pronounced *Birming-gum,* with a silent *h* and a hard *g* sound. Birmingham was at the heart of the United Kingdom's industrial revolution.

Ray attended Paget Road School from the age of 6 until he was 14. His musical interests began when his father taught him to play the harmonica at the age of 9, and he sang in both the school choir and the

Birmingham Youth Choir. "My grandfather, who used to conduct choirs, said to me, 'So you still sing?' I said, 'Oh, yes.' He said, 'Tenor,' and I said, 'No. I'm not a tenor, I'm a baritone.' And he said, 'No you're not.' I said, 'Yes, I am.' He said, 'We're all tenors in this family.' I said, 'Well, I'm not, I'm a baritone.' He said, 'OK. You're a bass tenor.'"

Because Birmingham was a factory town, the schools divided students among three occupation-oriented groups called "streams." The "A" stream students generally became tradesmen; the "B" stream students were primed to be semi-skilled tradesmen; and the "C" stream students were destined to become the laborers. Ray graduated in the top of the "A" stream and became a skilled toolmaker like his father, who was a foreman in an industrial toolmaking shop.

Ray graduated from Paget Road School at the age of 14, but had to wait until after his 15th birthday in December 1956 to go to work at Lemark in Birmingham to begin his six-year apprenticeship producing the tools that stamped Rolls Royce car parts out of sheet metal. "When I went to work in the press shop, one of the guys came over and said, 'Let me look at your hands,' and he counted my fingers and said, 'You're no toolmaker.' If someone had lost a finger, they'd get 250 pounds for a thumb, 150 pounds for an index finger, 100 pounds for the next finger, 120 for the ring finger, and 75 pounds for the pinky."

His foreman at Lemark was an old guy nicknamed Billy "Brabazon" because he made the tools for the Brabazon long-range bomber aircraft that the Bristol Aeroplane Company developed. "Billy used to tell me the way to stand, the way to use a file. Then he'd come up and say, 'No. You're doing that wrong.' And if he came by the third time and I was doing it wrong, he'd smack me around a bit," said Ray. "He called me 'Domino,' and I answered to it for years until one time I asked, 'Billy, why do you call me Domino?' and he said, 'Double blank!' What Billy didn't know wasn't worth knowing. He was a very, very old man, and he should have retired long before I got there, but he taught me pretty well."

Weekdays, Ray worked at the factory and on the weekends he performed with a band called Saints and Sinners, a skiffle group inspired by Lonnie Donegan that Mike Brassington, another Brummie about Ray's age, formed in March 1958. Together Thomas and Brassington built a one-string, electric double bass they called "The Coffin," which Ray played "until we lost it one night coming back from a show. We left it on the roof of an old van, and the damn thing took off," Ray chuckled. "When it hit the main road, it just disintegrated. We never even bothered to stop." The Saints and Sinners played gigs in and around Erdington, a suburb of Birmingham, until disbanding in June 1959.

Ray then formed a band called El Riot and the Rebels, which included bass player John Lodge, lead guitar player Bryan Betteridge, rhythm guitarist Mike Heard, drummer Ricky Wade (and later keyboard player Mike Pinder and Rob Sheward, who replaced Wade on drums). Calling himself El Riot, Ray dressed in a green satin Mexican toreador suit and began his trademark entrance of sliding across the stage on his knees. The group landed several spots on ATV's popular midday entertainment show *Lunch Box*. On their first appearance on November 14, 1962, the group played Cliff Richard and the Shadows' "Guitar Tango" and Frank Ifield's "I Remember You." That same year, the group made their first recordings, "Blue Moon" and "Down the Line" – on a 78 rpm demo.

"In the beginning, we were playing clubs, and pubs, which we shouldn't have been in. In Birmingham, they have these huge assembly rooms that they open on Friday and Saturday nights when the guys get paid, and they'd take their wives there. We used to rent these rooms and stage our own shows," said Ray. "John [Lodge] and I had the cheek of the devil, and we would go in and ask, 'Can we hire your room on a Tuesday or Wednesday?' So they would make 100 pounds on the bar, which was a huge amount of money then, because all of the people who came to see us play drank a lot of beer, including us. So we ended up playing a different pub or club five nights a week."

On April 15, 1963, El Riot and the Rebels performed at the Riverside Dancing Club in Tenbury Wells, about 40 miles southwest of Birmingham near the border of Wales, as the opening act for a band from Liverpool – the Beatles. By October 1963 Ray decided it was time to quit his day job and pursue music as a full-time career. He already had finished his apprenticeship at Lemark, so his father gave him his blessing. "My dad said, 'If this goes belly up, at least you've always got your trade to fall back on,' recalls Ray. "That's why John [Lodge] wasn't in the original Moody Blues, because his dad said exactly the same thing to him. John was a tool maker, too, but I'm 18 months older than him. So with Mike, I formed the Moody Blues, and when Clint left, I found John. He had finished his apprenticeship, so he joined the band."

Before establishing the Moody Blues, Thomas and Pinder had formed the Krew Kats in 1963 and set off to establish themselves in Germany, where Mike had been stationed during his year-long stint in the British Army. Some gigs had been lined up for them at the Top Ten Club in Hamburg (made famous by the Beatles), but a couple of months into it they discovered the clubs had been run by some shady characters who failed to pay them. Flat broke with no passports, they had no choice but to walk the 417 miles from Hamburg, Germany, through the Ardennes Forest to Oostende, Belgium, where they would eventually catch a ferry back to the U.K.

"We did the Battle of the Bulge on foot," said Ray. "It was December 1963, and we had two suitcases and a guitar case with us, and we just went as the crow flies, basically. We hitched one ride, and the guy took us about a half-mile down the road and said, 'I turn off here.' It was so cold at the seafront that we sat in this bus shelter and Mike was saying, 'I'm going to go to sleep, I feel really warm.' And I started to shit myself, thinking 'If he goes to sleep, he isn't going to wake up.' We'd been sleeping rough for weeks. So I kept him awake."

The journey took Ray and Mike more than seven days to complete, with little sleep and only a few snacks to eat. They limped into Oostende and straight to the British Consulate that, reluctantly, gave them a loan of just enough money to get them safely back to Birmingham.

"It was a very tough road trip, but we did eventually make it back to Birmingham and home to our parents," said Ray. "That bad experience did nothing to dampen our spirits toward making music and starting another band. It was probably a lucky road trip in that once back in Birmingham we teamed up with Denny Laine, Clint Warwick, and Graeme Edge to form the band that would be the beginning of a 40-year love affair with making music for me." It also marked Ray's transition to the flute, which he taught himself how to play at 22 years of age. By the spring of '65 he felt comfortable enough to play flute on the Moodys' recording "From the Bottom of My Heart (I Love You)."

Ray recalls the first time he visited America with the Moody Blues. "We played Murray the K's Rock and Roll Review at the Brooklyn Fox with Wilson Pickett, Cannibal and the Headhunters, and the Fortunes. It was really weird because it went all day long, and in the morning and in the afternoon shows, all the white acts and the bands were going down great and all the black acts weren't. But as the day progressed the audience got blacker and blacker, so Wilson Pickett was going down like a storm and we were getting polite applause by then.

"It was bloody hard work. We played only two songs in each show – "Go Now" and "Bye Bye, Bird," the Sonny Boy Williamson song. But we had to be there for the overture, and at the end we all had to get on stage and do this bloody stupid walk for the audience. We did that about two nights, then started going down to the pub instead. You could never find the English acts, we were all down the road at the pub."

Another trip to America was a memorable experience for Ray. He said, "The first time we came across 'hash' brownies, we were scheduled to play a show in Los Angeles, and our plane got diverted with all of our gear on board. And we couldn't open the plane to get our instruments or gear. It was the only show we ever missed. We were supposed to do a show with Jefferson Airplane. So we said, because we missed the show, we'll do a free concert in Griffith Park, and we got two flatbed trucks to make a stage and the place was packed. The Airplane said, 'If you're playing it, we will, too.' We got this great big basket of what we thought were biscuits. They were throwing them out to the audience and everybody was high as a kite. That was the thing back then, playing indoors you didn't have to smoke the stuff yourself, you got it from the audience. You could see the bluish fog in the air," he laughed.

Two and a half years after Ray's group El Riot and the Rebels first opened for the Beatles, he met up with them again in December 1965, when the Moody Blues were an accompanying act on the Beatles' last British tour – a nine-city excursion starting in Glasgow, Scotland, and ending in Cardiff, Wales. "We opened for the Beatles. They were good mates of ours by then. Half the time, it was half the Beatles in our car, and half the Moodys in their car."

By the time John Lodge and Justin Hayward had joined the Moody Blues, the other members already had conceived writing a stage show. "At the time, we could not get money for enough studio time. We used to get three hours to do the A and the B side, and everything had to be three minutes or less. We decided we were going to do a stage show with a theme, so we got ideas for it before we went into the studio to do *Days of Future Passed*."

Ray, who wrote about two dozen songs that the Moody Blues recorded, including "Another Morning," "Twilight Time," "Dr. Livingstone, I Presume," "Dear Diary," "Lazy Day," and "Floating," described his composing process for the *Days of Future Passed* album. "Justin would come into the broom closet with a guitar and he'd work out the chords, and I had a little glockenspiel, and I'd sing the song and we'd just write while the guys were recording something else. None of us read music. Peter Knight did all of our transcription for the music. We never actually played with the orchestra, we were just using the Mellotron. Peter did the overture and all of the bridges and links," Ray recalled. "Peter [Knight] wouldn't let us go into the studio when he was mixing, but when he finished, he phoned us all up and said, 'Get your ass up here!' We all went with our families, and when we got in there he set up the studio itself, with two big speakers, rows of chairs, and we all sat down, and he pulled the lights, it's pitch black, and kicked it off. We'd obviously heard all the individual tracks, but we'd never heard it in its entirety. Peter was a lovely man."

Ray's favorite flutes are those made by German manufacturer Conrad Mollenhauer, and he's adamant that there's no better make. Ray recalls, "In 1968 we were working in Frankfurt, Germany. I had broken my flute and walked into this shop one morning and, strangely, the shopkeeper thought I was American, so he came out with this American Armstrong flute. I don't mean to be insulting, but that's bloody awful. The balance is not right, and I don't like the sound, and I said, 'I don't want that.' So I looked in this glass case in the counter and said, 'Let me look at that one,' and he wouldn't even sell it to me. He was still holding the Armstrong and said, 'No, this one's for you,' And I said, 'No, I'm not buying it.' So then, I think he just wanted to get rid of me, and he got the Conrad Mollenhauer out of the glass case and put it together. And the bottom end of that flute is really rich in tone. So I said, 'This is the one I want.' I paid him and left with it, but he didn't want to sell it to me because he didn't want anyone but a German playing it."

These days Ray regularly plays three favorite flutes: a C flute, an alto flute, and a bass flute. "The bass flute is like a big walking stick. You have to have a curve on it, otherwise your arms wouldn't be long enough," he says. "I played it on loads of our albums. I used to play on my own in the studio against a backing track."

Ray recalls that years after Peter Knight's death in 1985, the Moodys needed the original scores for *Days of Future Passed*, so they hired composers to listen to it, decipher it, and put it in written form. "We had a team of people transcribing, because we needed different scores for different orchestras. It was time-consuming and tedious," he said. "One of the composers commented, 'The oddest thing about the whole thing was the bell tree [a percussion instrument that consists of a stack of tuned metal bowls in a chromatic scale].' And we asked, 'What bell tree? We never used a bell tree.' He said, 'Well, there's a bell tree on there.' And we said, 'Not unless the bloody studio cat knocked it over.' It took him weeks to write this bell tree that the bloody studio cat had knocked over," Ray laughed.

When the Moodys began their four-year hiatus from recording and performing in 1974, Ray was ready for a break. "We lived in each other's pocket, literally. Everything I saw, they saw. Everything I heard, they heard, because they were with me all the time. It became a bit claustrophobic, so we needed a break," he said. "Also, people wanted to play with other people and try other things, which is what happened."

In July 1975, Ray released his first solo album, *From Mighty Oaks,* recorded with guitarist John Jones, keyboard player Mike Moran, bassist Trevor Jones, singer and percussionist Nicky James, and drummer Dave Potts. The album reached No. 23 on the U.K. albums chart, and No. 68 on the *Billboard* albums chart. "I had a great band," said Ray. "They're all Welshmen, so that helped. Nicky James signed on the Threshold label as a soloist. He had an incredible voice. Nicky always worked hard, but he never really made it, and he used to write some lovely songs. He wrote one song called 'The Troubadour,' and he wrote it while he was on holiday. The thing is, nobody could sing it as well as Nicky. I would have to do a different slant on it to get away with it. We worked well together."

In June 1976, Thomas released his second album with Nicky James, called *Hopes, Wishes and Dreams.* The album, which ranked 145 on the *Billboard* chart, produced one single, "One Night Stand," which was the "B" side of the single "Carousel." Thomas remastered and reissued both *From Mighty Oaks* and *Hopes, Wishes and Dreams* in 1989.

The Moody Blues regrouped in January 1978 to begin recording their eighth album, *Octave.* While they had a beautiful, well-equipped studio in England, the government was taking 85 percent tax at the time. "So we all got on a plane and did it in L.A., which was a joke because we left a better studio and our engineers were doing absolutely nothing for 12 months. We had to rent homes and rent a studio in L.A., pay for all the airfare there and back, and my youngest daughter was born there. It wasn't easy."

Following the recording, the Moodys were scheduled to do a world tour to promote their new album, but Mike Pinder's refusal to leave his family created another rift. "Mike and I didn't speak for about 20 years," said Ray, "but we're great mates again. It's water under the bridge." The band continued to record albums and toured extensively, with a huge fan base in the United States.

Ray recalls the last time he performed with the Moody Blues in Birmingham, Alabama. "It was about the time people started bringing glow sticks to concerts and they were throwing them on the stage. Earlier, I had asked if they wouldn't do that because we can't see them and they could put someone's eye out. When we got toward the end of the concert, we saw this thing swinging around somebody's head in the audience. I was looking at Justin, and he was looking at me, thinking 'What the hell is that?' And all of the sudden this guy just let it go, and it came whizzing over everybody's heads and landed on the stage between Justin and myself. It was somebody's artificial leg, and it's got a sock and a sneaker on it! I was about cracking up because I had just come off a solo on the flute and you can't laugh and play flute. When you think you've seen it all, you haven't. Justin threw it back out into the crowd like an American football player, and someone caught it and threw it back up in the air. Someone asked, 'Did you see who threw it in the first place?' and I said, 'Yes. He was the last to leave.'"

In 1999 the Moodys traveled to Italy to record their self-produced album *Strange Times*. "The reason we recorded in Italy is because Justin, who lives in Monaco, had done some work in a studio in Recco, and he really liked it. The engineers spoke good English and the guy who worked on the computer spoke good English, so that wasn't a problem at all. The studio was in a big house and the engineer's mother cooked one day, and his auntie came in and cooked the next. We had lunch and dinner, but after a month, I was quite sick of pasta."

It would be the last album on which Thomas would perform before his retirement in 2002 because of a neurological condition called cerebellar ataxia, which causes him to lose his balance and fall. Ray describes it: "It's the cerebellum, which is your balance box, and I've blown a fuse. My brain has to go through a different route, whereas yours is instant. By the time I know that I'm going to fall down, I've already fallen down."

Ray Thomas in 2010
(photo by Carlos Chiavacci)

He uses a walking stick, and likes to joke and have a little fun with his situation. He said, "When I'm standing in line with a guy in front of me and a woman is in front of him, I can goose her with the stick and he gets the blame," he laughs. "Also, in a crowded room, if you wave it about, people get out of the way."

Ray's American-born wife, Lee (née Lightle) had been a single mother, working as a bookkeeper and living in St. Louis, when they first met. "I first saw the Moody Blues in 1970 in St. Louis. I'm from Illinois, but I spent my adult life working in St. Louis," she told us. "A disk jockey named Radio Rich Dalton on radio station KSHE in St. Louis had started playing progressive rock music on Sunday afternoons, with no break between the songs. He would play the entire album. That's where I first heard the Moody Blues. I love rock 'n roll, I don't play any musical instruments, I don't sing, can't dance, but I like live concerts, and I went to a lot of them, not just the Moody Blues – Led Zeppelin and Eric

Clapton were among my favorites.

"After taking 18 years off to raise my daughter, I started going back to concerts and found out there was this huge Moody Blues fan base, and it fascinated me because they were middle-aged people. So after my daughter graduated, I started going to Moody Blues concerts and other concerts – the Grateful Dead, you name it, I went to them," Lee said. "I met Ray in New Orleans in 1998. He asked me if I wanted to have a drink, and I thought, 'okay I'll have a drink, and you've probably got an ego bigger than a house.' It turned out that he's the most down to-earth-person you'd ever want to meet. We don't lead a rock 'n' roll lifestyle, our friends are ordinary people, and he's been that way all his life. He's a...."

As she paused in search of an aptly descriptive word, Ray piped in, "a chick magnet!"

Laughing, she agreed. "Chick magnet, yes, I have to watch him." Lee moved to England in 2003, and the two were married on July 9, 2009, in a 14th-century church in Ceredigion, Wales. Ray, who identifies himself as a Welshman, said, "When the clergyman was filling out documents for us before the wedding, he was thrilled because he had never married an American before. It was a tiny little chapel by the sea. My great grand-father made all the pews for this chapel. My granddad and great uncle George repaired them. I was a little kid when they did that. There is a strong family connection with the church there. So the clergyman said to Lee, 'I've got to put down "citizen of the United States of America for you," and then he turned to me and asked, 'Now with you, do you want me to put down "English" or "Welsh"?' I said, 'Welsh.' We say we're Brit-ish born, but Welsh by the grace of God."

Lee interjected, "There was no electricity in the church, so we had an organist who had a pump organ brought over from the States, and she was quite honky-tonk – it was great! As we left the church, she swung into her version of 'He's Got the Whole World in His Hands.' It cracked us up."

Ray and Lee live on seven acres, which has become a sanctuary for various types of wildlife, including ducks, owls, and birds. They have two natural lakes, which they stock with fish. Ray, who has always loved fishing, said, "I used to get a lot of ideas when I went out fishing, because that's my big passion. I've fished all over the world. The idea and all of the bits and pieces of 'Nice to Be Here' were put together while I was fishing. I composed it all in my head. I considered it to be one of my kids' songs."

While Ray is catching and releasing fish (he doesn't eat them), Lee is tending to her ducks and other wild birds. "We take in rescue ducks that have been orphaned or injured," said Lee. "We have probably the biggest population of Mandarin ducks in the U.K. I think we've got about 75. There's a rescue center close to us and they take them in. Once they're ready to be released, they bring them over to our lake. And owls – we had 16 owls, and the BBC came down and filmed one release that looked like Harry Potter's mail call."

They also have a greenhouse and grow a lot of flowers and vegetables on their property. "We grow Yankee corn, because British corn is god-awful," said Lee. "They asked the Americans to give them some corn, and

This oak tree, on the first page of Ray's website, was photographed on his property. The tree actually has the door, lantern, windows, and gnomes. Look closely and you can read "From Mighty Oaks" – the title of his 1975 solo album.

we gave them what we feed the cows. Most people don't know the difference. But you come over from America and eat the corn here, the first thing you say is 'What's wrong with the corn?'

Ray, who is the cook in the household, enjoys making his own jams and marmalade, which he ships to friends all over the world. It's made from Seville oranges from Spain, which are available in late January or early February. "I've been shipping out marmalade for two weeks now," said Lee in February 2012. "I keep Mike Pinder supplied with it. I got an e-mail from him with a picture of a sad empty jar," she laughs. "The marmalade has gone to Montreal, Quebec, The Netherlands, Florida, California, Indiana."

Ray has three children, Adam, Nancy, and Zoe, from his marriage to his first wife, Gillian; and Lee has one daughter, Jennifer. Together they have five grandsons and two granddaughters. Adam and his family live in England, and the others live in the United States.

Ray and Lee are so appreciative of the fans. When Ray turned 70 years old on December 29, 2011, two of their friends, Maggie from Indiana and Sue from Ohio, rented a post office box and posted on Facebook that anyone who wanted to send Ray a 70th birthday card could send it to that address. Maggie brought them to Ray at Christmastime, and it took Ray more than two hours to open his cards. "I think it kind of amazes Ray that he's still remembered. He doesn't believe it," said Lee.

"I try to keep the ego down," Ray chucked.

"The fans have really been wonderful," Lee said. "I think Ray thought when he retired, that would be the end of it. When we did the box set signing in September 2010 at Threshold Records in Cobham, there were over a hundred people from all over the world standing in the rain to get to see him again, and get their box set signed. It was very moving, and we appreciated it. It was an amazing outpouring." Ray added, "I'd like to let my fans know that I'm very happily married, and I'm enjoying my retirement. I'm doing all right. And I want to give them a great big *thank you!*"

Ray's continued popularity exceeded their expectations when his website www.raythomas.me went live in 2010. It had so many hits that it overloaded and shut down. His webmaster was truly amazed and had to switch to a higher capacity connection to accommodate broader bandwidth.

"I don't think Ray always realizes the respect and the esteem people hold for him. I took his grandsons to the Hard Rock Café in London a couple of years ago. There's always a line to get in, whenever you go. It was winter, and the guy at the door said to me, 'It will be 45 minutes.'

I pulled out Ray's lifetime Hard Rock card issued to artists and showed it to him, and he said, 'Oh. Ray Thomas, the Moody Blues. That will be 5 minutes.' So our little grandson said to me, 'What did you do?' I said, 'I showed them grandpa's card.' He said, 'How does that move us from 45 minutes to 5 minutes?' I said, 'Well, your grandpa is famous,' and he said, 'He is?' I answered, "Yes, he is." He yelled over to his mother, 'Did you know that grandpa is famous?'"

RAY ThOMAS

Visit www.raythomas.me and enjoy the animation inside Ray's tree house.

Donnie Brooks in 1960 (photo courtesy of Donnie Brooks)

Mission Bell

Donnie Brooks

In the autumn of 1959, months before Chubby Checker catapulted a cover version of Hank Ballard's "The Twist" to the top of the charts and launched a dance craze that sent teens as well as their parents into gyrations, a then-unknown session singer went into a Hollywood recording studio to croon a demo version of a newly written love song. His name was Donnie Brooks, and he turned in a star performance of the lilting ballad called "Mission Bell." On the strength of that song, as well as his ability to demonstrate how to do the twist, Brooks built a career that kept him – and dozens of other performers – working for more than four decades.

Donnie, whose real name was John Faircloth, had come to Los Angeles in 1957 as an aspiring singer. He was making the rounds, performing "Granada" and other standards at local nightclubs, when he met music arranger Jesse Hodges, who thought they could make money together by producing demo records. Normally songwriters and publishers would expect to pay $100 per musician to cut a song. A four-piece band, a vocalist and three backup singers would cost $800. "We figured out how to bring the cost down to $300 per song. We'd wait until we had five or more songs to record, and then produce them all during a single session," Brooks explained. With the promise of mass production, Hodges and Brooks paid musicians $25 per song. "Since we did five or 10 songs at a session, the musicians made a lot of money, the background singers made a lot of money, and we made money."

William Michael, a stockbroker who was drawn to music publishing, began to engage the services of Hodges and Brooks regularly. "Jesse would do the charts and I would work with the background singers and I'd do the lead vocals," said Brooks. Michael paid them $100 per tune. They'd crank out songs, back to back, often working with guitarist Neil LeVang, who at the time was a featured performer on the *Lawrence Welk Show* television program.

Hodges, who later founded Hollywood Sound Recorders and made a name for himself as a recording engineer, singer and songwriter, expanded his collaboration with Brooks when they began producing background music for aspiring singers who wanted record producers to hear them perform. For $200 per song, they'd record the would-be singer doing vocal tracks over a prerecorded instrumental background – somewhat like karaoke. The package price included record pressings for the singer to shop around to record companies.

Meanwhile, Donnie continued to cut song demo tracks on Fable Records, Jolt, Surf Records and other labels under various names. He used the name Johnny Faire for three 1957 Fable Records releases: "If I'm a Fool," "Make Up Your Mind Baby," and "You Gotta Walk the Line." On other releases he was Johnny Jordan or Dick Bush. His first record to generate radio airplay came to him via the late Johnny and Dorsey Burnette, brothers who each went on to pop music stardom but were working as songwriters when they first befriended Donnie. After Johnny Burnette wrote a song called "Bertha Lou," he sold it for $50 to songwriter John Marascalco, who with Robert "Bumps" Blackwell had written the Little Richard songs "Good Golly, Miss Molly," "Rip It Up," and "Ready Teddy." Marascalco took the song to an acquaintance named Kenny Babcock, owner of the small Surf Records label. Because Johnny Burnette already had signed with Coral Records, he was prohibited from recording for Surf, so Babcock and Marascalco instead recorded Dorsey singing the rockabilly-style "Bertha Lou" backed with "'Til the Law Says Stop." When Dorsey signed with Coral, Marascalco and Babcock realized that they had to bring in another singer to overdub and muffle Burnette's vocal track.

"I had sung for Babcock, who owned a tool and die place and pressed his own records. Babcock told Marascalco, 'I know a guy who does "Granada." He sings real good.' They brought me in to the studio and I sang 'Bertha Lou,'" Donnie said. The overdub was no easy task, because Brooks had not previously attempted a rockabilly style, yet had to match and overpower Dorsey Burnette's staccato phrasing syllable by syllable. But he had fun with the suggestive lyrics "Hey, hey, Bertha Lou, I want to conjugate with you," and "If I could hear you moan on Mr. Bell's telephone, ain't no tellin' what'd I'd do, Bertha Lou." Marascalco produced that Johnny Faire recording session. The Surf label pressed and issued the high-energy rocker in December 1957, and London Records released it in the United Kingdom.

"Good song. It got a lot of play," said Brooks. Donnie was parked at Scrivener's Drive-In at Sunset and La Brea the first time he heard "Bertha Lou" on the air. "I couldn't believe it, man. KFWB was playing my record. I cranked it up and began screaming in the car and nobody knew what the hell I was yelling at," Donnie laughed. Both songs – particularly "'Til the Law Says Stop" – were purely in the rockabilly vein that the early Sun Records recordings by Elvis Presley, Carl Perkins, and Roy Orbison had tapped. "I heard that rockabilly music is popular in Europe now and that 'Bertha Lou' is a big thing again," Brooks said in 1997.

Surf Records released one more Johnny Faire single, a swingin' pair of rockabilly tunes called "Betcha I Getcha" and "I Fell for Your Line, Baby," in February 1958, before Donnie connected with Era Records, for which Gogi Grant, Art and Dottie Todd, Dorsey Burnette, the Castells, Larry Verne, and Johnny Rivers also recorded. At Era, Donnie mischievously adopted the name Dick Bush, under which he recorded a novelty tune called "Hollywood Party" backed with "Ezactly," both of which were written by Lee Redman and Jesse Hodges. The record attracted less attention when Era released it in May 1958 than it did during a resurgence in the late 1990s. "Back in 1958 it took off in El Paso but that was all. It never happened anywhere else. Now it's big in Europe because people are collecting these old crappy records," Donnie told us in 1997. After Donnie recorded "Hollywood Party," he next became Johnny Jordan for Jolt Records, which in October 1958 released one single, "Sweet, Sweet, Sweet," written by William Michael, backed with "Don't Cry Little Baby," written by Doris Ellner.

Era Records owner Herb Newman called on Donnie again, in the summer of '59, to record a couple of sides – "Li'l Sweetheart" and "If You're Lookin'." Songwriter Dave Taxe wanted to disassociate the release from songs recorded under the names Johnny Faire, Johnny Jordan, and Dick Bush. Taxe concocted a name inspired by the term "donnybrook," referring to an Irish free-for-all. That's when John Faircloth became Donnie Brooks. "I like to fight. That's a good idea," said the young singer, who happily adopted the new moniker Donnie. He followed that with other Era releases – a song called "White Orchid," and another one called "The Devil Ain't a Man." In the fall of 1959 William Michael contacted

Jesse Hodges with ideas for about five songs, one of which was called "Put Another Nickel in the Wishing Well." Though incomplete, the song captured the imagination of Hodges, who began to tinker with it. Dorsey Burnette, who by then had signed with Era, strode into the room, took a look at the work-in-progress, and sang, "my love is taller than the tall oak tree." A few months later, Burnette would score a hit of his own on Era, "(There Was a) Tall Oak Tree." But Burnette's improvisation gave Hodges an idea. The result was "Mission Bell," backed by a choral group with musical arrangement by Danny Gould, and released on the Era Records label in early May 1960. (Although William Michael initially was given sole credit for writing the song, Jesse Hodges shared songwriting credit in subsequent releases). On the flip side of "Mission Bell" was a song called "Do it for Me," written by Carmino Ravaso and Jon Shepodd. London Records released the single in the United Kingdom and Australia.

Radio stations in a few small markets put "Mission Bell" on their playlists, and momentum began to build. It broke onto the charts in June, and rose steadily to No. 7 on the *Billboard* Hot 100, and remained on the chart for an enviable term of 20 weeks. Within two delirious months, "Mission Bell" transformed Donnie Brooks from a lounge singer into a headliner. Marathon Pictures hired Donnie under the name Johnny Faire as a singer for two 1960 motion pictures: *Date Bait* and *High School Caesar* (in which Brooks sang "I Fell for Your Line, Baby").

Era rushed Brooks back into the studio to record a follow-up single, the bouncy love song "Doll House" backed with "Round Robin," returning him to the charts at the close of the year. As "Doll House" climbed toward No. 31, Donnie went on tour throughout the Midwest and Canada, playing halls and community centers with the Fendermen (who were promoting their hit "Mule Skinner Blues"), Bobby Vee (who had just begun his hit recording career with "Devil or Angel") and the Fireballs (who had scored with "Torquay" and "Bulldog"). In February 1961 Era issued another Donnie Brooks single, "Memphis" – not the Chuck Berry tune that Johnny Rivers and Lonnie Mack recorded, but rather a different tune that Jesse Hodges wrote. Donnie's "Memphis" disappointingly went no higher than No. 90. Era released an album titled *The Happiest Donnie Brooks* in 1961 and seven more Brooks singles before he left the label in 1963 and subsequently signed with Reprise Records, just about the time Frank Sinatra sold the label to Warner Bros. Reprise released three Donnie Brooks singles – easy rockers, arranged and conducted by Jack Nitzsche and Ernie Freeman – in 1964 and '65. Then he signed with Challenge Records, which released two of his singles in 1966. But he had no chart successes with either of those labels.

Brooks' friend P.J. Proby (James Marcus Smith), meanwhile, recorded a brassy arrangement of "Mission Bell," which became a top-10 hit in Australia in 1965. Others who recorded the song included Gene Pitney (on his 1967 album *Golden Greats*), Fleetwood Mac (on the 1970 album *Kiln House*) and Tiny Tim (with whom Brooks developed a fast friendship). Although the twist craze, surf music, and the emergence of Motown artists shunted the recording career of Donnie Brooks, he continued to polish his stage act in the casinos of Nevada during the remainder of the decade. Since the 1970s, Donnie Brooks songs have been issued on more than two dozen compilation CDs and vinyl albums.

Television and Hollywood film studios also called. Donnie won an acting role in the 1964 MGM comedy film *Get Yourself a College Girl,* which starred Mary Ann Mobley, Joan O'Brien and Nancy Sinatra, and musical performers the Standells. Donnie was signed to play himself in the 1965 United Screen Arts musical comedy film *A Swingin' Summer,* with James Stacy and Raquel Welch in starring roles. Righteous Brothers Bill Medley and Bobby Hatfield also appeared in the film. Donnie was cast in the 1967 Columbia Pictures release *The Love-Ins,* in which he played an entertainer. That film, in which Richard Todd, James MacArthur, and Susan Oliver starred, also included appearances by the rock band the Chocolate Watch Band and talk show host Joe Pyne. In the spring of 1971 Donnie was cast in the role of Jesus Christ in a live staging of a rock opera titled *Truth Of Truths* at the Greek Theatre in Los Angeles, which prompted Oak Records to release a soundtrack album. The dramatic songs Brooks performed in the show included "He's the Light of the World" and "I Am What I Say I Am." Donnie continued performing pop music as well, and evolved into a significant force in the preservation of his fellow recording artists of the 1960s through show production. From the late 1980s into the early 2000s, Brooks was among the nation's most active packagers of oldies music shows, where he often took to the stage to sing "Mission Bell."

U.S. HIT SINGLES BY DONNIE BROOKS

Debut	Peak	Title	Label
6/60	7	Mission Bell	Era (20 wks)
11/60	31	Doll House	Era (10 wks)
3/61	90	Memphis	Era (2 wks)

Billboard's pop singles chart data is courtesy of Joel Whitburn's Record Research Inc. (www.recordresearch.com), Menomonee Falls, Wisconsin.

Epilogue: Donnie Brooks

Singer and show producer
February 6, 1936 – Feb. 23, 2007

Oldies music fans throughout California's San Joaquin Valley were preparing to head to Oakwood Lake Resort in Manteca the evening of Saturday, July 5, 1997. By noon that day, show promoter and entertainer Donnie Brooks already had been on the job for two hours. Work crews were unloading two truckloads of sound gear and setting up the barren stage. Security guards reviewed their plans. Caterers had just delivered a bounty of food.

In a little building just offstage that housed two dressing rooms, a kitchen and a seating area, Donnie Brooks set up shop on a sofa into which he sank his 6-foot-2 frame. His bulging black briefcase was his mobile office. Munching a cold chicken leg, Brooks discussed sequencing of the show with his band's lead guitarist and musical director, Jerry Cole. As they talked, a late-model Cadillac crunched to a halt in the gravel parking lot. Out stepped one of the Drift-

Donnie Brooks in 1990s (photo courtesy of Donnie Brooks)

ers. When he entered the doorway, he and Donnie exchanged warm greetings, clasping hands and slapping each other on the back. Donnie spewed a series of topical one-liners and silly jokes, sending his guest into deep tremors of laughter. And then, before going further, Donnie did what other show producers often save for last: he wrote out a paycheck and handed it over. On the performing circuit, Brooks was widely admired and respected among legendary recording artists because of his fair treatment. He, in turn, modestly told us that he was merely provid-

111

ing the accommodations that his fellow performers deserve – a perspective he derived as a working performer himself. For Brooks adeptly performed a dual role: that of entertainer as well as show producer.

As more performers arrived – other members of the Drifters and Thomas Turner, Bobby Sheen and Randy Jones of the Coasters – Donnie heartily embraced each, laughing and joking. They sat, they ate, they talked. But not about business. Donnie asked about how they were doing, about their children and grandchildren, about new developments in their lives.

Onstage, the band started warming up. Donnie headed to the stage and ran through his set of tunes while the sound engineers checked and adjusted the audio equipment. Dressed in their street clothes, the Drifters took to the stage to rehearse their 40-minute set, followed by the Coasters. They needn't have. The acts performed like clockwork, with tightly synchronized dance routines and well-patterned harmonies.

With two hours remaining before showtime, Donnie headed for his rented minivan in the parking lot and led a caravan of Coasters, Drifters, musicians and their family members to the Stockton, Calif., hotel several miles away where he had reserved rooms for them. There, Donnie learned that the hotel reservations desk had shorted his order by one room. And now the place was full. Without hesitation, Brooks surrendered his room to one of the Coasters. Donnie would find other accommodations for himself elsewhere.

"Anyone hungry?" Donnie asked the performers as they stood in the hotel hallway. "Let's go eat!"

Brooks ushered a procession to a coffee shop across the road. He and a group of a dozen performers and spouses took over a quadrant of the restaurant and spent most of the next hour telling outrageous stories about themselves and mutual friends, bantering with each other and with a good-natured food server. With an hour remaining before showtime, Brooks finished his cold roast beef sandwich, slapped his hand on the table, announced, "It's time, folks," took his wallet from his jacket pocket, and peeled off four $50 bills – three for the tab and one for the food server's tip.

Back at the Oakwood Lake Resort concert arena in Manteca, the Drifters dispersed to the dressing rooms, as Donnie used the restroom to change into a sharp black suit. When he emerged, he exchanged a few timing points with the Coasters, who lounged in the seating area.

Six o'clock. Showtime.

Donnie straightened his tie, strode to the flank of the stage out of view of the audience but in line of sight with musical conductor Jerry

Cole. Brooks nodded his readiness. Cole hit the downbeat. Brooks bounded onto the stage and up to the microphone.

"Good evening and welcome!" he announced to the audience. "My name is Donnie Brooks." For the next 20 minutes, Brooks engaged the audience with a high-energy mix of stand-up comedy and songs, including his top-10 hit "Mission Bell" and tunes by other performers ranging from the Isley Brothers to Elvis. It was an act he'd polished over the past three decades, in small nightclubs and Nevada lounges.

The San Joaquin Valley heat that summer evening drenched the performers in droplets of sweat on the outdoor stage, but Brooks barely noticed. He was doing what he always wanted to do. Something he loved to do. Something he had literally fought to do.

Donnie Brooks was a parochial school student in San Diego when a nun who discovered his natural singing ability placed him in the choir. And almost immediately, Brooks became a target of tough kids who ridiculed his singing. They hadn't figured that the "sissy singer" would not only fight back, but also beat the daylights out of them. "My arms were really long, so I could stand back and punch a guy all day long and he'd never hit me," Brooks told us in October 1997. He had to repeatedly prove himself – one kid at a time. "Every time a guy picked a fight, we'd meet after school in a vacant lot about two blocks away and I'd beat his brains out."

Brooks says he learned to fight on the streets. But he may have picked it up from his father. "I think my father was a prizefighter," Brooks recalled hazily. "I remember seeing him in the ring when I was very little, one of my first memories." Brooks wasn't sure of that. Nor was he certain that the man he called his father really was his father.

Donnie's mother, Albina "Mary" Chernoch, was 13 when she left her family's farm in Terrell, Texas, married a guy named Scott and moved with him 25 miles west to Dallas. After enrolling in a beauty school there, she dropped Scott and started seeing a Syrian man named Dee Abohash. She left him to take up with a newspaper delivery man named Jim Faircloth. Donnie, born John Dee Abohash in Dallas on February 6, 1936, was uncertain who among those three men was his real father. He did know that he was 5 years old when he moved with his mother and Jim Faircloth to Southern California after Faircloth enlisted in the U.S. Marines and was assigned to Camp Pendleton. Jim Faircloth adopted young John, but shipped out to Guadalcanal after the United States entered World War II. That's when John and his mother moved 40 miles south to San Diego. There she found a job as a beautician but she was unable to properly care for her son.

"So she put me in the care of a lady named Mrs. Craft," said Brooks. It was not the first time he was placed in the care of strangers. "When my mother was working in Dallas, she left me with my 'Aunt Shirley' who wasn't my aunt. I had lots of 'aunts' and 'uncles' who weren't relatives. Mrs. Craft was a divorced lady who was raising her daughter, and my parents paid her to raise me," Brooks explained. Mrs. Craft's daughter went to Catholic school, and even though Donnie's Polish-American mother was a Baptist, he was enrolled in parochial school – as John Dee Faircloth. Every day, Mrs. Craft would drive her daughter and Donnie from her modest home on Iowa Street in the North Park area to the local public school during kindergarten, then to Sacred Heart School during the remainder of his elementary school years. "I became part of Mrs. Craft's family, and I lived with her all the way through the eighth grade." During the summers, Donnie would sometimes stay with his mother, who lived in the Navy housing projects in Linda Vista.

Donnie experienced discord even as a kindergartner. "A kid would put sand in my oatmeal, so I'd put sand in his and the teacher would make both of us eat it." One day he ran off and climbed a wooden water tower, where he was spotted by a neighbor who called the fire department. When fire crews arrived, Donnie was not in sight. "They drained the water tower. There was no body. Well, nobody had seen me climb down. I was at home hiding under the bed at Mrs. Craft's place," Brooks confessed. He hadn't anticipated the punishment he would receive the next day from the school principal. Telling Donnie his behavior had embarrassed the school, the principal offered him his choice of punishment: a belt whipping or hot mush. "Well, I get hit with a Marine belt all the time by my mom, so I'll take the hot mush," he told the principal. He hadn't anticipated how hot the mush would be. "He boiled that mush, and it burned my mouth and gave me blisters on my tongue. To this day I don't eat hot food," Brooks told us that July day in 1997. "I take chicken and put it in the icebox. It was a cruel beginning for a kid."

The parochial school kids who picked on Donnie were toying with a pit bull. They had no idea of his underlying torment and bitterness. "Bitter? You don't know what bitter is, to be raised all your life and not know who your father is," said Brooks. "Of all three of those men, my stepfather is the only one who actually worked and supported me. He's was the only one who has really been a father to me, but even he was busy all the time, working and in the Marine Corps. So I was raised around boarding schools and Mrs. Craft, and by the time I moved in with my parents when I was 13, I didn't know them."

Through it all, Donnie found comfort and escape in his singing. As a preteen, he had a crisp soprano voice that brought him singing leads in local variety productions and appearances on local San Diego variety television programs.

The summer of 1950 was a time of dramatic change for Donnie. His stepfather had been discharged from the Marines and took a civilian job at Port Hueneme in Oxnard, 175 miles up the coast from San Diego. Jim and Mary enrolled Donnie in Villanova High School, a boys' boarding school in Ojai Valley. As if that change were not difficult enough, Donnie lost his youthful soprano range as adolescence deepened his voice. "It was really traumatic for me when I lost my voice. My freshman year in high school was terrible. No more boy soprano, no more big star. It was devastating to me," Brooks said. "I thought my life was over."

But life went on, and by his junior year he regained sufficient confidence in his voice to resume singing as a tenor. "I took lessons from a lady named Mrs. Reardon in Ventura. Her brother owned Reardon Mortuary. She was a good teacher," Brooks said. She must have been, because when he entered a talent contest sponsored by the Ventura Junior Chamber of Commerce, he won. He tried out for the school's football team. He made the squad as a 180-pound tackle and rose to team captain. His high school yearbook described him as a "glass-shattering tenor" and as "sparkplug of the football team." After graduation from high school in 1954, he enrolled at Ventura Junior College with a major in music. There, he studied everything from light opera and jazz to folk stylings, pop, rhythm and blues, and dance.

He put himself through school with a night job at Camarillo State Hospital, a mental health treatment facility that has since been closed. He also sang with a little band composed of a man who played saxophone and his wife who played piano. They did gigs at a little Navy beer bar in Oxnard, where Donnie would sing and dance to "Chattanooga Choo Choo," "Kansas City," and other swing tunes. He sang "I'm Looking Over a Four-Leaf Clover," "When Irish Eyes Are Smiling," and other standards for senior citizens in retirement homes. Speaking and singing in Spanish and English, he purposely uttered malapropisms just to get a laugh. "Buenos noches, damas y caballos," he'd say – "Good evening, ladies and horses."

When he completed his college course of study in 1956, he packed his belongings and drove down to Los Angeles to study with musical arranger and producer Al Berkman. "He had a place at 8500 Melrose Avenue, corner of La Cienega. He wasn't a vocal coach. He taught stage presence, lighting techniques, microphone technique, timing, hand motions, how to bow. Techniques that singers nowadays don't seem to have," Brooks explained. "They just don't know what to do with their hands." Berkman, who died in May 1996 at age 82, had worked with singers Eddie Fisher and Vic Damone, and was an arranger for Sammy Kaye and Cab Calloway. He taught his students to view hand motion as a picture frame for what you're going to say. "He taught us that hand motion should precede what you say. If I say 'you' and then I point to you, then I'm late. But if I point to you and say 'hey you' or if I gesture toward myself and then say, 'look at me,' then the hand motion provides a descriptive framework."

While studying with Berkman, Brooks supported himself by working at a place called Rapid Wire, where he got an education of another sort. At its plant in Culver City on L.A.'s west side, Rapid Wire fabricated metal stays for brassieres and bathing suits by Jantzen and other garment manufacturers. Donnie performed two jobs at Rapid Wire. "In the afternoons I drove truck. And in the mornings I would heat wires." He was on the crew that would apply heat to wires to produce desired curvature. "After the wires were chemically treated to prevent rusting during laundering, I would put them in an oven for a certain amount of time. The stays had to fit patterns for the specific sizes. As the stays were heated, they would draw into a curved shape. And I had to stop the heating process at just the right point. The size is measured underneath a woman's breasts, and the size indicates the width of the curvature. If a woman is a double-A, she's small-framed. But if she's a double-D, she's wide chested and this wire has to go all around the bottom of her breast. So the wires I heated had to fit those patterns. So every once in a while you'd open the oven, pull one out, dip it in cold water and put it on the pattern to see if it closed up the proper way. I got so I could look at a girl and say, '36D'. Or '34C.' And they'd say, how do you know that? It was because I knew these patterns and I could just cup my hands as I looked at them from a distance and I'd know their size."

With that skill in hand, Donnie would take to the road in the afternoons, delivering the stays that he helped produce. That gave him the opportunity to schedule afternoon singing auditions at recording studios where songwriters and music publishers went to produce demo versions of new songs. His audition for Sandy Stanton at Fable Records was productive. "The first pressing I ever had was on his label," Brooks recalled.

And then he heard about a place called the York Club on Western Avenue. "It was a strip joint, and they had a Monday talent contest. The prize was 50 bucks and the chance to work the weekend for 50 bucks a night. I entered the contest and sang 'Long Tall Sally' and 'Granada,' so it was plain to see I didn't know what I was doing," Brooks chuckled.

Nevertheless, he won the contest and sang his set in between striptease performances. He quickly became a regular at the York Club. "I did three 15-minute shows a night. As soon as the strippers would walk off I'd do the three songs, someone else would do a couple of songs, a comic would do a few jokes, and then they'd bring the strippers back on." His act included "Long Tall Sally," "Granada" in Spanish and "On the Sunny Side of the Street." Brooks confessed, "The selection of songs made no sense at all. When I'd come on the patrons would get up and go to the bathroom, then they'd order another beer and watch the strippers for the next 45 minutes. But I didn't care. It was show business to me. My goodness, I worked all week driving truck for 100 bucks. But I could pick up another 150 bucks working weekends and Monday nights. It was more money than I knew what to do with," Donnie told us in July 1997.

Donnie worked his way into other gigs, including standing weekend appearances on Latino-flavored rock and roll bills at El Monte Legion Stadium, sharing the stage with Ritchie Valens, who was then on his rise to fame. Other acts with whom Donnie appeared included the Penguins, the Shields, the Medallions, and Johnny Otis and the Masked Phantoms Band. The shows were staged by local disc jockey Art Laboe, who later launched the Original Sound oldies label. "The Phantoms Band consisted of Johnny Otis, two beautiful girls dressed up like cats in little skin-tight phantom outfits, and musicians wearing purple outfits with hoods like the Phantom. The reason was the guitar player, a guy by the name of Don Preston, was only 16 years old. And minors were not permitted there. Don went on with Leon Russell, he appeared on the Bangladesh tour with the Beatles, and he sang 'Youngblood' on that benefit album. He's also written a lot of songs for different people, and he's still a great guitar player."

Brooks was paid $14 per night for the shows, but he made a lot more as a result. "Red Gilson, who ran the door at El Monte Legion Stadium, liked to gamble. On Saturday nights after he got his take from the door, he would drive me over to his house, pay me my 28 bucks, and he would say, 'You deal.' We'd start out playing poker at 2 bucks a hand. He'd play seven hands and lose. He'd raise it to 10 bucks, then to 50 bucks a hand. By 8 o'clock in the morning his wife would come out and tell us, 'go home, go to bed, get out of my house.' And I'd leave with 300 bucks."

By that time, he got the urge to see the bright lights of Las Vegas for the first time. Vegas in '58. The El Rancho. The Sands. The Thunderbird. The Desert Inn. The Tropicana. He anticipated being awestruck. He never expected to become lovestruck. Penny was a dancer who had

117

spent years with the New York City Ballet, before going west to dance with Jimmy Durante's show troupe. After her show, Donnie introduced himself to her. They talked. They enjoyed each others' company. Penny subsequently signed on to dance in the acclaimed *Vive les Girls* revue at the Dunes Hotel and Casino, while Donnie returned to L.A. But as Penny and Donnie pursued their separate show business careers, they remained in touch with each other.

Back in L.A., as Brooks made the rounds of the studios, he met musical arranger and songwriter Jesse Hodges. Their work together led to Donnie's success with "Mission Bell" and "Doll House" in 1960.

Subsequent releases on Era failed to repeat his earlier successes, but Brooks by then had developed a new interest: the twist. As the dancing craze began sweeping America in 1961, Donnie and his new manager saw opportunity. With the twist as the basis of a song-and-dance act, he started working nightclubs. He'd perform a song like "What'd I Say," as he jumped out into the audience and persuaded a couple of young women to twist with him on stage, demonstrating the steps. Then Donnie would get a couple of guys to join the women on stage, and as they danced he'd put other dancing couples in motion on the floor. Among those who caught his act at the Palomino in North Hollywood were Milton Berle, who was instrumental in securing a long-running booking for Donnie at Le Crazy Horse (formerly Ciro's nightclub) on Sunset Boulevard in Hollywood. "And I became the West Coast king of the twist." He acquired the skill in an afternoon. "I watched the dancers on Dick Clark's *American Bandstand* and learned how do to it." He learned his lesson well, because before long he was invited to the homes of Jimmy Durante and other celebrities to teach the twist at Hollywood parties.

As the twist lost its appeal in 1962, Donnie refined his act, blending standards and pop tunes in a musical-comedy repertoire that took him to the lounges and showrooms of Reno, Lake Tahoe, and Vegas. The Mint Hotel & Casino booked him for eight weeks, and he performed at the Silverbird Casino for four weeks, at the Desert Inn for eight weeks, and the Tropicana held him over for 12 weeks. He opened for Louis Prima and Keely Smith, and went on Frank Sinatra's payroll at the Cal-Neva Lodge, where he opened for Buddy Greco, and for Diahann Carroll. There were often more stars in the audience than on stage. Donnie played to Marilyn Monroe, David Janssen, Phil Harris, Joe E. Brown, and other actors and entertainers. In Reno, Donnie played the Mapes Hotel while Penny danced at the Riverside in 1963. They married that year, and remained together until death did them part.

118

At the time he married, Donnie was making about $2,000 a week playing the lounges and $300 to $500 per evening at nightclub engagements. Realizing that multiple-star bills have substantially more drawing power than single-performer shows, he hatched an idea. Donnie, who knew the Platters, approached the owner of an L.A. nightclub. "How would you like to have the Platters play your place Monday night?" Brooks asked. The club owner was interested. So Brooks called the Platters' manager to see if they'd consider working on a Monday night for him for 10 percent less than their usual $5,000 fee. The group's manager thought for only a moment, then said, "Sure, why not?" Donnie's concept was to charge the club owner the group's usual amount, then keep the difference as a service fee for making the arrangements.

Donnie headed back to the nightclub owner. "I can get the Platters for you next Monday night for $5,000, and I'll perform on the same bill for $200." The club owner agreed. It added up to a fast $700 for Brooks for pulling together a one-night show. Next he called the Drifters, also friends of his. Although they normally commanded $4,000 per appearance, they agreed to do a Monday night show for 10 percent less. They figured they weren't working then anyway. Brooks booked the show, appeared on stage along with the Drifters, and took home a $600 paycheck.

All of a sudden, he was more than a performer. He was a show producer. That, he discovered, is what he wanted to do. And that's what he continued to do for more than 30 years. In December 1984, Brooks began an eight-year business relationship with talent manager and producer Ron Kurtz. Together they staged a New Year's Eve show called "Rock in '85" at the MGM Grand Hotel & Casino in Reno. The show was a hit, and Richard Sturm, the hotel's entertainment director, booked Kurtz and Brooks to repeat it for two more years. After Bally Manufacturing Company acquired the MGM Grand properties, Sturm became entertainment director at Bally's in Las Vegas, where singer Dean Martin had been booked for an appearance in the spring of 1987. Martin cancelled the appearance after his eldest son, Dean Paul Martin, was killed in the crash of a California Air National Guard fighter jet he was piloting. Sturm called Kurtz and said he needed to know immediately if he had a show available to substitute. "Out of the blue, I answered, 'here's one that's available: "The 30th Anniversary of Rock and Roll."' Richard said, 'That sounds good. Who's in it?' So I just started making up names. And they bought it. Then Donnie and I put the show together," Kurtz told us in March 2012. It worked — so well that Kurtz and Brooks decided to package a "30th Anniversary of Rock 'n' Roll" tour.

They lined up dates across the country, in concert halls, at county fairs, in nightclubs and at business conventions, and hit the road with busloads of entertainers and truckloads of equipment. Performers they booked for the tours in 1988 and '89 included Lesley Gore, Mitch Ryder and the Detroit Wheels, Gary Lewis, the Tokens, the Buckinghams, B. J. Thomas, Merrilee Rush, Micky Dolenz (of the Monkees), Dennis Yost (of the Classics IV), Gladys Horton (of the Marvelettes), Pat Upton (of the Spiral Starecase), Len Barry, Spencer Davis, Al Wilson, Tiny Tim, the Coasters, the Rivingtons, Bobby Day, Jewel Akens, Bobby "Boris" Pickett, and Cannibal and the Headhunters. "Donnie was always a tre- mendously fun person to be around, and always had a joke ready. In fact, he never stopped telling jokes. He was a consummate performer," Kurtz said. The bus tours were arduous, though, and Kurtz and Brooks scaled back the show's schedule to weekends in 1990 and '91 before going their separate ways in 1992.

Brooks continued packaging shows on his own. He was booking $18,000 shows and did quite well, but it was a lot of work. "I contact every one of the acts, set a price with each, arrange and pay for their air and ground transportation, pay for their overnight accommodations, arrange for all the stage and sound equipment, set up rehearsals, bring in caterers." It's not brain surgery, he acknowledged, but involves a lot of legwork that many others were unwilling to do. "It's a lot easier for them to just give me the money and tell me, 'you handle it all. It's too much trouble.' So I book them, I make sure the performers get there, make sure they get checked into the rooms, make sure they're all happy. That's what I do. Everything from Johnny Cash to the Kingston Trio to Engelbert Humperdinck. I'm an order filler."

But to the artists, Donnie was much more than an order filler. He was a respected colleague and a friend. He was one of them.

"They regard me as another entertainer. I know exactly what they want. And that's difficult to know if you're not in the entertainment busi- ness yourself," Brooks explained. "It's important for singers to know that they'll be backed by a good band that knows their material, that the band reviewed and rehearsed their songs, so that the singers don't look like fools on stage. They deserve to be treated well when they're picked up at the airport. They shouldn't have to worry about making arrangements for meals. My acts know I'll take them out to dinner afterwards. It's a matter of creating a feeling of camaraderie, like a family. Artists don't get that in a lot of shows. They're more often treated like pieces of meat." Brooks used humor liberally among his performer-friends, poking fun at them as well as himself. "All right, all you pieces of meat over here…" he'd tell a group of performers before a show. "Well, what are you then?" a singer may ask. Laughing, Brooks was likely to reply, "Me? I'm the baloney."

Donnie booked performances at concert halls, fairs, corporate parties, amusement parks and business conventions. "I love producing shows," he said. "And I book my friends, people who are fun to be with. When someone becomes a pain in the ass, I just don't work with him anymore."

Although Donnie's production firm in Burbank, California, was a one-man operation, he occasionally collaborated with other producers and worked regularly with Mario Sanders Management in Las Vegas. Brooks was honored by induction into the Rockabilly Hall of Fame in Burns, Tennessee, in 2003. But the close of that year brought tragedy. While driving south on Interstate 15 on his way home from Las Vegas, where he had been attending a conference of the International Association of Fairs and Expositions, Donnie fell asleep at the wheel. His car slammed into the rear of a truck and he sustained serious injuries, from which he never fully recovered. He gradually, painfully resumed work, seated in a chair when he sang on stage. With his big frame ravaged by the ongoing effects of his injuries, he died at age 71 of congestive heart failure on February 23, 2007, at Mission Community Hospital in the San Fernando Valley community of Panorama City.

Donnie and Penny raised two children: Shad, born in 1970, and Saji, born in 1973. Shad entered food service management for several Southern California golf courses, and Saji concentrated on raising her own daughter, born in 1995. "Our granddaughter is the joy of our life," Donnie said lovingly, clearly savoring the family closeness that he was denied as a child.

If there's one thing that he did derive from his own childhood, it was admiration for his stepfather. "When he worked as a civil servant, his job was to find parts for the Navy. If the Seabees wanted a bolt for a certain tractor, he would know how to get it in stock. He worked at those salt mines until the day he died. He called them the salt mines. But he never took a day off, and he was always there on time. He was a hard worker," Brooks said.

As Brooks readied for one of his lively stage performances in the 1990s, in which he would once again sing "Mission Bell," he was energized to pack as much enthusiasm into his show as he did on tour in 1960.

"That song is like a calling card for me," he had told us. "That's my one claim to fame, my 15 minutes of glory. And so it's not at all hard for me to sing it with feeling."

121

Sam and Dave (photo courtesy of Joyce and Sam Moore)

Hold On, I'm Comin'

Sam and Dave

By the time the Blues Brothers characters created by portly John Belushi and then-gangly Dan Aykroyd burst from Saturday late-night television onto the big screen in 1980, their rendition of the song "Soul Man" already was a fixture of their act, a top-20 single culled from their 1978 album *Briefcase Full of Blues*. Resembling, as Aretha Franklin said in the *Blues Brothers* movie, "two honkies dressed like Hasidic diamond merchants ... like they're from the CIA or somethin'," the blank-faced Belushi and earnest Aykroyd exuberantly performed R&B classics with a conviction that gave nary a hint of the tongue-in-cheek notion of two white guys proclaiming themselves "soul men." But in truth, both men shared deep respect for soul music, rhythm and blues, and jazz, and their performance of "Soul Man" paid homage to the originators of the 1966 hit: Sam and Dave, who by then had dissolved their act. Belushi and Aykroyd recognized the musical contributions of Sam and Dave, whose string of hits during the 1960s celebrated the gospel roots of Southern soul music.

Sam Moore and Dave Prater Jr. were for a time among the world's most popular recording and performing artists, and with their frenzied stage appearances established themselves as the most electrifying duo in the history of rhythm and blues music. Between 1966 and 1969 they accumulated an impressive succession of hits on the R&B and pop music charts for the Memphis-based Stax label, which had a stellar roster of artists that included Otis Redding, the Mar-Keys, Rufus and Carla

Thomas, the Bar-Kays, Eddie Floyd, and Booker T. & the MGs. Packing their gritty, forceful vocals with raw emotion and energy, Sam and Dave worked primarily with material developed by the songwriting team of David Porter and Isaac Hayes Jr. Backed by the powerful horn-driven Stax rhythm section, their singing drew heavily from the chords of black church hymnals. Their powerfully intense live performances in the Stax-Volt Revues infused the call-and-response testimonial tradition of black church congregations, and earned the duo the affectionate nicknames "the Sultans of Sweat" and "Double Dynamite," when their album of that name was high on the charts.

They drew the gospel undertones of their music from personal experience. Sam Moore had sung in church choirs as a child growing up in Miami, and performed with several gospel vocal ensembles, including the Gales and the Melionaires. He'd become so proficient and well-known among gospel groups that he was asked to join the Soul Stirrers as the replacement for Sam Cooke as that singer's solo career began. Dave Prater moved from his native Georgia to Miami to join his brother's gospel group, the Sensational Hummingbirds. But just as they loved gospel music, Sam and Dave also were intrigued by popular music, which drew them together by chance at an amateur singing contest at the King o' Hearts nightclub on Northwest Seventh Avenue at 62nd Street in Miami one summer night in 1961. Prater had chosen to sing "Doggin' Around," a tune that Jackie Wilson had recorded. When, in the glare of the spotlight, Prater stumbled over lyrics he momentarily forgot, Moore prompted him by singing along.

The club's owner, John Lomelo, was struck by their spontaneous synergy on stage and prompted them to develop a stage act. With Lomelo functioning as their manager, they landed a recording contract with the small Alston label, which released a single, "Never Never" – which never went anywhere. A move to Marlin Records produced two more singles: "I Need Love and "No More Pain." The duo signed in 1962 with much larger Roulette Records, the pop and jazz-oriented roster of which at the time included Joey Dee and the Starliters, Dinah Washington, Jimmie Rodgers, the Regents, Joe Jones, and Sarah Vaughan.

Roulette sent Sam and Dave to Bell Sound Studios at 237 W. 54th Street in New York City. During the next two years, they recorded six singles for Roulette, beginning with "I Need Love," as well as an album titled *Sam & Dave,* but they remained hitless. "We hadn't done well with Roulette because they didn't know what to do with us," Sam Moore explained. "We were more like gospel singers." Their recording career languished until Atlantic Records executive Ahmet Ertegun and producer

Jerry Wexler saw them perform at the King o' Hearts. Sensing that the only thing standing between them and huge success was the right material, Wexler signed them to New York-based Atlantic in late 1964, but sent them to Memphis to record for Stax, for which Atlantic served as distributor. That was the right choice. Sam and Dave fit the Stax mold like a pair of feet in comfortable old shoes. They entered the studio for their first Stax session on March 19, 1965. They missed the mark with their first two Stax singles, "A Place Nobody Can Find" (written by David Porter) and "I Take What I Want" (a collaboration by Isaac Hayes and Porter with Mabon Lewis "Teenie" Hodges – who later co-wrote several hits with Al Green). They hit the bull's eye when they went into the studio on October 25, 1965, and recorded a Hayes-Porter gem. "You Don't Know Like I Know," two and a half minutes of jumping, jubilant, finger-snapping Memphis funk produced by Stax co-owner Jim Stewart, entered the soul music charts the first week in January 1966 and peaked at No. 7. Sam and Dave were on their way.

They developed a sound that was distinctly their own, but through which glinted reflections of the influence of Sam Cooke, the Impressions, Rufus Thomas, Bobby "Blue" Bland, Ben E. King, and Solomon Burke. Most of their recordings were thumping hand-clappers, as was their first "crossover" pop hit, "Hold On, I'm Comin'," which they recorded March 8, 1966. That Hayes-Porter tune (to which Sam Moore also made unacknowledged contributions, and which was shown as "Hold On! I'm A Comin'" on some pressings) hit No. 1 on the soul chart (and remained on that chart for nearly five months), and reached No. 21 on the pop chart. It spawned an album, *Hold On, I'm Comin'*, which hit No. 1 on the R&B album chart. Delivering the high-potency instrumental power behind Sam and Dave were Stax's cadre of top-notch musicians: guitarist Steve Cropper, bassist Donald "Duck" Dunn, drummer Al Jackson Jr., Isaac Hayes on keyboards and organ, saxophonists Charles "Packy" Axton and Andrew Love Jr., and trumpet player Wayne Jackson. Other members of the "Memphis Horn Section" who backed them on some tracks included trumpet and trombone player Jack Hale, and baritone sax player Floyd Newman, and even Isaac Hayes played on some sessions.

Sam and Dave were in the studio on August 8, 1966, when they recorded a superb track of strutting funk, "Said I Wasn't Gonna Tell Nobody," which was another Hayes-Porter tune. Back in the studio on November 4, they laid down the Hayes-Porter composition "You Got Me Hummin'" – which in reality got their growing number of fans humming.

In contrast to those pulsating tracks, the pleading ballad "When

Something Is Wrong With My Baby," recorded on November 15, 1966, sounded as if it were scored using a page ripped from a church hymnal. That became their first chart record of 1967. It hit No. 2 on the soul music charts and a respectable No. 42 slot on the pop chart. Sam and Dave followed that with a Sam Cooke composition, "Soothe Me," recorded while they were performing live on the Stax-Volt tour in Paris. The label had flown producer Isaac Hayes and renowned recording engineer Tom Dowd to Paris to capture Sam and Dave's dynamic performance on tape. "Such an expenditure was particularly exceptional for American black artists touring Europe in 1967," Sam noted. The track opened with a bluesy instrumental bed, sensual humming and soft finger snaps – before Sam and Dave burst forth with a passionate plea for love. ("Soothe Me" later would be used in the *Blues Brothers* movie in a sequence in which Belushi and Aykroyd's characters Jake and Elwood Blues were listening to a Sam and Dave eight-track tape while cruising after dark along the streets of Chicago in the '74 Dodge Monaco "Bluesmobile.") Stax released a second album, *Double Dynamite,* containing "Soothe Me" and three other hit singles that the duo recorded between August 1966 and May 1967. "Dan Aykroyd, who has introduced Sam as 'super voice' on several occasions, considers 'Soothe Me' his favorite Sam and Dave song," Sam's wife Joyce told us.

On the strength of those successes, Sam and Dave hit the road in the spring of '67 with the Stax-Volt Revue, an energetic five-week concert performance tour inaugurated with a seven-night stand at the legendary Apollo Theater at 253 W. 125th Street in New York City, before taking Europe by storm. With the great Otis Redding as headliner and Sam and Dave in second billing, the entourage included Booker T. & the MGs, Eddie Floyd, Carla Thomas, Arthur Conley, and the Mar-Keys. Sam and Dave ignited every stage on which they appeared into a sweaty soul inferno. The performers intoxicated audiences in England, Sweden, Norway, and Denmark.

"We had a couple of years of touring with other Stax acts, then we started doing tours ourselves," Dave Prater said in an interview on May 19, 1983, with Toronto-area FM station CFNY disc jockey Dave "Daddy Cool" Booth, who now operates Showtime Music Archive in Toronto. "Sam had a plane and we'd play two countries in one night. Keep on truckin'. But the Apollo Theater was the toughest. That was like a proving ground. If you couldn't satisfy the people in Harlem at the Apollo Theater, you could forget it. We used to work all day and half the night there. Man, we used to do sometimes ten, twelve shows back to back. We used to work like dogs in that place – I'm not kidding," Prater told Booth.

On August 10, 1967, Sam and Dave recorded what would become their signature song, the celebratory "Soul Man." Another Hayes and Porter composition, it was inspired by the hand-lettered "soul" and "soul brother" signs that black business owners posted on their storefronts to protect their property from destruction during the July 1967 Detroit riots in which 43 people were killed, more than 400 others were injured, and 2,500 businesses were looted or incinerated. The song affixed the term "soul" as synonymous with black identity and pride. Sam's spontaneous exclamation "Play it, Steve," hailing the guitar riffs of Steve Cropper, is a standout moment in the track. The horn-driven "Soul Man" resonated with fans in the fall of 1967, who sent it to the No. 2 position

Cover from Sam and Dave's 1967 album *Double Dynamite* (photo courtesy of Atlantic Records/Warner Music Group Archives)

on the pop chart and No. 1 on the soul music chart. The Recording Industry Association of America awarded a gold record for "Soul Man" on November 22, 1967. The song, which prompted an album, *Soul Men,* also captivated the attention of the industry at large, earning Sam and Dave a Grammy Award on February 29, 1968, for Best Rhythm & Blues Performance by a Duo or Group during 1967. "Soul Man/ Soul Men" became the branded identity of the duo and later of Moore as a soloist. "That unfortunately has been one of the most invaded and misappropriated identities as the years have progressed, requiring me to mount some heavy litigation to protect the legacy," Moore said.

The new year began with another productive recording session. On January 5, 1968, Sam and Dave recorded Hayes and Porter's tune "I Thank You," which oozed with funky self-confidence and reveled in the pure joy of rhythm. The song opened with a rap that Sam wrote: "I want everybody to get up off your seat, and get your arms together, and your hands together, and give me some of that ooooold soul clapping." The recording, however, would become their last formidable hit.

Although Sam and Dave had an impeccable sense of timing and tightly choreographed interplay on stage, that *Double Dynamite* album title came to define them in unintended ways. Their professionalism during concert performances concealed their explosive personal relationship, which disintegrated under the pressure of frequent and often bitter clashes. Their unrelenting squabbles contributed as much to their eventual split as the dissolution of the distribution arrangement between Atlantic and Stax in 1968. That presaged an end to the magically creative working relationship with their production team of Porter and Hayes and the recording backup work of Booker T. & the MGs, whose work Sam Moore praises. "David was the lyricist, and Isaac was the composer and arranger, and if you want to talk about the Memphis sound, it was Isaac Hayes' sound. He *is* the Memphis sound," Moore emphatically declared. "Isaac Hayes was the *man* – he was the Quincy Jones of Stax."

Sam and Dave's 1968 album, *I Thank You,* seemed to be an appreciative nod to their fans. In addition to the title track, it included their follow-up single, "You Don't Know What You Mean to Me," which Eddie Floyd and Steve Cropper wrote, with an introduction penned by Sam Moore. It was only the second Sam and Dave chart single in more than two years that had been written by anyone other than Isaac Hayes and David Porter. And it marked the duo's shift from the Stax label to Atlantic Records.

Atlantic singles that followed included "Can't You Find Another Way (of Doing It)," written by Homer Banks and Raymond E. Jackson (who also co-wrote Johnnie Taylor's "Who's Making Love"), and "Everybody Got to Believe in Somebody," a Hayes and Porter composition. "Born Again," the last Sam and Dave single produced by Hayes and Porter at the Stax studio in Memphis, was also their last single to make the charts, coinciding with the release of another album, *The Best of Sam & Dave*. Working with producers Jerry Wexler and Tom Dowd in New York beginning in 1969, Sam and Dave recorded three more singles, "Ooh Ooh Ooh," "Baby, Baby, Don't Stop Now" and "When You Steal From Me." When those failed to chart, they began working with another producer, Dave Crawford, with whom they recorded their last two

Cover from Sam and Dave's 1968 album *I Thank You* (photo courtesy of Atlantic Records/Warner Music Group Archives)

Atlantic singles, "Knock Out in the Park" and "Don't Pull Your Love Out," released in 1971. By then Sam and Dave had already split.

Atlantic signed Sam Moore as a solo artist and in 1970 and '71 released three singles, "Tennessee Waltz," "Stop" and "Shop Around." Dave Prater signed as a solo act with Alston Records, which in 1972 released a single, "Keep My Fingers Crossed." None of those releases, however, made a dent on the charts.

During successive years, they did manage to stage several reunions – "if you could call them that," Sam interjected. "We did some dates here and there over the years to support our habits. We were both in such bad shape we couldn't really be counted on, and the word about our being 'undependable' was out there." In 1974 they signed with United Artists Records, which released two new Sam and Dave singles, "A Little Bit of Good (Cures a Whole Lot of Bad)" and "Under the Boardwalk" (with which the Drifters hit the charts in 1964) along with a companion album, *Back At'cha,* which Booker T. & the MGs guitarist Steve Cropper produced at the studio he owned. The musicianship was solid, with bassist Donald "Duck" Dunn, guitarist and arranger Danny Kortchmar, trumpet player Wayne Jackson, and drummers Willie Hall and Al Jackson Jr. Even so, the 1976 album release did not attract sufficient attention. After another hiatus, Sam and Dave were back again in 1977 with a new single, a rendition of John Lennon and Paul McCartney's "We Can Work it Out" recorded for the British label Contempo. But like their other post-1968 recordings, it lacked the chemistry that had made their Stax recordings so vibrant and potent. On the strength of the Blues Brothers' revival of "Soul Man," Sam and Dave paired once again for a tour in 1979. They performed together for the last time, however, in San Francisco on New Year's Eve at the close of 1981. "Sam already had started the process of 'cleaning up' from his addiction and knew that the only way he could survive was to break free, at least for a time, from the duo, from their manager Jeff Brown, from New York City, and from the road," Joyce Moore explained. *I Can't Stand Up For Falling Down,* a 1984 Edsel Records album consisting of previously unreleased tracks that Sam and Dave had recorded between 1969 and '71, was a treat for fans in the United Kingdom who hungered for more music by the "Soul Men."

After the breakup Dave began performing with other singers – including singer Sam Daniels, a school teacher. Despite Moore's objections, Prater and Daniels also recorded a single, *A Sam & Dave Medley,* for 21 Records. The 1985 release contained a seven-minute medley of "You Don't Know What You Mean to Me," "Soul Sister (Brown Sugar)," "Soul Man," "Hold On, I'm Coming," and "I Thank You," on side A, with a compressed four-minute version on side B. On a second pressing, the singers' name credit was changed to "Stars On 45, Featuring the New Sam and Dave Revue." Prater's partnership with Daniels rubbed open old wounds. Sam Moore, asserting that his trademark and identity had been hijacked, initiated legal action. "Atlantic Records released *Stars on 45 – The Sam and Dave Medley* and claimed it was by the original artists, but that was not me singing. They had Sam Daniels singing a medley of songs that I made famous with Dave," Moore said. He filed legal action against Atlantic. "They were ordered to recall all the records from the stores to re-label them, indicating that the 'Sam' on the records was not the original 'Sam' – me." However, until Prater died in a car crash in April 1988, he continued performing with Daniels.

Sam Moore and Dave Prater Jr. were inducted into the Rock & Roll Hall of Fame in 1992. On July 17, 1995, the Recording Industry Association of America (RIAA) finally recognized Sam and Dave's 1966 hit "Hold On, I'm Coming" with a gold record award, and in 1999 conferred its Grammy Hall of Fame award honoring "recordings of lasting qualitative or historical significance" to Sam and Dave's "Soul Man." In a nationwide selection process that the RIAA and the National Endowment for the Arts concluded in March 2001, "Soul Man" was chosen among 365 historically significant "Songs of the Century" that embody the musical and cultural heritage of America.

U.S. HIT SINGLES BY SAM AND DAVE

Debut	Peak	Gold	Title	Label
1/66	90		You Don't Know Like I Know	Stax
4/66	21	Δ	Hold On, I'm Comin'	Stax
9/66	64		Said I Wasn't Gonna Tell Nobody	Stax
12/66	77		You Got Me Hummin'	Stax
2/67	42		When Something Is Wrong With My Baby	Stax
6/67	56		Soothe Me	Stax
9/67	2	Δ	Soul Man	Stax
1/68	9		I Thank You	Stax
5/68	48		You Don't Know What You Mean to Me	Atlantic
8/68	54		Can't You Find Another Way (Of Doing It)	Atlantic
11/68	73		Everybody Got to Believe in Somebody	Atlantic
12/68	41		Soul Sister, Brown Sugar	Atlantic
3/69	92		Born Again	Atlantic

Δ symbol: RIAA certified gold record (Recording Industry Association of America)

Billboard's pop singles chart data is courtesy of Joel Whitburn's Record Research Inc. (www.recordresearch.com), Menomonee Falls, Wisconsin.

Epilogue: Sam Moore

Singer

Record labels didn't know what to do with Sam and Dave. The Alston label didn't know in 1962. Neither did Roulette Records in 1963. When Sam and Dave signed with New York-based Atlantic Records in late 1964, that label decided to send them to Stax Records in Memphis, for which Atlantic served as manufacturer and distributor. And on their first meeting with Stax personnel in March 1965, Sam Moore and Dave Prater didn't quite know what to do. After checking into their hotel room upon their arrival in Memphis, Moore and Prater went to the label's headquarters, a former movie theater

Sam Moore in the 2000s (photo courtesy of Joyce and Sam Moore)

on East McLemore Avenue, south of the downtown area. There they met Stax co-owner and producer Jim Stewart, drummer Al Jackson Jr., and guitarist Steve Cropper of Booker T. & the MGs, which functioned as the Stax house band for its recording sessions. Next to arrive was lyricist David Porter, who at the time was working full-time as an insurance salesman. They were waiting for one more member of their production team.

Sam Moore glanced down the block and what he saw stunned him. "Walking up the street toward us was a young man wearing a pink shirt, chartreuse pants, a white belt, pink socks, and white shoes," recalled Moore. "I didn't say anything to anyone else, but I thought to myself, 'Oh my God! Why did Atlantic send us here?' That man in the chartreuse pants and pink socks was Isaac Hayes. I didn't know who he was, and when he and David Porter started playing their new songs for us to record, I didn't like any of them. My head was all set into Jackie Wilson, Sam Cooke, Little Willie John, the "5" Royales, the Drifters, and Ray Charles. The material that Hayes and Porter were playing for us wasn't at all like that, and wasn't anything like the songs that I was writing at the time, either. And no one asked us if we wrote music. I said to Dave, 'What is happening here?' I didn't think we were going to go anywhere with those people."

Raised in the gospel tradition, Sam by that time had become enamored with popular performers after attending a performance by Jackie Wilson (with whom Sam subsequently developed a close friendship after moving to New York). That concert changed the direction of Moore's career. He was on his way to Chicago to replace Sam Cooke in the Soul Stirrers Gospel Group, but instead decided he wanted the adulation and respect that he saw in Jackie. So Sam left that lead singer slot open for Johnnie Taylor, who eventually became another Stax label mate. Sam was so disenchanted with the new material Hayes and Porter presented that he approached recording sessions with indifference. "I didn't like 'I Take What I Want,' our second single," Moore acknowledged. "The way I phrased it made it sound more like country than soul. I was so angry and upset, so I just phrased it like I wanted because I didn't care. I just didn't have enough power at that time to turn anything down."

But the team at Stax, especially Isaac Hayes, heard a quality in Sam Moore's singing that they were trying to coax out of him – something that he at the time was trying to deny – the fire, brimstone and passion of his gospel roots. Just as Sam's earlier record labels hadn't been sure what to do with him, Sam hadn't exactly been sure of what to do himself either. Despite being raised on gospel music, he had considered a career as a football player. He became a father at age 16. He joined a circus troupe for a while. He hustled pool. And he had thought about becoming a professional prize fighter. But even as he pursued those other whims, music always remained the foundation of Sam's being.

Sam's voice was distinctly different from Dave Prater's low-register baritone. Sam's was the sweeter, smoother tenor of the duo. He discovered his musical talent in the bathroom one day when he was about 11 years old. "The acoustics sure sounded good in the bathroom," he chuckled.

Sam was born during the depths of the Great Depression on October 12, 1935 – the same day on which another gifted tenor, preeminent Italian operatic singer Luciano Pavarotti, was born halfway around the globe. For most of his life Sam was under the impression that he had been born in Miami. But after requesting an original copy of his birth certificate so he could register for Social Security benefits at age 65, he was astonished to learn that he was born at Winchester Station, a train whistle stop two miles south of Marshallville, Georgia. His mother, Louise, had attended nearby Fort Valley State College and was employed as a teacher when she became pregnant and gave birth to Sam. "My dad worked on the railroad at one time as a porter," Sam told us in July

2000. "Who knows what he did after that?" When Sam was an infant his mother and birth father moved to the Miami area, then separated. Louise subsequently met and married Charlie Moore, an architect, who legally adopted Sam. At Dillard High School in Fort Lauderdale, Sam's band teacher was Julian Adderley – who played trumpet at the time but subsequently developed renown as preeminent jazz saxophonist "Cannonball" Adderley. But Sam got into trouble with a girl named Ora Lee, who became pregnant and gave birth to a daughter, Deborah, in 1952. So Sam was a father before he was out of high school. "Yeah, man! She conceived in ninth grade and I was a dad in about tenth grade," he acknowledged. The teenagers did not marry. After Deborah's birth, Sam resumed his education at Booker T. Washington High School in Miami.

After his bathroom acoustics revelation, Sam got together with some Washington High School friends of his who also enjoyed singing. After school, they'd practice singing doo-wop harmonies – in Sam's bathroom. Their singing caught the ear of John McArthur, an older friend of theirs who happened to be walking past Sam's home during one of those bathroom singing sessions. "At the time I liked the Coasters, the Drifters, the '5' Royales, the Platters, and Billy Ward and his Dominoes," Sam told us in 2000. "John McArthur was a black person, but he had a big, robust Irish tenor singing voice. He would do 'Danny Boy,' and we would go, 'Wow!' He told us we sounded good." McArthur asked Sam and his friends if they would like to sing background in his doo-wop group, the Majestics, which typically performed at high school dances. That was fine with Sam, who was by then in 11th grade. "I wasn't interested in stepping out front to sing. I *never* thought about being a star." Together, McArthur and Moore wrote two songs, "Nitey Nite" and "Cave Man Rock." The Majestics (later to become known as the Gales) approached the independent Marlin label, which agreed to record the group and released their doo-wop ballad "Nitey Nite" backed with "Cave Man Rock" as a single in 1954. Moore also sang on Sundays with a gospel group composed of several of his high school friends, who first called themselves the Mellow Fellows, then became the Melionaires.

Sam had set his sights on attending college, and he decided to try for a football scholarship. He signed on with the high school football team, felt good in all the gear, but quickly found that it wasn't for him. "The first day a big ole linebacker knocked me into the next century, and I came home with a big gash over my eye. My mother said, 'That's no good. Take all that stuff back, you can't play that.' And that was that," Sam laughed. "Then I thought I wanted to be a boxer. I went to a gym on the beach in Miami to work out, and people like Cassius Clay, Joe Lewis, and Sugar Ray Robinson were down there. I got to be a good punching bag fighter. Then they gave me my first fight, and I held my own until the second round. Then I got knocked out, and I came home with my money. I think they paid me $40." Deciding to find a more suitable, safe way to earn spending cash and help support his mother, Sam got a job at his church. He tended the lawn and flowers, cleaned the pews, and did other maintenance work. On his way home from work one evening in 1954 after being paid, Sam suffered severe leg injuries when he was jumped and shot by a robber. As a result of his long recuperation from the injury to his muscle tissue and his splintered bone, he missed much of the school year. He resumed school in his senior year at Booker T. Washington High, from which he graduated at age 19 in 1955.

The following year, Sam and the Mellow Fellows left home and joined a circus troupe called the World of Mirth, out of Orlando, Florida. "It was an all-black circus, and we traveled by train. We had to sing at night, and in every city we were different acts. In one city we were the Drifters, and in the next we might be the Coasters. When we came to a city where we were locally known, we went back to being the Mellow Fellows. We didn't think we were hurting anybody by using other names," Sam explained. Loneliness set in during Sam's seemingly unending travels with the troupe. "I was like a vagabond." On a stop in Jacksonville, Sam met a young woman who charmed him. When the train pulled out of town, Sam remained in Jacksonville and moved in with the woman, who was the single mother of "about nine babies," Sam grins. "My mom wasn't very proud of that." After a year in Jacksonville, Sam returned to Miami in 1959, when his mother became ill. He moved in with his grandmother, mother, and his daughter.

Sam rejoined the Melionaires gospel group, stepping out in front as lead singer just as the group began to land some good bookings. "I gotta tell you, we opened up for some very prominent gospel groups, including the Caravans, the Gospel Harmonettes, and the Soulsters. That's history, my friend," Sam told us in July 2000. Sam's more visible role with the Melionaires, unfortunately, coincided with the death of his mother in 1960. He also began singing solo, competing in Miami-area amateur talent shows for prize money. "I think first prize was about $25. Second prize was about $15," he recalled. Upon the death of his grandmother in 1961, Sam had full responsibility for raising his 8-year-old daughter, as well as caring for his ailing stepfather. Sam was walking with some friends in the old neighborhood that spring when they paused in front of the King o' Hearts, a nightclub that had for many years been a country music hangout. "No blacks could go there," Sam said. But

we didn't know it had turned into a predominantly black club. So on a
dare, I opened the door and the owner, Johnny Lomelo, was sitting there
with his son. The son asked me what I do, and I told him I sing. I lived
within walking distance of the club, so I came back that Wednesday for
a live audition, and I opened with a song, 'Danny Boy,' attempted to tell
a couple of jokes, and then I said 'We're going to bring on the amateurs
tonight.' The son came to me and said, 'You've got the job. But do me
a favor and drop the comedy.'" Even though the job paid only $7 per
night, Sam needed the money, and he gladly accepted. "So I played pool,
and I worked at the club. It wasn't a lot of money, but it was enough to
support us."

Sam had been working at the King o' Hearts for about three months
when Dave Prater walked into the club one evening in the summer of
1961 to compete in the amateur hour segment. Prater said he was going
to sing "Doggin' Around," a Jackie Wilson tune. Moore began the evening's
show, as usual, with "Danny Boy" and a couple of other songs. Then
he introduced the first "amateur hour" contestant of the evening, Dave
Prater. Before Sam had glided off the stage, Dave hit a snag, momentarily
forgetting a verse. "The crowd was booing Dave, and they were very
vicious," said Sam, who idolized Jackie Wilson and knew his music
intimately. "So I stepped up behind Dave and told him, 'I know the words
to this song, so when you get to the verse, I'll be standing behind you and
mouth the words so you can hear me.' So he went into it again and when
he got to the verse, he repeated everything I said. But I didn't see the cord
of the microphone and I was trying to step back and I stepped on the
chord, which pulled the microphone down to the side. Dave jumped to the
floor to grab the mike and so did I. We came up at the same time and the
house went berserk because it looked like a dance move."

After the show, Sam went to the bar to retrieve the money for
the prize-winning contestants, including Dave Prater, who won the
second-place prize of $20. Johnny Lomelo called Sam aside and said,
"Look, look, look. Why don't you and Dave Prater get together on the
weekend and practice some songs? Sing some songs like 'I'll Never
Smile Again' or something. I'll pay you." Prater couldn't linger that
night because he had to get to his job as a bread baker on the midnight
shift at the Miami Bakery Bread Company. Prater ultimately agreed,
and Sam and Dave became the house act at the King o' Hearts. "And I
noticed something. I realized that all you've got to do to get the girls
is to be on the stage," Sam laughed. He and Dave remained the house
act at the King o' Hearts until 1963, by which time they were on the
Roulette Records roster of artists.

137

The course of their career changed dramatically in 1964 when Atlantic Records signed them to the Stax label. And it changed nearly as markedly four years later. When Atlantic Records pulled Sam and Dave from Stax in 1968, their creative output and popularity plummeted. "Our career went into the toilet," Sam says flatly. "With any artist, there comes a time when you have a drought. But I gotta tell you, with us it was a combination of a lot of things. We didn't have the right components to get it together. Then the '60s drug scene had also raised its hand for both of us. We were so screwed up, so drugged up. A lot of times Dave would show up for a gig and I didn't, and vice versa." After the breakup of Sam and Dave in 1970, Sam remained with Atlantic Records, signing as a solo artist. Atlantic released three singles, "Tennessee Waltz," "Stop," and "Shop Around," but none made the national charts. King Curtis and Dave Crawford produced those songs, along with enough other tracks for an album, but Atlantic shelved the project and kept the unreleased album tracks in the vaults for more than 30 years – thereby crippling Sam's career as a soloist.

Fresh opportunity came about in 1979. "We got back together after John [Belushi] and Danny [Aykroyd] did 'Soul Man' [as the Blues Brothers]. I remember Dave and I were working at Martha's Vineyard at Carly Simon's place, the Hot Tin Roof, and John came by to tell me the *Blues Brothers* movie had gone into production. And he was telling me what the scenes were like. He and Judy, his wife, had a home there. He was talking about Dave and me going out on tour with them. That never came about. The Blues Brothers did go out and tour, but we didn't. Our manager, Jeff Brown, was controlling, he was incompetent, he was unscrupulous, and he completely screwed up the deal. Soon after that, the addiction got worse for both of us," Sam said. The drugs? "The same thing that killed John [Belushi] – heroin and cocaine."

Belushi's death came just as Sam was about to battle his own addiction head-on. The real impetus for his conviction to rid himself of drugs came from one of Sam's longtime friends, Joyce Greenberg McRae. Back in the 1960s, when she lived in Chicago, Joyce had a pretty serious affair with Jackie Wilson. When she moved to Los Angeles and signed a record deal with legendary producer H.B. Barnum, she became friends with Judy Gilbert, who was then Dave Prater's girlfriend and later became his second wife. Joyce had first met Sam in 1967 when Judy brought her and a bunch of girlfriends to the Cheetah nightclub in Santa Monica, California, where Sam and Dave were performing. Sam told Joyce, "We're doing a gig with Jackie Wilson tomorrow night in the Bay Area, so why don't you fly in with us and surprise him?" Joyce agreed, joining them on their flight to San Francisco. "I was involved with Jackie at that time, or I should say I was, along with several other women, most of whom I knew nothing about. But Jackie and I were very close. He had told his mother and other family members that he wanted to marry me," Joyce said.

Joyce became Jackie's main caretaker after he suffered brain damage as a result of oxygen deprivation due to a major heart attack that struck in September 1975 while he was performing "Lonely Teardrops" on stage in Cherry Hill, New Jersey. Joyce had been subpoenaed to testify at Jackie's guardianship hearing in March 1976 to help determine his legal marital status, and she was permitted to visit Jackie in the hospital. In his semi-comatose state, Jackie appeared to recognize and respond to Joyce. After months in a comatose state, Jackie was unable to speak or walk when he regained consciousness in June 1976. Dysfunction of his major motor skills required massive amounts of rehabilitative therapy, but he was allegedly deeply in debt, mired in a financial dispute with his record company, Brunswick Records. Nat Tarnopol, the label's president and controlling stockholder, along with other record company executives, had been indicted as part of a federal payola investigation and were charged with conspiracy, mail fraud, wire fraud, and evasion of personal and corporate income taxes. (An appellate court later cleared Tarnopol of the charges due to a legal technicality.) But the label's fiscal problems obstructed Wilson's medical coverage, and entangled him in a legal battle between his present and former wives, both of whom claimed they were legally married to Jackie. Amid the legal dispute, Jackie was withering without proper medical care or a court-appointed guardian. "Jackie's charge nurse called me because Jackie was depressed and appeared to be losing the will to live," Joyce said. In response, Joyce moved from her home in Chicago to New Jersey near the nursing home to which Jackie had been transferred. "There, after Jackie had shown signs of recovery, I advocated vigorously to obtain his essential rehabilitation therapy that had been suspended by his second guardian and terminated by his 'wife,' Harlean, from whom he had been estranged since 1968," Joyce declared. Joyce expended nearly all of her own savings in medical expenses and legal fees in Jackie's behalf.

After Joyce began dating Sam in August 1981 and realized that he needed help with his drug problem, she likewise remained by his side. "Joyce was already living in Encino [a Los Angeles suburb] and I had moved to L.A. The day after John [Belushi] passed, I was on my way to a clinic in Oxnard that Joyce had learned about and got me into. We went there to see about an experimental drug to help me conquer the heroin addiction," explained Sam. The then-experimental medication, naltrexone, has since been approved by the U.S. Food and Drug Administration as an effective anti-addiction therapy. "When I had been detoxed enough to kick the legal methadone maintenance I had been on for six months, I was weak and Joyce had to help me get dressed. I weighed only about 118 pounds. At the clinic the doctors told Joyce, 'We'll put him on the program, but he's not going to make the next year.' But I went on and off drugs – back and forth, as we moved back and forth between New York and L.A. The last time I was on drugs I almost died, and I prayed to God, 'Let me hang on.' I came too close that time. So I cleaned up." Joyce's devotion to Sam, and his appreciation for her caring, turned into love. Sam and Joyce married on March 26, 1982, in Sardinia, while Joyce was detoxing Sam under the Oxnard clinic's directions while he was on tour with Carla Thomas, Eddie Floyd, and Wilson Pickett. After that successful detoxification treatment with the assistance of the opiate blocker naltrexone, in April 1982, Sam publicly acknowledged that the tensions between him and Dave Prater had been intensified by drugs. Sam has remained free of drugs since that public statement 30 years ago.

Ironically, a new and final lawsuit that Sam Moore was bringing against Dave Prater seeking a cease and desist order for unauthorized use of the "Sam and Dave" name was due to be filed in federal court in New Jersey the day after Dave died. Sam says he would not have brought the suit if only Dave had billed his act more clearly. "If he would have said 'Dave Prater, formerly of Sam and Dave' or even 'Dave Prater's Sam and Dave' I wouldn't have said anything. I may not have liked it, but I would have respected it more than him using the name 'Sam and Dave.' I was very sad because I didn't want it to be that way," Sam said solemnly. "If we would have worked hard to try to get ourselves together, I would have loved to do some stuff together. But it never came about. It's a sad ending for a dynasty to have ended like that. There was no glorious ending."

Sam and Joyce by then were living in Scottsdale, Arizona, where they had moved in 1987. Soon after they settled in to their new surroundings, Joyce helped launch the campaign to remove Gov. Evan Mecham for his positions that she and many other people regarded as racist. Joyce co-produced a gala musical concert titled "Celebration For Young Americans" that was staged Saturday, January 21, 1989, at the Washington Convention Center as part of the presidential inauguration ceremonies for George H.W. Bush. Performers in the inaugural program included Stevie Ray Vaughan, Jimmie Vaughan, Ronnie Wood, Bo Diddley, Percy Sledge, Willie Dixon and Lafayette Leake, Eddie Floyd,

William Bell, Carla Thomas, Dr. John, Billy Preston, Steve Cropper, Donald "Duck" Dunn, and, yes, Sam Moore. She currently manages the career of Sam as well as the legacy of the late musical genius Billy Preston, and acts as a talent coordinator for television programs.

Working with Joyce, Sam resurrected his performing career, appearing with former Motown recording star Junior Walker in the 1988 film *Tapeheads*. Sam sung harmony on several tracks of Bruce Springsteen's 1992 album *Human Touch*, and in 1993 performed a duet version of "Rainy Night In Georgia" with Conway Twitty for MCA Records' top-10 "various artists" album *Rhythm, Country, and Blues*, which paired country and R&B musicians. The album also teamed Vince Gill with Gladys Knight, Clint Black with the Pointer Sisters, Little Richard with Tanya Tucker, Patti LaBelle with Travis Tritt, and George Jones with B.B. King. In early June 1993, shortly after recording the duet with Sam Moore, Twitty died of an abdominal aneurysm while in Missouri on a concert tour.

Sam and Joyce did not have children together, but Joyce has a daughter, Michelle, who was born a year and a half before she first met Sam. "Joyce was nice and kind enough to let me share in helping raise her daughter," said Sam, who has an indeterminate number of children of his own. "Quite a few. I could give you a number – not too high, not too low," he teased. "I have quite a few girls. And I'm a great grandfather," he boasted with a big grin.

One of Sam's most important contributions to music took place not in the recording studio or on a stage, but on in the U.S. Congress. There, on May 21, 1998, Sam offered testimony before the House Judiciary Subcommittee on Courts and Intellectual Property over proposed changes to the Lanham Act of 1947 involving impersonators who masquerade as musical celebrities. Sam spoke on behalf of Artists & Others Against Impostors, a nonprofit organization that his wife Joyce formed in an effort to help protect recording artists whose names and personas are commandeered by imitators.

"All the way back in 1968, at Dave's request, I had bought Dave's rights in a corporation we owned and therefore the name 'Sam and Dave.' I alone am the holder of the trademark of the name. As a result, legally I can or could have taken anyone with me, advertised and promoted as such and been 'Sam and Dave' on stage or otherwise. To me, it wasn't the honest thing to do to the audience who would then come and pay money to see a performance that was half a lie," Sam told the committee. "That decision cost me a lot. I know there were a lot of well-paying dates I could have played with a 'Dave,' trading on the name and fame of 'Sam and Dave,' and there were even record contracts I could have gotten. Believe me, I badly needed the money from those offers because I had lost all I had made in the '60s and never got a chance to put anything aside for a rainy day. There were no new 'Sam and Dave' hit records."

Sam described his legal battles to bar Dave Prater's appearances with other singers masquerading as Sam. "They fooled some very smart people. The State of Arkansas declared a 'Sam and Dave Day,' in the mid-1980s, but, that wasn't me at the ceremony with then-Governor Clinton, a self-professed 'big fan'. "I pursued Dave and the 'fake Sams' to protect my name and reputation, to enforce my rights and to increase my ability to get some work in the marketplace. I chased them from state to state and court to court. I got injunctions, contempt citations, and even arrest warrants against them, but the laws are such that I found myself playing 'catch me if you can' with them from one end of this country and the world to the other. The legal bills were staggering. At this time there was very little work for me," said Moore.

"These fights cost my new wife nearly everything she had. She lost her house. We moved from a four-bedroom Encino townhouse into a one-bedroom motel, paying weekly, with her daughter, my daughter, and one of our grand babies," said Moore in reference to Joyce. "For years she attempted to educate agents, artists, and others in the industry that their practices were not only hurting 'Sam and Dave' but all the other artists who were being invaded by phonies. She worked tirelessly to accomplish the objective of change, and she's done this because it is the right thing to do and it had to be done." Sam told the committee that some promoters and others justify passing off imposters as original performers by claiming that audiences come to hear the music rather than to see the performers. "To me, that's like looking at a Picasso and saying, 'Oh! It's just the paint.'"

Moore beseeched the committee to enact corrective regulations. "We need your help. We need to fix the broken laws that allow, tolerate and reward these practices. I speak here today for those who cannot be here to tell you their story. I speak on behalf of Johnny Moore, lead singer of the Drifters on some of their greatest hits like 'Up on the Roof', 'On Broadway' and 'Under the Boardwalk.' Unable to call himself a Drifter here at home, where he made those hits, Johnny must work in exile in Europe. I speak for Dennis Yost, the lead singer of the Classics IV, who cannot make such reference when he wants to sing in public. I speak for Chuck Blasko, who can call himself a Vogue, a group he helped make famous, only in a small part of western Pennsylvania. I speak for Gladys Horton of the Marvelettes, Dennis Edwards and Ali Woodson, both famous lead singers of the Temptations, Alex Chilton, Gary Talley and Bill Cunningham of the Box Tops, and for dozens more, some of whom are sitting behind me this afternoon. Impostors are everywhere, taking away opportunities that belong to the real acts. Why, there were even impostors at the 1996 Clinton Inaugural. That just isn't right. We are here to petition this committee to give careful consideration to a change in the law that will permit the artists who created the histories by their recordings, to declare who they are to the world, and to make the impostors admit what they are so as to make sure that the buyers, promoters, agents, and the millions of fans know who is who when money is being exchanged, regardless of if it's to buy, sell, or see a show."

A 2002 documentary motion picture called *Only the Strong Survive,* which celebrated Stax recording artists, included segments on Wilson Pickett, Rufus and Carla Thomas, Isaac Hayes, and Sam Moore. Joyce Moore also was included in the film, in which Sam performed a towering version of "When Something Is Wrong With My Baby." When *Only the Strong Survive* was exhibited at the Hamptons International Film Festival in October 2003, the film's co-producer Roger Friedman was seated alongside former Atlantic Records vice president and producer Jerry Wexler, and seated at Jerry's left side was Joyce Moore. Sam, who avoids seeing himself on film, was chatting with others outside the theater. "Jerry looked at me and tears streamed down his face as he wailed, 'Oh my God, what did I do to Sam?' Later he embraced Sam and pleaded, 'Can you ever forgive me?' because he realized how magnificently talented Sam is, and at that moment Wex confronted the fact that he had screwed up Sam's solo career," Joyce told us in September 2012. "Jerry had been in a position to singlehandedly make or break artists of that era, but chose to throw Sam under the bus in 1971. Jerry Wexler caused the failure of Sam's career and put a brilliant album into a vault. Jerry's emotional plea for forgiveness gave Sam if nothing else some sense of vindication and peace of mind."

Sam had been told that those solo tracks he had recorded for Atlantic Records in 1970 had been destroyed in a storage facility fire. But a pleasant surprise awaited him. Rhino Records researchers unearthed the material, and Warner Bros. Special Products division gave the Moores' trust the exclusive license rights to the album, which a British label released in 2002 as *Plenty Good Lovin': The Lost Solo Album.* In addition to top-notch session musicians, the performers include guest appearances by Aretha Franklin and Donny Hathaway, and King Curtis on saxophone.

In 2006 Sam was at work on an ambitious project, an album of duets called *Overnight Sensational* for Rhino Records. Overseeing the project was producer Randy Jackson, who was bassist with the band Journey in the mid-1980s. He gained widespread renown as a judge alongside Simon Cowell and Paula Abdul in *American Idol*. The CD, released in the summer of 2006, showcased Sam in duets with Bruce Springsteen, Jon Bon Jovi, Garth Brooks, Mariah Carey, Seals and Crofts, Wynonna Judd, and other performers.

The National Academy of Recording Arts and Sciences honored Sam by choosing him to perform at the 2010 Grammy Celebration, an exclusive invitation-only event at the Los Angeles Convention Center on January 31, 2010, immediately following the 52nd Annual Grammy Awards public ceremony. The organization also recognized him with its NARAS Heroes Award.

"Sam has returned to congress to testify before a House Judiciary Committee hearing in an attempt to finally secure broadcast performance rights to pay recording artists, not just the writers and producers of your favorite songs, when you hear them on AM or FM radio," Joyce said. "This fight against the NAB [National Association of Broadcasters] and the station owners against the artists costs American singers nearly $200 million a year in lost income just from all of the foreign money alone being withheld from the U.S. artists because we don't have a reciprocal broadcast right for their artists. This really is life-changing money for the legacy groups and their families," she asserted.

Sam added, "The real problem here is just about everyone – our fans and even the advertisers buying radio spots who spend about $16 billion a year – think that when they hear their favorite song on the radio the artists get paid. We don't and we never have, as shocking as that is to learn, and it's got to change," Sam implores.

In his late 70s, Sam remains a live wire. "Besides making everyone around me crazy," Sam jokingly told us in July 2012, "I enjoy reading mysteries, watching bios on TV, and I swim and play golf – which I am not good at."

Although Sam is semi-retired, he continues to perform in public selectively. While on the road, he did detour to Fort Valley, Georgia, to have a look around at the countryside where he was born. In the summer of 2012 Sam and Joyce were negotiating a prospective new recording contract. Sam says that despite his long battle with drug addiction, the disappointment over the far-too-short career of Sam and Dave together, and the sad death of Dave, Isaac Hayes, Stax saxophonist Andrew Love, his dear buddy Donald "Duck" Dunn and his precious Billy Preston, he is a content man and gives thanks for his experiences. "I've been lucky to have had good people around me, and I've had a good time. I've been able to do things I never thought I'd do, and sing with people that I had no inkling that I would ever sing with. I've done movies, concerts, and I've had a wonderful time."

Visit **www.sammoore.net/** on the web for more information about Sam Moore.

Epilogue: Dave Prater Jr.

Singer

May 9, 1937 – April 9, 1988

When Dave Prater sang the "Soul Man" verses about walking on a "dust road" to see his honey, and getting what he got "the hard way," he didn't have to concoct an imaginary picture. He simply relied upon his memories of growing up dirt-poor as the son of sharecroppers on a farm in Irwin County, Georgia. Fields of peanuts, cotton, corn, wheat, soybeans, tobacco, rye, berries, melons, collard, onions, mustard, cucumbers, peas, sweet potatoes, tomatoes and other crops, along with pens of cattle, hogs, goats and chickens, made a patchwork quilt of the surrounding landscape. Dave was the seventh of 10 kids that his parents, Mary (Pressley) and Dave Prater Sr. raised in a little house on that farm, where they

Dave Prater as an adolescent (photo courtesy of Sarah Caruthers-Jackson)

turned over a portion of their crops to the landowner as rent. The wood-fired stove in the kitchen that the family used for cooking and heating inexorably altered the childhood lives of Dave and all his siblings.

Dave Prater Jr., the husky-voiced baritone half of Sam and Dave, was born May 9, 1937, in the Irwin County town of Ocilla, in south-central Georgia 110 miles south of Macon. Dave came along 13 years after his eldest brother, James Thomas ("J.T.") Prater. Jannie, Bertha, Bruce, Evelyn, Lillie, and Dave were next in succession, followed by siblings Helen, Robert, and Sammie. Another child died at birth.

His parents, who had married in the early 1920s, had settled in Ocilla after previously living in Sarasota, Melbourne, and Willow, Florida. The senior Dave Prater was a barber, but relied primarily on farming for income. As the eldest children gained the ability to perform chores, they helped with farming.

"My brothers and sisters and I walked four or five miles to school every morning, and then the children helped with the farming," recalled Lillie, who was Dave's elder by four years. "Then in the evenings, my brothers and sisters and I went out in the yard and played ball in the moonlight. We had a basketball, but we didn't have a hoop. We just tossed the ball around to each other, and we all had fun. Dave was a good brother." Television broadcasting hadn't yet begun in Georgia, but the Prater family had a radio receiver. "Only one station was on that radio, and that was WLAC from Nashville, Tennessee," Lillie said. During that era, WLAC was among the first high-powered stations to broadcast gospel and rhythm and blues programming, during the nighttime hours. Although Nashville was more than 400 miles away, the distant WLAC signal reached a large area of the South, including Ocilla, after dark. Dave Prater said that the radio was tuned exclusively to the music of the Highway QCs, the Mighty Clouds of Joy, and other gospel groups. "When we were growing up we couldn't listen to blues in my house," Dave said in an interview on May 19, 1983, with Toronto-area FM station CFNY disc jockey Dave "Daddy Cool" Booth, who now operates Showtime Music Archive in Toronto. "If you didn't listen to gospel, you didn't listen to nothing. Every so often I'd ease on out to my friend's place and we'd listen to whoever was big in blues – B.B. King, you know. I'd listen to country and western, too. I used to listen to the guys that *sing* – Roy Hamilton, Johnny Ace – 'Cross My Heart.' I used to love that song," Dave said.

The family members also sang together and their mother taught them a valuable skill. "My mother taught all her children how to cook," Lillie said. Later in life, Mary Prater became a food service worker at Ocilla High and Industrial School. The Prater family regularly attended services at Mount Olive AME (African Methodist Episcopal) Church at 207 East Seventh Street in Ocilla. Mary Prater served as treasurer and a missionary for the church. Dave's Methodist upbringing gave him a foundation not only in spirituality, but in music and singing technique because his family was too poor to afford the music lessons he had always wanted. "My daddy was a singer," Lillie told us in July 2012. "He and my oldest brother sang spiritual songs for us. And most all of us, including Dave, sang in the church choir."

Life for the family took a devastating turn in the summer of 1944, just after young Dave turned 7 years old. Mary, accompanied by all of her children except J.T., had traveled by train to Newark, New Jersey, to visit her sister. Lillie said that she and her siblings and her mother learned about the accident by telegram.

"We always kept a five-gallon can of tractor fuel in the kitchen to start a fire in the stove. My brother J.T. said my daddy was starting a fire in the stove to cook breakfast. He put the wood in the stove, and he poured the fluid over the wood, and he scratched a match. He didn't see no flame, so he turned the can on it a second time, and it exploded. They had to run and catch him and put out the flames on him," Lillie explained. "They sent a telegram to my older sister saying my daddy had got burned very bad and the doctors say he wasn't going to live. And then later my sister got a call saying my daddy was dead. So we caught a train and went back to Georgia." More bad news awaited them upon their arrival. "They didn't tell us that the house got burned down. So we got there, and there was nothing but the chimney standing up. The man that mother was working for, he built the house back, and told my mother she could stay there as long as she wanted to."

Mary and her children remained, and farmed crops together, but one by one during the following years the Prater children left to find their own way in life. The postwar building boom that was occurring 500 miles to the south in Miami, Florida, was a powerful lure. Previously a playground for the wealthy, Miami began to cater to young families. New hotels were on the rise, and in the decade between 1940 and 1950 the population of Miami nearly doubled. Among those new arrivals was J.T. Prater, who moved to Miami in 1948 and found work in the hotel construction trades. All of J.T.'s brothers and sisters eventually followed him to Miami.

A photo that Dave Prater (seated) signed for Sarah Jackson's oldest son, Michael Corbitt (photo courtesy of Sarah Caruthers-Jackson)

As a student at Irwin County High School in Ocilla, Dave pursued music with an instructor who taught singing. "Dave sang in the glee club in high school. So did I,"

Lillie told us. "At his graduation he sang 'You'll Never Walk Alone.'"

Dave's relatives in the region included Sarah Ann Caruthers, a second cousin on his mother's side of the family. Sarah lived in Fitzgerald, a larger town nine miles north of Ocilla. "We were together quite often. Dave's family would come to visit us at our house," said Sarah, who was born a year before Dave. "We had a good, happy childhood. We really did. And we were close. Of all the cousins, I think I was closest to Dave." Some of the Prater kids stayed with the Caruthers family for extended periods when they began working for Norris Pressley, one of Sarah's uncles who owned restaurants and nightclubs in Fitzgerald. "I think Janney was the first to come to stay with us and to work in my uncle's club, until she had saved enough money to move to Miami." Bertha and Evelyn soon relocated to Miami as well. Lillie, who lived with Sarah's family while training in a nurses' aide program at Ben Hill County Hospital in Fitzgerald, moved to Miami in 1955. "My brother had lost his wife, and I came down here to help him with his seven children," said Lillie, who then attended nursing school and subsequently worked as a nurse at Jackson High School for 31 years.

The opportunity to perform attracted Dave to Fitzgerald. "We had a lot of black clubs there – the Savoy, the Country Club, Paradise Inn, John's Place and MIC Club," Sarah said. "When Little Richard was starting out, he was playing piano and dancing with a traveling medicine show. When the show came to Fitzgerald, Little Richard quit the medicine show because he saw many opportunities for performing in the clubs there. And he moved into a lady's house named Mrs. Butt, right in the next block down from us." Young Dave Prater likewise began performing in one of Norris Pressley's clubs while staying with Sarah and her family.

Dave headed for Miami in 1959 and moved in with his brother J.T., who helped him land a job as a construction worker. He also joined a gospel group called the Sensational Hummingbirds, in which his older brother, J.T., was a member. The group toured throughout the region, performing wherever gospel acts could get bookings.

To augment his income, Dave had begun working as a short-order cook in a restaurant, and as a bread baker at the Miami Bakery Bread Company. He also began entering amateur singing competitions at nightclubs around Miami. Lillie said that her deeply religious mother found the contrasts between nightclub entertaining and gospel singing unacceptable. "Our mother told him 'If you're going to sing for the Devil, you sing for the Devil, but if you're going to sing for the Lord, you sing for the Lord.' She told him you can't serve the Devil and the Lord at the same time." To please his mother, he had to decide on a career path. "Yeah, he made a choice," Lillie said. Dave already had won a few competitions by the time he decided to enter an amateur talent show at the King o' Hearts club in Miami, where he would meet Sam Moore in 1961.

Before Dave left Ocilla, he had fathered a daughter, Deborah Paschal. He married his first wife, Annie Belle, in March 1962 – the year that Sam and Dave signed with Roulette Records. Together Dave and Annie Belle had five children: David (born in 1961), Anthony (1962), Sharon (1964), Timothy (1966), and Christopher (1967). The couple divorced in 1967. That year he fathered a son, Bruce Latson, in Miami. In December 1969, Dave wed Judith Gilbert, but that marriage also ended in divorce.

Sarah said that Dave remained close to her and other family members throughout the years that Sam and Dave were recording and touring. When concert tours brought Dave through Jacksonville, he often visited Sarah, who was chair of the natural sciences department at Florida Community College (since renamed Florida State College). Known now by her married name, Sarah Caruthers-Jackson, she conducts research about classroom teaching practices. "When Dave come to Jacksonville, he would end up in my house. Every time he walk through the door, he going to shed his shirt, find a comfortable chair, and put his legs up," Sarah said, giggling. "Then Dave would be fussin' about 'Let's go shop for food,' and then I would cook – not only for him, but I cooked for the band, too."

Dave initially gave some thought to launching a solo career following the breakup of Sam and Dave, and in 1972 signed once again with Alston Records, with which he and Sam had launched their recording partnership 11 years earlier. Alston released a single, "Keep My Fingers Crossed," but it did not generate sufficient attention to make the charts.

Dave was performing the weekend of July 4, 1972, at the Chatterbox Bar, a club on the boardwalk at Lincoln Avenue in Seaside, New Jersey, when he met the woman who would become his third wife. Rosemary Grish had gone to the Chatterbox to see the show. "Dave and the band members were sitting at the bar after the show, and my girlfriends and I were just sitting around, talking among ourselves, when one of my friends got up and began talking to the musicians and Dave. Then Dave came over to meet the rest of us, and that was the beginning," Rosemary said. "We talked, and then he started calling me, and when he came to the area we began seeing each other."

Rosemary had lived all of her life in Paterson, New Jersey, where she attended Catholic school and her mother owned a luncheonette. "As a

14-year-old going to high school I used to work there afternoons to help her out," Rosemary said. Her emphasis in school was business, which led her to jobs as a typist and stenographer – taking dictation in shorthand, in those days before personal computers transformed offices. "I worked for a packing company right down the street from where I lived, and I worked for a trucking company where other members of my family worked. Then I got a position managing the office of a wholesale fruit and vegetable distributor, where I worked for 37 years. After meeting Dave, I began helping him manage bookings and money." Dave moved in with Rosemary in 1974. "Then some of his kids came to stay with us," she said.

Dave and Rosemary married on November 21, 1982, at the Wayne Manor in Wayne, New Jersey. It was Rosemary's first and only marriage. "At that time we were living in Lodi, New Jersey, but the following April, we bought a two-family house in Paterson," Rosemary said.

Dave Prater's struggles with drug dependences over many years are widely known. "He went through treatments, and he achieved recovery," Sarah Caruthers-Jackson told us. Rosemary added, "I was instrumental in getting him into a rehab program, and he did very, very well. He did some treatment time, and he did some hospital time, and he came out and it seemed like everything was going to be OK. But it's a tough industry to exist in without being exposed to drugs. So he probably had his ups and downs through that."

Sarah Caruthers-Jackson said that through it all, Dave found family relationships more compelling than drugs. "Throughout his career, he used to call me from various cities when he was on tour, to see whether or not we had cousins in that city. And if we do have cousin in that city, he invited them to see him," Sarah said. "In Chicago he learned that two first cousins lived there. I gave him their number, and he called them. And although they knew Dave was their cousin, they didn't expect Dave to call them to invite them to his concert. But that's a family value that we have, because we are close knit."

Rosemary said that Dave liked people, enjoyed the company of family members and friends, and he liked kids, even though the couple had no children together. "He liked to cook, and he did like to eat. Eating was a very substantial part of his existence," she chuckled. "He wasn't the kind of guy who could go to a barbecue and have only a hot dog. If he went to a barbecue, it was going to be steak and potatoes. It had to be a filling dinner. Here in this area we have places that sell 'hot dogs all the way.' It's hot dogs with mustard, onions, and sauce. For anybody else, two hot dogs and an order of fries would be dinner. For him that was a snack." She said that Dave remained trim because he was always active, and liked to dance whenever the opportunity presented itself. "I'm not saying he was an angel. I'm saying he was a good, decent guy," Rosemary said.

Dave's singing style was influenced not only by other R&B greats, but also by rockabilly and country music performers. "Sam Cooke influenced a lot of people with the style and quality of his voice, and when he did his lyrics you could hear everything he said perfectly. It wasn't muffled, fumbled. It just came together, and everybody tried to sing like him, including me," Dave Prater told Dave Booth of Showtime Music Archive. Rosemary added, "Dave was a big fan of Elvis Presley, and he liked

Autographed 1967 photo of Sam and Dave (right) from the collection of Sarah Caruthers-Jackson

Willie Nelson's song 'You Were Always On My Mind.' Dave wanted to do a rendition of that, and he had begun working on an arrangement of that song. He was a good singer, he was a good dancer. He had a lot of ability."

Dave performed in public for the last time at a Stax Revue reunion show in Atlanta on April 3, 1988, before heading south to visit his mother. During the early morning on Saturday, April 9, near Sycamore Georgia, 160 miles south of Atlanta, Dave exited Interstate 75 and headed down the rural road toward Ocilla. The Chevrolet he was driving overshot a turn, barreled off the road and slammed into a tree. Only 20 miles short of his destination, Dave died when he was ejected from the car and catapulted into a tree. He was exactly one month shy of his 51st birthday. "At Dave's funeral in Ocilla, his seven children got their first chance to be altogether and spend some time with each other. His funeral was held in the church where he sang and grew up, and more than 500 people attended," Rosemary said. His body subsequently was flown to New Jersey for another funeral service for the benefit of family members and friends in that region. Dave was buried in Holy Sepulchre Cemetery in Totowa, New Jersey. His gravestone is carved with the words "Soul Man" within a five-pointed star. Tragically, his son Timothy died at age 44 in March 2011 after suffering a brain aneurysm while driving his car. Bruce also is deceased.

Sarah Caruthers-Jackson says Dave's fame did not affect his relationships with family members. "Dave and I, we just had a lot of fun. When we got together, we were just family. Dave didn't talk about anything he was doing that could be classified as fame. We talked just like cousins should talk. So I don't think fame really affected him," Sarah said.

Dave remained proud of the recordings that he made with Sam Moore. In August 1987, Dave Prater told an *Atlanta Journal-Constitution* newspaper reporter, "You can play one of our records now and it sounds like a brand-new record. The songwriters and producers Isaac Hayes and David Porter were writing ahead of the time. Besides, rhythm and blues never dies."

Courtesy of Ray Stevens

ON AIR

CHAPTER 6

Everything Is Beautiful

Ray Stevens

Numerous recording artists of the top 40 era attained popularity with romantic ballads. Others gained fame by singing ditties that made people laugh. Some performers became known for channeling the power of music for social commentary. Others infused gospel influences into mainstream pop. Some singers crooned standards from the big-band era. One performer, Ray Stevens, has done all of that, and more. He's been a recording session producer, a music publisher, a session musician, a disc jockey, a musical theater owner, and a television program host as well as a recording artist whose songs have topped both the pop and country music charts. Throughout his 55-year career, Ray Stevens has been anything but predictable. No two Ray Stevens songs have been alike. Some of his recordings have been sentimental, others introspective, but most of them have been flat-out wacky – none more so than his feathers-flying impression of chickens clucking out Glenn Miller's classic tune "In the Mood," under the name the Henhouse Five Plus Too. Most recently, he has concentrated on scathing political satire. And although he casts himself as a bit of a bumpkin in the comedic videos he has made during recent years, he is a shrewd, experienced, multi-talented, Grammy-winning entertainment professional who has earned respect in the music industry.

Ray Stevens is a "crossover" recording artist who achieved popularity among country music fans as well as pop music audiences. During four decades Ray racked up 52 chart singles: 18 releases that reached the *Billboard* Hot 100 chart, 25 that were exclusively country hits on the *Billboard* Hot Country chart, and nine others that registered in the top 100 on both pop and country charts. He recorded Kris Kristofferson's bitterly tender song "Sunday Mornin' Comin' Down" before Johnny Cash did. As a session musician, he played trumpet on an Elvis Presley track. Years later Ray's company published "Way Down," the last hit that Elvis had before dying in 1977.

Despite Ray's predominantly country-pop repertoire, he cut his musical teeth on rhythm and blues in the southern Georgia town of Albany. As a teenage disc jockey on Albany radio station WGPC, he helped introduce new rock and roll and rhythm and blues records to that region. He and Mary Dale Vansant were co-hosts of "The Record Hop," a Saturday afternoon radio program broadcast from the station's studio in the New Albany Hotel. "I loved the Clovers, the Drifters, Ray Charles, the Moonglows, Fats Domino – all those R&B acts," Stevens said. "Mary Dale was more into traditional 'white bread' music, and we'd have some debates from time to time about what to play. She liked Hugo Winterhalter and his Orchestra, and we played a little of that, but by and large we played stuff like 'Work With Me Annie' by Hank Ballard & the Midnighters."

At age 15, eight years after Ray started taking piano lessons, he began performing in public with the Barons, a band that he formed. As he entered his senior year of high school in the autumn of 1956, his family moved to Atlanta. He learned that Atlanta radio personality Bill Lowery had formed a music publishing company that had published Gene Vincent's 1956 hit song "Be-Bop-a-Lula" and Sonny James' early 1957 hit "Young Love." When Ray heard in the spring of '57 that Lowery Music Company was soliciting material from composers, he introduced himself to Bill Lowery and said that he wanted to write songs. Lowery was encouraging, so Ray set about writing a song with a high school classmate. He made a demo of the song, called "Silver Bracelet," on a tape recorder he borrowed. He played the tape for Lowery, who was sufficiently impressed to call his friend Ken Nelson, a producer for Capitol Records who worked frequently in Nashville. Nelson signed the teenager to the label's new Prep Records subsidiary, which released the song. "Silver Bracelet" got some airplay on Atlanta-area radio stations, but nowhere else.

Disappointed but not dissuaded from a career in music, Ray enrolled as a freshman at Georgia State University in the autumn of 1957 as a music major, studying classical piano and music theory. While attending college, he wrote and recorded a song called "Sergeant Preston of the Yukon" for Lowery's independent National Recording Corporation label. The song was about a Canadian Mountie, a character from a television adventure program that was popular at the time. On the novelty record, Ray barked like Preston's dog, Yukon King. While disc jockeys and record-buying kids liked the song, the producers of the TV program didn't. "It was taking off like gangbusters when lawyers from King Features Syndicate got in touch with Bill Lowery and told him we couldn't use their character in a song and issued a 'cease and desist' order," Stevens said. "I think if Bill had lawyered up, we might have gotten away with it, but he didn't want to mess with it. It broke my heart to kill a hit record like that, but it gave me the clue that if I wrote another nutty song, I had a shot."

That opportunity presented itself when he was performing in a show in East Point, Georgia, broadcast live on the radio. "It was in an auditorium, like a little Grand Ole Opry," Stevens explained. Mercury Records producer and talent promoter Shelby Singleton happened to stop by, and caught Ray's act. They kept in touch and, during Ray's junior year of college in 1961, Singleton (who would produce Jeannie C. Riley's 1968 smash hit "Harper Valley P.T.A.") signed Ray to a Mercury Records contract. Ray went into the studio with a novelty tune that he had written, published through Lowery Music, called "Jeremiah Peabody's Poly Unsaturated Quick Dissolving Fast Acting Pleasant Tasting Green and Purple Pills," a poke at television commercial hucksterism. At 22 years of age, Ray had a hit record on his hands – the first of 27 of his singles to reach the pop chart. "Jeremiah Peabody" premiered on the *Billboard* Hot 100 on August 21, 1961, peaked at No. 35, and remained on the chart for six weeks.

That autumn, Singleton was appointed head of the Mercury Records A&R (artists and repertoire) department in Nashville. He called Stevens to ask him to work for the label, along with record producer Jerry Kennedy. Stevens asked, "How much does the job pay?" Singleton replied, "$50 per week." Stevens responded, "I can't live on $50 a week." Singleton said, "I'll let you play on all the sessions, too." Ray responded, "I'll be there." Stevens moved to Nashville on January 2, 1962. Seventeen days later, he became desperate. He was scheduled to record some tracks, including the next planned Ray Stevens single, the following day, January 20 – four days before his 23rd birthday. Nearly five months had passed since "Jeremiah Peabody" was released. He had a list of songs to record, but he didn't like any of them. Then an idea came to him.

"When I was a kid, my mom insisted that I read books, so I did. I read *Arabian Nights* and I thought that was pretty cool. Then there was *Ali Baba and the Forty Thieves*, with 'open sesame' and all that," Stevens explained. "So I thought I'd write a funny song about an Arab with a camel, and make a camel noise like I did the dog sound on "Sergeant Preston." I pronounced it *A-rab* on purpose – not knowing that it would be considered a slur, because there's a town in Alabama called Arab, which is pronounced that way." In Stevens' song, Ahab wore rings and a turban, had a scimitar – a curved sword – and rode a camel named Clyde who made loud noises – with Ray translating the "camel talk." The real story, though, was about Ahab's romantic interest. Ray needed a name for her, and thought of Fatima Cigarettes, made with Turkish tobaccos. "Fatima just seemed like a good name for an Arab lady to have, so it worked for me. I wrote it late the night before the session in about 45 minutes. I was desperate. I needed something that was going to rattle some cages out there."

It did. While Ray was at work as a session pianist, arranger, and background singer on numerous sessions for other Mercury recording artists, the label pressed "Ahab the Arab," two minutes and 47 seconds of silliness produced by Shelby Singleton with credit to the Merry Melody Singers and Jerry Kennedy as orchestra conductor. Released in May, it premiered on the *Billboard* Hot 100 on June 30, 1962, got persistent radio airplay throughout the summer, peaked at No. 5, and remained on the chart until mid-September. It also hit *Billboard's* rhythm and blues chart, on which it ranked as high as No. 9. Mercury released a Ray Stevens album titled *1,837 Seconds of Humor,* which included "Jeremiah Peabody" and "Ahab." Stevens' next single was a song called "Further More," about a guy who has finally made the difficult decision to break up with his lying, cheating girlfriend by trying to convince himself that he doesn't really love her – even though he probably still does. The record, which premiered on the chart October 13, 1962, went no higher than No. 91, and remained on the chart for only three weeks. Stevens, who acknowledges that he was influenced by the Coasters' "Yakety, Yak," "Charlie Brown," and "Along Came Jones," realized that his fans expected zaniness from him. He delivered with his follow-up, a seasonal ditty, "Santa Claus Is Watching You," in which Clyde the camel and a couple of extra stand-in reindeer named Bruce and Marvin helped pull the sleigh after Rudolph dislocated his hip in a twist dance contest. The madcap tune began a three-week stay on the *Billboard* Hot 100 that December 15, and reached No. 45.

With Bill Lowery as his manager and music publisher, Ray wrote "Funny Man," his first single of 1963. It was a serious song that described a jokester's inner turmoil and sadness about the painful rejection by a girl whom he had loved. Its topic is similar to that of Bobby

Goldsboro's "See the Funny Little Clown," but "Funny Man" was a hit first. Stevens insists that "Funny Man" was not autobiographical. "I was too young to be smitten that badly. Plus I was married with a daughter. I was just trying to see what I could come up with as a songwriter. I did a lot of things for no good reason," he said. After its chart debut on March 30, "Funny Man" went no higher than No. 81 and remained on the chart for only three weeks. It was time to return to silly stuff, and Ray had one ready. It was "Harry the Hairy Ape," another rib-tickling tune, reminiscent of "Ahab the Arab," with Ray supplying simian sounds. It premiered on the *Billboard* Hot 100 on June 15, 1963, and took Ray into the top 20 for the second time. The Mercury recording peaked at No. 17, and remained on the chart for nine weeks. It went even higher on the R&B chart, to No. 14. His follow-up release, "Speed Ball," about a motorcyclist and his girlfriend who learned a happy-ever-after lesson about recklessness, presaged a slowdown in Ray's performing career. The record, which premiered on the *Billboard* Hot 100 on October 12, 1963, peaked at No. 59, and remained on the chart for three weeks. "Bubblegum, the Bubble Dancer," a single that Mercury released in July '64, did not reach the charts.

By then, Ray no longer was with Mercury Records; he had left the label in late 1963. He had become primarily occupied with arranging and producing sessions for other recording artists, and began a self-imposed three-year absence from the charts. "I was in love with the studio situation in Nashville at the time. There were half a dozen studios and the musicians were great, so that's what I was doing. I accepted a position at Monument Records as a producer," Stevens said. The artists for whom he produced sessions included Dolly Parton, who at 18 years of age had just moved from her hometown of Sevierville, Tennessee, to Nashville. "We didn't get a hit, but we tried hard and had a lot of fun. I cut her more R&B than she was used to. She wanted to cut cornball country stuff, and I should have listened to her. I shouldn't have called it 'cornball country,' but back in those days, that's what I thought of it. Later, I became more educated about what country music is and what it's about." The Dolly Parton tracks that Stevens produced included "Happy, Happy Birthday, Baby," "Busy Signal," and "Don't Drop Out."

At Monument, Stevens arranged and played on sessions for Brenda Lee, Brook Benton, Patti Page, and other performers. "Shelby would bring all these people in and try to cross-collateralize their New York R&B roots with the Nashville guitar sound, and sometimes it worked good. I remember we brought in Clyde McPhatter, who was the lead singer with the Drifters when they had the original record of 'Ruby Baby.'

Clyde was one of my heroes, and I had a great experience meeting him. He was such a nice guy," Stevens said.

By the spring of 1966, Ray felt ready to get back into the game as a performer. He wrote and recorded another comedic song, "Freddie Feelgood (and His Funky Little Five Piece Band)," which he licensed through his own publishing business, Ahab Music. "Freddie" premiered on the *Billboard* Hot 100 on July 16, 1966, on the Monument label, but rose no higher than No. 91, and was on the chart for only two weeks. Ray resumed his focus on musical arrangement and production. But his observations about the business world prompted him to make a dramatic turn to social commentary. "Unwind," Ray's ninth chart single, advised people caught up in the chaos and bustle of the workday to slow down, relax, and enjoy life. Ray was credited with the song's brassy musical arrangement, and he shared production duties with Fred Foster. The Monument release, which premiered on the *Billboard* Hot 100 on April 20, 1968, peaked at No. 52, and spent nine weeks on the chart. He remained in that vein with his follow-up composition, which was prompted by an unpleasant encounter. "I had gotten the short end of a business deal, and I was kicking myself because I should have known better. So instead of punching the guy in the nose, I wrote a song to vent my frustration and anger," Ray told us in July 2012. The song, "Mr. Businessman," was an indignant denunciation of greed, dishonesty, and immorality in pursuit of ego-driven financial success. Stevens forcefully condemned misplacement of personal priorities that subjugated family life to career pursuits. The powerful message of the song remains as resonant today as it was upon its chart debut on August 3, 1968. "Mr. Businessman," his 10th chart single, peaked at No. 28, and remained on the chart for seven weeks.

Ray's penchant for nuttiness surfaced again in the spring of '69, just after he turned 30 years of age. When Bill Justis happened to put the word "guitar" and the name "Tarzan" together, that sparked Ray to write another comic story song, "Gitarzan," his 11th chart single. The song about an ape who rocks out in the jungle premiered on the *Billboard* Hot 100 on April 5, 1969. The label credits Justis under the name "Bill Everette" as co-writer. "Gitarzan" sent Ray into the top 10 for the second time and brought him his first gold record certification from the Recording Industry Association of America (RIAA). The recording, on the Monument label, peaked at No. 8, and remained on the chart for 13 weeks. He followed that with "Along Came Jones," a cover version of the Coasters' wacky 1959 hit. Ray's version, which hit the chart on June 28, 1969, peaked at No. 27, and remained on the chart for eight weeks. That summer, a song by a struggling new Nashville songwriter came to the attention of Ray, who became the first to record it – Kris Kristofferson's "Sunday Mornin' Comin' Down." Ray's recording, which premiered on the *Billboard* Hot 100 on October 25, 1969, reached No. 81, and remained on the pop chart for three weeks. Meanwhile it became Ray's first song to cross over to the country chart, where it rose to No. 55. It also was his last single on the Monument label. Johnny Cash subsequently recorded a version of "Sunday Mornin' Comin' Down," which reached No. 46 on the pop chart and No. 1 on the country hit list 11 months later, in the late summer of 1970.

In early 1970 Ray received a phone call from Don Williams, brother of singer Andy Williams. "Don was managing Roger Miller at the time. Roger had given my number to Don, who was with a management firm called Bernard-Williams-Price. Don called to ask me if he could manage me, and we made a deal. He signed me away from Monument to Barnaby Records," Stevens said. That began a long relationship; Don remained Ray's personal manager for about 25 years. Andy Williams had established and incorporated Barnaby in the summer of '69, and arranged for distribution through CBS Records. Barnaby artists included Claudine Longet, the Osmonds, and Jimmy Buffett. "The inducement for me to sign with Barnaby was to host the Andy Williams summer show on NBC television," Ray explained. He acknowledges that hosting a nationwide telecast was a big leap for him. "I was scared to death. I did the best I could at the time, and it was okay, I guess. I'd like to do it over with the experience I have now," he confides. The program, titled *Andy Williams Presents Ray Stevens,* consisted of skits and songs, with a cast that included singers Mama Cass Elliot and Lulu, and comedian Steve Martin.

"I wrote 'Everything is Beautiful' to be the theme song for the TV show, and it was my first record on Barnaby. And sure enough, it was a successful song," Ray said. It was as unexpected as it was successful, because the spring of 1970 was a turbulent time. The violence at the Rolling Stones' Altamont Speedway Free Festival concert was still fresh in people's minds, the Chicago Eight trial was creating nationwide friction, the Vietnam War was raging, the American public had learned recently about the My Lai Massacre, the U.S. invaded Cambodia in pursuit of Viet Cong troops, and increasingly strident antiwar protests were leading to a deadly climax at Kent State University. Stevens is uncertain why he wrote "Everything Is Beautiful" amid that sociological chaos. "I don't know. I think there are ideas floating around in space, and every once in awhile, I zone out and tune in and I can get those vibrations. I'm not trying to go weird on ya. It has come to my attention over the years that a lot of songwriters will write the same damn song at the same time, and that's because of the ideas that are floating around in what some people call 'the universal mind.' I just think I was able to tap into some ideas that were floating around in space," Stevens explained. "Everything Is Beautiful," which premiered on the chart on April 4, 1970, became his first No. 1 hit. It also took Ray onto the British charts for the first time, peaking at No. 6, and earned his second RIAA gold record. Ray arranged and produced the recording through Ahab Productions, and published the song through Ahab Music.

During the following 18 months, Barnaby released six more Ray Stevens singles that registered on the pop charts. "America, Communicate With Me," which hit the chart July 25, 1970, and peaked at No. 45, was a quest for middle ground between extremist protesters and politicians, and a confirmation that Ray still had faith in his country, despite its deep divisions. "Sunset Strip," a tempo-changing bouquet to the hip nightclub sector of Sunset Boulevard in West Hollywood, made its chart debut on November 7, 1970, but went no higher than No. 81. A month later Ray returned to the strip with a zany tune about entertainer "Bridget the Midget (the Queen of the Blues)," which rose to No. 50 in the U.S. after its December 19 debut. It especially tickled the fancy of the Brits, who sent it to a No. 2 ranking in the U.K. "A Mama and a Papa" appeared on the chart May 1, 1971, but stalled at No. 82 and dropped off after three weeks. Stevens took a spiritual turn with his next two recordings. "All My Trials," Ray's take on a traditional folk lullaby that Pete Seeger, Harry Belafonte, and Joan Baez also recorded, premiered on the chart on August 28, 1971, and reached No. 70. His lively gospel-inspired version of Albert E. Brumley's "Turn Your Radio On," an appeal to make divine connections, made its chart debut on November 20, 1971, reached No. 63, and remained on the pop chart for seven weeks. It hit No. 33 in the U.K., and No. 17 on the U.S. country chart.

Ray was absent from the charts for two and a half years after that, but in the spring of 1974 he headed a new direction that streaked him to the top of the charts. Amused by the fad of "streaking" – the act of dashing naked in crowded public places on a dare or for the fun of disruption – Ray wrote "The Streak." It was a hot topic when it hit the charts on April 13, 1974, less than two weeks after a streaker dashed across the stage at the Academy Awards presentation during a live telecast on NBC. The labels of some pressings of "The Streak" displayed Ahab Music's new camel silhouette logo. On May 18, "The Streak" knocked Grand Funk's version of "The Loco Motion" from the No. 1 spot, held that lofty position for three weeks, remained on the chart a total of 17 weeks, and became Ray's third RIAA gold record. It also hit No. 1 in the U.K. and No. 23 on the U.S. country chart. Ray's follow-up, "Moonlight Special," was a spoof on another social phenomenon, NBC-TV's *Midnight Special* late-night rock music platform. "Moonlight Special" made its chart debut on July 27, 1974, reached No. 73, and remained on the chart for seven weeks.

In 1975, Ray's music took a nostalgic turn. He resurrected the Erroll Garner-Johnny Burke composition "Misty," which Garner had recorded as a tender jazz instrumental in 1954 and Johnny Mathis had crooned in 1959 – but he gave it a rollicking bluegrass twist with a banjo, fiddle, and steel guitar. Ray's lively version of the standard, which he arranged and produced, made its debut on the *Billboard* Hot 100 on April 26, 1975. The Barnaby release peaked at No. 14, and remained on the chart for 16 weeks. It performed even better on the country chart, where it hit No. 3, and in the U.K., where it peaked at No. 2. That success prompted Ray to dredge up a really moldy oldie, "Indian Love Call," which Rudof Friml, Otto Harbach, and Oscar Hammerstein II had written for the 1924 Broadway musical production *Rose-Marie*. In the 1936 motion picture version of the musical, Nelson Eddy and Jeanette MacDonald immortalized the song, which yodeling country singer Slim Whitman also recorded in 1951. Ray's soaring interpretation landed the song on the chart on October 11, 1975. It reached No. 68 on the Hot 100, remained on the chart for five weeks, and hit No. 38 on the country chart. He endeared himself so much to country audiences that by 1976 his records began to perform more consistently on the country charts than on the pop charts.

As Barnaby Records prepared to shut down, Ray signed with the Warner Bros. label. There he dusted off one more old standard, but ran it through his loony filter. He wondered how Glenn Miller's "In the Mood" would sound if performed by a chorus of strutting, rhythmic chickens. The result, by the Henhouse Five Plus Too, hit the *Billboard* Hot 100 on January 8, 1977. The "Plus Too" consisted of a bass player and a drummer; the "Henhouse Five" was all Ray, who played the piano, overdubbed other instruments, and clucked and warbled his way through the hot big-band dance tune. The recording, which marked Stevens' debut on the Warner Bros. label, reached No. 40, and remained on the pop chart for seven weeks. It also hit No. 39 on the country chart and No. 31 in Great Britain. "One radio station in Louisiana received a call from a farmer who said, 'Please don't play that anymore, because every time you play it, my dog attacks the henhouse.'" Ray remained in the comedy vein for "I Need Your Help Barry Manilow," about a down-in-the-dumps guy whose psychiatrist was out of town, but who takes solace in the wistful songs that Manilow was cranking out at the time. The Warner Bros. release, the last of singer Ray Stevens' 27 chart singles, made its debut on the *Billboard* Hot 100 on March 24, 1979. Its picture sleeve, with a high-contrast photo of Ray playing a piano against a dark blue background, mimicked a Barry Manilow album cover. Ray's recording reached No. 49, and remained on the chart for eight weeks.

Later that year Ray signed with RCA Records. His singles for RCA included "Shriner's Convention," Ray's comedic impression of the loopy misadventures of conventioneers that he witnessed at a motel where one guest's motorcycle wound up submerged in the swimming pool. The single hit No. 7 on the country music chart. In 1984 Ray signed with MCA Records, for which he recorded and released several singles, including Buddy Kalb's "The Mississippi Squirrel Revival," which hit No. 20 on the country chart, "The Haircut Song," a No. 45 country record, and the Margaret Archer-Chet Atkins song "Would Jesus Wear a Rolex," which reached No. 41 on the country chart.

Stevens has continued to record through the years, but he views his most recent project as his crowning achievement – the *Encyclopedia of Recorded Comedy Music,* an expansive collection of songs he regards as the best comedic songs of all time. He spent two years in the studio recording tracks for the box set, released on Clyde Records in February 2012. The project reflects Ray's dedication to perpetuating the memory of Spike Jones, the Coasters, the Olympics, Roger Miller, Sheb Wooley and other entertainers who recorded comedic songs. It encompasses 108 songs on nine CDs, accompanied by his carefully researched liner notes about the history of the selections, and a reference book.

In addition to running his successful music publishing enterprises – Ahab Music Inc., Ray Stevens Music, Grand Avenue Music, and Lucky Streak Music – and audio and video production facilities in a building that occupies a half block of Nashville's Music Row, Ray continues to make periodic concert appearances. Unlike that guy whose naked dash across the Academy Awards stage in 1974 lasted only five seconds, Ray Stevens has made people think, hum along, and laugh for more than five decades. Now that's a *streak.*

U.S. POP HIT SINGLES BY RAY STEVENS

Debut	Peak	Gold	Title	Label
8/61	35		Jeremiah Peabody's Poly Unsaturated Quick Dissolving Fast Acting Pleasant Tasting Green and Purple Pills	Mercury
6/62	5		Ahab, The Arab	Mercury
10/62	91		Further More	Mercury
12/62	45		Santa Claus Is Watching You	Mercury
3/63	81		Funny Man	Mercury
6/63	17		Harry The Hairy Ape	Mercury
10/63	59		Speed Ball	Mercury
7/66	91		Freddie Feelgood (and His Funky Little Five Piece Band)	Monument
4/68	52		Unwind	Monument
8/68	28		Mr. Businessman	Monument
4/69	8	Δ	Gitarzan	Monument
6/69	27		Along Came Jones	Monument
10/69	81		Sunday Mornin' Comin' Down	Monument
4/70	1	Δ	Everything Is Beautiful	Barnaby
7/70	45		America, Communicate With Me	Barnaby
11/70	81		Sunset Strip	Barnaby
12/70	50		Bridget the Midget (the Queen Of the Blues)	Barnaby
5/71	82		A Mama and a Papa	Barnaby
8/71	70		All My Trials	Barnaby
11/71	63		Turn Your Radio On	Barnaby
4/74	1	Δ	The Streak	Barnaby
7/74	73		Moonlight Special	Barnaby
4/75	14		Misty	Barnaby
10/75	68		Indian Love Call	Barnaby
1/76	93		Young Love	Barnaby
1/77	40		In the Mood [as the Henhouse Five Plus Too]	Warner Bros.
3/79	49		I Need Your Help Barry Manilow	Warner Bros.

Δ symbol: RIAA certified gold record (Recording Industry Association of America)

Billboard's pop singles chart data is courtesy of Joel Whitburn's Record Research Inc. (www.recordresearch.com), Menomonee Falls, Wisconsin.

Epilogue: Ray Stevens

Singer, musician, composer, arranger, producer

As the Great Depression took hold in 1931, the Clark Thread Company, with origins dating to early 19th-century Scotland, took the bold step of establishing a sewing thread manufacturing facility near Austell, Georgia, in rural Cobb County, 20 miles west-northwest of Atlanta. The three-story spinning mill was built atop a gently sloping knoll, and dominated the local landscape. The factory, in which baled cotton was spun into thread for clothing manufacturers, created jobs for 650 employees. To house the workers, the Clark Thread Company hired contractors to build a village named Clarkdale at the base of the hill. The mill town

Ray Stevens (photo by Shannon Fontaine)

included 138 homes as well as retail stores. The factory's textile workers included Willis Harold Ragsdale, who married Frances Stephens and settled into one of the trim little company-owned homes in Clarkdale. There, on January 24, 1939, they welcomed the birth of a son, Harold Ray Ragsdale – whom the world would come to know 22 years later as Ray Stevens. "On my mother's side, one of the family names was Ray. It's Scottish, I think, and so I was named after the Rays in the family. In school I went by the name Ray Ragsdale. My nickname was 'Rags.' It wasn't used in a derogatory way, though."

Clarkdale was a close-knit community. "Everybody had a pretty good life there," Stevens said. "My dad started out sweeping floors in the mill, but he ended

166

up at a desk with a slide rule. He was in the rate section, which decided what kinds of machines to buy, where to put them, how many men to hire – logistics as far as the manufacturing process is concerned is the best description of what he did that I can make out. I remember asking when I got a little older, 'What does daddy do?' and that was kind of the fuzzy explanation I was given, but he wound up at a desk in the office of the company."

Ray's parents lived in a three-room duplex in the company housing village. "I was told that when I was born the doctor was on his way, and the nurse in the village did the delivery. The doctor finally showed up and told her she did a good job," Stevens said. "They were great houses. In those days in North Georgia, slate was abundant and inexpensive, and they roofed all of the houses in the village with slate. The houses were all painted white and some of them had black shutters, and the clapboard was, I think, cedar. Those houses are still there. They were very well built."

Clarkdale had some nice conveniences that, at the time, many rural places in Georgia lacked, including electricity and indoor plumbing, along with a public swimming pool, a community center for public gatherings, and a baseball diamond that the Clark Thread Company's team used. "My dad was a great baseball player on the team," said Stevens. "The Clarkdale team played the other towns around North Georgia. There were 10 or so towns around there that Clarkdale played against. I loved it. I was a bat boy from time to time. I got to get all the broken bats and glue and tape them back together, and we kids would use them on the mill hill to play our own games of baseball."

Ray has one brother, Johnny, who is five-and-a-half years younger. "He's retired now, and building a house on an island off the coast of Panama. In the past, he was in the Air Force, and he worked with me at my publishing office," said Stevens. "He was also a musician and moved to Nashville and represented other publishing companies that wanted to have a presence here – companies from New York – people like the Goodman Group. Benny Goodman's brother Gene had a publishing company, and John represented them here. About 20 years ago, John went to Branson with me when I built a theater there, and he managed the concessions and the gift shop, and made a lot of money doing that."

While Ray's parents weren't particularly musical, his mom encouraged him to take piano lessons at the age of 7. "My mom thought that's what I should do, and she wouldn't take 'no' for an answer. I didn't want to do it, but now I'm glad I did. I wanted to become a baseball player. But I would have been a lousy baseball player," he chuckled. "In the beginning I played popular songs of the day on the piano, just getting familiar with sheet music. The first song I remember learning was the *Marine Hymn*. This was right after World War II. I think I started piano in 1945 or '46, and all of the military songs were very popular during that period."

Clarkdale kids took a school bus to a public school in nearby Austell, Georgia, where Ray attended elementary school through the fourth grade. He was studious in school – not a distracting class clown. His family then moved 180 miles south to Albany, Georgia, when his father was transferred to the Clark Thread Company's mill there. "'All-Benny' it's called," said Ray. "There's a joke about it. A guy named Benny was working down there and when he finished somebody said, "that's all Benny," and that's how Albany got its name." Shortly after Ray's family moved there, Clark Thread Company merged with J. & P. Coats and became known as Coats and Clark.

Ray continued with piano lessons in Albany, switching from popular music to the classical music of Bach and Beethoven. While in high school in 1954, Ray assembled a rhythm and blues band called the Barons, for which he was lead singer and played piano. At the time, he was thinking of a career in architecture rather than music, so he was performing with the Barons only for the fun of it. "We would play for the school dances and local functions around Albany," said Ray. "After my dad was transferred again from Albany to Atlanta, I re-formed the Barons with all new guys, and I finished my last year of high school at Druid Hills High School in Atlanta."

After moving to Atlanta at the age of 17, Ray met radio personality and Georgia Tech football broadcaster Bill Lowery. "Bill had all types of shows. He was on several different radio stations around town, and he had started a music publishing company. He encouraged all the kids around Atlanta to write songs. Jerry Reed was one of them. A guy named Ric Cartey was one of them and he wrote a song called 'Young Love' which was another big hit by Sonny James. Tab Hunter also had a hit out of it, but I can remember thinking, 'Boy, this guy cannot sing.' Sonny James could sing, and he had a huge hit on Capitol.

"So I went out to Lowery's house and I said, 'My name is Ray Ragsdale, and I'm going to learn to write songs for you.' He said, 'Okay, lad, go to it.' Ray set about composing a song with a Druid Hills High School classmate, Will Rogers Jr. – unrelated to the famous Oklahoma cowboy and humorist. Their song, called "Silver Bracelet," was about a boy giving his girlfriend a bracelet engraved with her name to demonstrate his love for her. "I borrowed a little tape recorder from a friend, and I got the key to the lunchroom from the principal. The room had a very high ceiling and a piano on a little stage. I went there one Sunday by myself and made a demo of 'Silver Bracelet.'"

Although Bill Lowery's friend Ken Nelson of Capitol Records liked the song, he thought Ray's surname Ragsdale was unsuitable for a recording artist. When Ray asked why, Nelson replied, "When I was a kid, I read a book that talked about a dog named Rags, and it reminds me of that, so we gotta change your name." Ragsdale said, "You're gonna make my mother mad." Nelson asked, "What's your mother's maiden name?" The teenage singer replied, "Stephens." Nelson said, "That's a good name, Ray Stevens [spelled wtih a "v" instead of "ph"]." The young man said, "Wait a minute, you're gonna make my dad mad." Nelson responded, "Do you want to make a record, or not?" Young Ray didn't hesitate. "Yes sir!" From then on, he was Ray Stevens. At RCA's studio "B" in Nashville, Ray recorded "Silver Bracelet." Ray disliked the result of that recording session. He had conceived a bluesy sound similar to the Penguins' "Earth Angel." Instead, the arrangement sounded like a bubbly pop song that Marty Robbins, Guy Mitchell, or Johnny Ray might have recorded. "I wasn't strong-willed enough to insist on my ideas," he said.

But after he began asserting his own ideas and achieved seven Hot 100 hits during his first two years on the charts, Ray established Ahab Music Company in 1963 to start producing other recording artists. "You have to shepherd the song – if it's a new song, you make a demo, you pitch it, you try to get it cut, and after it's cut you get deals for sheet music, you register with all of the agencies to get your money, you represent the writer and make sure all of the i's are dotted and t's are crossed when it comes to making deals for any other use of the song, such as movies or advertising. That's a big source of income on some songs," he said. A good example of that is a song called "Rub it In," which Layng Martine Jr. wrote and published through Ahab Music. Billy "Crash" Craddock's version of the song hit No. 16 on the Billboard Hot 100 pop chart and No.1 on the country singles chart in 1974, but the tune took on new life in a long-running radio and TV commercial. "It made more money from S.C. Johnson on the Glade Plug-In room deodorizer commercials than it made as a hit record," Stevens said.

Ray counts guitarist, composer and musical arranger Bill Justis among the people who have been most influential in his life. "Bill was a great friend and great musician, and he taught me a lot about arranging," Ray said. "Although I never graduated from Georgia State, I spent three years there studying music theory and composition. But I learned more in three days from Bill Justis than during all that time in college. He was the first guy who showed me how to lay out a score, and it all just fell into place. In the basement of his house he showed me a big table laid out with score pages, and it was a revelation to me."

Another music business associate, Felton Jarvis, played a big role in Ray's life for another reason. Ray and his wife, Penny, met in Atlanta through Jarvis, who had worked with Bill Lowery during the mid-1950s. Penny had been visiting her sister, who was married to Jarvis. Penny and Ray married in 1960. "When Penny and I moved to Nashville in 1962, Felton and his wife moved here too, because he wanted to be in the music business." Felton Jarvis, who died in 1981, wound up producing most of Elvis Presley's recordings from 1966 to 1977. Jarvis also produced John Hartford's first six albums, as well as recordings by Carl Perkins, Jim Ed Brown, Skeeter Davis, Michael Nesmith, Mickey Newbury, Tommy Roe, Liz Anderson, Bobby Bare, and other performers.

Penny and Ray still live in Nashville, and have a vacation home in Gulf Shores, Alabama. They have two daughters: Timi Lynn (born in 1961), who is married and the mother of four children; and Suzi Ragsdale (born in 1964), who has a successful career as a songwriter, backup singer, and a performer in Nashville. Since 1990, Suzi has done vocal work on discs by country singers Suzy Bogguss, Pam Tillis, David Ball, Hank Williams Jr., Joy Lynn White, Tom Paxton, Ian Tyson, Jo-El Sonnier, and many others. During the same time period, her songs were recorded by Anne Murray, Billy Dean, Pam Tillis, Mila Mason, Suzy Bogguss, Lari White, Lisa Brokop and the band Nelson, composed of Ricky Nelson's twin sons Matthew and Gunnar. Since 1991, Suzi has collaborated in studio and on stage with singer and songwriter Darrell Scott (see www.suziragsdale.com for more information).

Thirty years after first attaining success as a recording artist, Ray took an adventurous step in 1991 – building and opening the Ray Stevens Theatre, a 2,000-seat showroom in Branson, Missouri. "My road show required more props and lights than was practical to carry around, so I wanted a sit-down place where I could assemble all of this material and produce a show with all of my strange songs, my comedy records, and I thought I had a following big enough to do that," Ray told us in July 2012. "I first went over to Pigeon Forge, Tennessee and talked to T.G. Sheppard, who had a theater over there, and then I got a call from a friend who said, 'Come to Branson, because I've been doing some leg-work over here and I found a place that would be great.' So I went to Branson, and bought the property and built the theater."

Ray conceived a stage show in which he was the starring attraction, and beginning at age 52 performed twice a day, six days a week for two years. "It was brutal. I did 1991, '92, and '93. By then I was whipped and I decided I gotta stop that," said Ray, who sold the theater in 1993 to give himself a much-needed break. As a show element, Ray had created music videos of several of his hits. The videos were so popular with theater audiences that Ray decided to release *Comedy Video Classics* through his newly established label, Clyde Records, and he promoted them through a mail order and television ad campaign. Video footage shot during his stage show resulted in production and distribution of *Ray Stevens Live!* in 1995. Ray resumed songwriting, returned to the recording studio in 1996, and created a new comedy album, *Hum It,* which MCA Records released. The album's tracks included "Virgil and the Moonshot," "Too Drunk to Fish," and "R.V." The following year, MCA released Ray's twisted Christmas album called *Ray Stevens – Christmas Through a Different Window.* As Ray signed with Curb records in 2000 and created a comedic musical album titled *Ear Candy,* he released a DVD called *Ray Stevens' Funniest Video Characters.* Ray harpooned terrorism in 2002 with his album *Osama, Yo' Mama.*

When Ray sold his theater in 1993, he and his business partners carried the financing. "The people who bought it made the payments for five years until the balloon payment came due. They couldn't afford that, so I got the theater back and I rented it to them after that for a while," Ray explained. He resurrected his stage show in the theater for two years beginning in 2004, and then sold the facility in 2006 to the RFD-TV cable channel. Meanwhile, he stepped up operations of his own label, Clyde Records, to produce recordings for retail sales and downloads. His first CD release on the label was *New Orleans Moon,* a tribute to the people of Louisiana.

In 1999 Stevens was diagnosed with prostate cancer, for which he underwent surgery. He's happy to report that he's had a clean bill of health since. "I got really lucky," said Stevens. "I found out about Dr. Patrick Walsh at Johns Hopkins Hospital in Baltimore, and he did my surgery. I flew up and talked to him and he said he couldn't do it. I said, 'Oh, come on, don't you know how important I am?' He laughed, and said, 'OK, get up here and I'll do it,' and he gave me a date. He did the nerve-sparing procedure on me and it was very successful. What a nice man!"

In 2007 Ray decided to record exclusively for his own label, Clyde Records, Inc., changing it from a direct-marketing outlet to a full-service label that would make releases available to retail and for download. His first release on Clyde Records was *New Orleans Moon,* the title track of which also was released as a single. The CD includes the fine old standards "Do You Know What it Means to Miss New Orleans," "Basin Street Blues," and "St. James Infirmary," along with Randy Newman's "Louisiana." The CD is Ray's tribute to the music, the culture, and the people of New Orleans, in response to the devastation that Hurricane Katrina caused as it plowed across the Gulf Coast in 2005.

Ray has concentrated on patriotic and politically themed CD and video productions since 2010, when he released *We The People,* followed the next year by *Spirit of '76.* He established a video channel on YouTube and a "Ray TV" section on his website (www.raystevens.com) to broadcast his biting political satire vignettes, including *Throw the Bums Out,*

The Skies Just Ain't Friendly, and *Obama Nation.* He also published a book, *Let's Get Political,* consisting of 34 essays in which he expands on themes he introduced in his recent social commentary songs and videos. We asked Ray if he would consider running for political office someday. He chuckled and replied, "I'm from the rural South and just a redneck Southern boy, but I'm way too smart for that."

Back in Clarkdale, the old thread mill shut down in 1983, a victim of increasing overseas competition that shredded the American textile industry. The mill remained unused until 1996, when a developer made extensive renovations with the intention of converting it into a shopping mall. But occupancy was insufficient, so the developer put the property up for sale. The city of Austell bought it, and reconfigured it as a mixed-

Ray Stevens (photo by Shannon Fontaine)

use building called the Threadmill Mall, combining government offices, retail shops, and restaurants. The old mill was added to the National Register of Historic Places in 1987, and the homes in the village are now privately owned and still occupied.

Since 1962, Ray Stevens has recorded more than 40 albums. The song that stands apart in his mind is "Everything is Beautiful," which he regards as his biggest song publishing success. "It's been recorded 200 to 300 times by other artists. And, of course, 'The Streak' was a huge hit. My record sold four to five million singles. That's back when singles were selling. I've been very lucky," said Stevens. "I've been able to make a living and make a career out of something that I really enjoy doing. And not everybody can say that."

Visit **www.raystevens.com** for more information.

The Grass Roots performing at The Trip nightclub in West Hollywood, 1965.
From left, David Stensen, Denny Ellis, Joel Larson and Bill Fulton (photo
courtesy of Joel Larson)

ON AIR

CHAPTER 7

Midnight Confessions
The Grass Roots

The epicenters of musical innovation have shifted over the years, with hotbeds of talent sometimes erupting in unexpected places, like a geyser suddenly spewing forth from a previously undiscovered subterranean geologic fault. So it was in the Los Angeles Basin in the mid-1960s, along a mile-long section of Sunset Boulevard midway between Hollywood and Beverly Hills. Known as the Sunset Strip, it was the locale for a cluster of nightclubs that began attracting restless youths from the surrounding safe suburbs. Increasingly wary of a presidential administration committed to escalation of the Vietnam conflict, kids converged at the "Strip" to hang out along the boulevard, to patronize the area's "head shops" that sold water pipes, incense, and strobe lights, and to hear the numerous bands performing in the Whisky à Go Go, Pandora's Box, Gazzarri's, the London Fog, the Sea Witch, The Trip, and the Galaxy. Unlike Ed Pearl's Ash Grove, Doug Weston's Troubadour, and other traditional folk hangouts in the Melrose Avenue-Santa Monica Boulevard district that tended to attract bohemian poets, philosophers, and intellectual college students, the Sunset Strip clubs served as a platform for rock performers who appealed to young people with outrageous attire and rebellious anti-war attitudes. Along with the Byrds, Buffalo Springfield, Love, Sonny and Cher, the Leaves, the Turtles, the Seeds, the Electric Prunes, and the Doors, the Grass Roots embodied the Sunset Strip music scene that heavily influenced young people throughout the nation.

Dunhill Records partner Lou Adler established the Grass Roots in 1965 as a band to record the songs of P.F. Sloan and Steve Barri, who were staff writers for the label's Trousdale Music subsidiary. Over time, the band and its sound evolved substantially, far beyond Adler's original folk-rock vision. Between 1965 and 1973, Dunhill Records released 23 Grass Roots singles, all but three of which made the national charts. The Grass Roots became consistent hit makers, landing 14 singles in the top 40, including three top-10 hits.

Sloan and Barri had first achieved success with Imperial Records in 1964 performing as the Fantastic Baggys (a reference to swim trunks for surfers) using recording studio overdubbing. Among the surf and hot rod-oriented tunes that Sloan and Barri wrote ("This Little Woody," "Wax Up Your Board," "Surfer Boy's Dream Come True"), one Fantastic Baggys release, "Tell 'em I'm Surfin,'" became a regional Southern California hit. Steve Barri (born Steven Barry Lipkin) and Phil "Flip" Sloan (born Philip Gary Schlein) were first brought together at Screen Gems Publishing, where they worked as writers under Adler – a producer who earlier had teamed with Herb Alpert as co-managers of Jan & Dean. "Lou felt my songs could use some help melodically, and I guess he felt Phil's songs could use some help lyrically, so he put us together. He thought we might be a pretty good team," Barri told us. "I played a little guitar – very little. To be real honest, Phil was much more of a musician, and far more talented than I was in songwriting. I knew just my basic four chords, but because he could play any instrument, he knew all the chords. My strength was song ideas and titles and lyrics. Lou would tell us, 'The Vogues are looking for a new song,' or 'The Turtles are looking.' In those days, songwriters like Goffin and King, and Mann and Weil, were writing for the various acts that were having hits. So Phil and I would get together at his mom's house, at the little dinette that they had in the kitchen, because it was a very ambient-sounding room, and we would try to come up with songs for different people."

They achieved their first success with a heavyset rhythm and blues singer named Round Robin who scored a Southern California dance hit called "Do the Slauson," followed by a national hit called "Kick That Little Foot, Sally Ann" in the spring of '64. More hits followed as producer Terry Melcher, who had recorded with singer Bruce Johnston as the Rip Chords and as Bruce and Terry, took a liking to tunes that Sloan and Barri wrote – including "Summer Means Fun." When Adler left Screen Gems and launched Trousdale Music in 1964, he recruited Sloan and Barri to serve as his writing staff. The following year, he established Dunhill Records with partners Jay Lasker and Bobby Roberts. Sloan and

Barri were pivotal in Adler's concept for the creation of a band to record songs published through Trousdale Music. "Lou's idea was to try to find a band that could do a group version of what Bob Dylan was doing," Barri explained.

Sloan and Barri's transformation to producers was serendipitous. They initially became involved in the recording process cutting demos of the songs they had written, working with a stable of L.A. studio musicians that included keyboard player Leon Russell, drummer Hal Blaine, bass player Joe Osborn, guitarist Glen Campbell, and keyboard player Larry Knechtel. Working at the hottest studio in town – Studio 3 at Western Recorders on Sunset Boulevard, where the Beach Boys recorded – Sloan and Barri learned the ropes quickly, and began producing demos of exceptionally high quality. Among them was Barry McGuire's powerfully angry condemnation of the Vietnam war, "Eve of Destruction," the lyrics for which Sloan wrote in one evening. "That was never meant to be a single. We really cut it to be a 'B' side of a record," Barri confided. "Once it started to explode as a hit in the summer of '65, we needed to finish an album quickly. Although Lou Adler was producing the album, he let Sloan and me lay down the tracks, to develop us as producers. But during the making of that record, Barry McGuire brought in friends of his who he asked to use as background singers. They turned out to be the Mamas and the Papas. When they sang 'California Dreamin" and 'Monday, Monday,' Phil and I looked at each other and said, 'My God. This is unbelievable.' We called Lou, who came down and flipped over them. So he said to us, 'Look, I'm gonna sign these guys and make a record with them. I want you two to get more involved in finishing up Barry McGuire's record.' That really was the first opportunity that we had to go in and test our chops as producers."

With his sights set on producing as well as writing, Sloan had in mind a name for a band to fulfill Adler's vision – the Grassroots. But it already was taken. At Bido Lito's, a small, out-of-the-way club off Vine Street south of Hollywood Boulevard, he had seen Arthur Lee fronting a group previously known as the American Four that recently had begun billing itself as the Grass Roots. Adler liked the name and, correctly assuming that Lee had not registered it, figured it was his for the plucking. Adler sent Sloan and Barri, along with session musicians, into the studio in the spring of 1965 to record some demo tracks. With Sloan singing lead, they recorded a demo of a composition of theirs, "Where Were You When I Needed You." Creation of the Grass Roots band was the next step.

Adler invited three bands to audition at the Whisky à Go Go, the club on Grant Street in San Francisco that he co-owned with Elmer Valentine and Mario Maglieri. The bands that had earned spots in the audition early that summer included a group called the Bedouins (pronounced BED-o-wins), consisting of rhythm guitarist Denny Ellis, bass player Dave Stensen, drummer Joel Larson, and guitar-playing lead singer Bill Fulton, all from the peninsula region near San Francisco International Airport. A "cover band" with a preference for tunes by the Rolling Stones and other blues-influenced "British invasion" bands, the Bedouins frequently performed for teen dances at roller rinks and so-called "rec clubs," sponsored by local park and recreation districts. They had been finalists on March 14 in a spring-break San Mateo Teenage Fair "battle of the bands" – the winner of which had been the Syndicate of Sound,

The Grass Roots at the Third Street Tunnel near Angels Flight in downtown Los Angeles in 1966 (L-R): Denny Ellis, Dave Stensen, Joel Larson, and Bill Fulton (photo courtesy of Dave Stensen)

which went on to record the hit "Little Girl" for Bell Records. At the time of the Teenage Fair, Larson had been in another band, the Intruders, which had placed fourth in the "battle of the bands," two positions higher than the Bedouins. Larson joined the Bedouins shortly afterward to replace drummer Bill Schoppe, who left the band due to illness in his family. "Also finishing above us was a band [the New Invaders] featuring an amazing young vocalist, Lydia Pense. She would go on to front the band Cold Blood," Ellis observed.

The Bedouins began associating with other musicians in the area, including the Beau Brummels, who often played at the Morocco Room on El Camino Real. "We weren't old enough to go in, but we watched the Brummels from the back door," Larson said. "The band members ended up being our friends, and we would hang out with them. We'd go up to a place called Searsville Lake, up behind Stanford in Menlo Park. There were a couple of electrical outlets, and we'd plug in and just play underneath the trees in picnic grounds. That's where I really learned to play, because these guys were older than me – they were real good musicians – and we learned a lot of skills from [Beau Brummels] Ron Meagher and Sal Valentino, and the others."

Dave Stensen recalls that Beau Brummels composer and guitarist Ron Elliott introduced the Bedouins to Tom Gericke, a college friend of his who was establishing himself as a talent agent. Ace Records music archivist and reissue consultant Alec Palao observes that Gericke had produced and released records by the Off-Beats, an Oakland surf band in which Ron Meagher had played before his Beau Brummels days. Gericke agreed to represent the Bedouins and, upon his instruction, the band members cut a four-track demo record at the Sierra Sound recording studio in Berkeley. Gericke managed to persuade Lou Adler of Dunhill records to give the band that important audition at the Whisky. The Bedouins had barely completed their third song when Adler said, "That's all I need to hear. You guys are it." What he had heard was Bill Fulton's voice, which happened to be nearly indiscernible from Sloan's. The band members had no idea at the time that "it" meant not only a recording agreement, but also a new identity as the "Grassroots" – the spelling of which was soon changed to two words: "Grass Roots." The allure of a recording contract overshadowed any trepidation about assuming a new identity.

At a meeting in Los Angeles in September 1965, the boys signed the recording contract on the dotted line. "About two weeks after signing the recording contract, we went into Studio 3 at Western Recorders with Lou Adler," Larson said. At the studio, the band members were told to sign a document giving Dunhill exclusive rights to the "Grass Roots" name.

179

"One of us asked, 'What if we don't want to sign that?' Lou flatly told us if we didn't we wouldn't record. We gave them all the power," Ellis said. Adler produced the session. Larson added, "The engineer was Bones Howe, and P.F. Sloan and Steve Barri were there also. We recorded vocals over some of the tracks that they had." At that session, Fulton recorded the vocal lead for an interpretation of Bob Dylan's scornful composition "Mr. Jones (Ballad Of a Thin Man)." Fulton and the newly dubbed Grass Roots gave the song an appropriately sullen reading. At that session they also finished the "B" side, the Sloan-Barri song "You're a Lonely Girl." Released as a single (Dunhill No. 4013) in the autumn of 1965, "Mr. Jones" garnered considerable airplay in Los Angeles and some other markets, but did not reach the nationwide top 100.

As McGuire's "Eve of Destruction" growled its way up the charts, Dunhill quickly sent Ellis, Stensen, Larson, and Fulton on the road with a new mission – back-up band for Barry McGuire. In concerts in a string of cities, beginning with an arena concert in Seattle, the Grass Roots were the opening act, and then remained on stage for headliner McGuire. They did the same for the Mamas and the Papas. On their own, the Roots did the TV pop show circuit – the *Lloyd Thaxton Show, Shivaree,* and *Shindig.* They also made a *Hollywood Palace* appearance in which guest host Don Knotts played Larson's drums.

The band members moved down to L.A., as they were installed as the house band at The Trip, a club that Elmer Valentine and Lou Adler had opened at 8572 W. Sunset Boulevard. The club's neon sign, on which the word "the" was upside-down, hinted at the club's hipness and irreverence. During their first week on the job, the Byrds were the headliners. The Grass Roots lived in an apartment on Santa Monica Boulevard, a couple of blocks from The Trip. "We would literally get our guitars and walk up the hill to The Trip. The steady club gig kept us in rent and food money," Stensen explained. "Each of us in the Grass Roots was making $200 to $300 per week at The Trip, which was pretty good money then," Fulton said. But Denny Ellis said that he, Fulton, Stensen, and Larson were unaware that the Grass Roots name had been hijacked until he and his band mates were confronted unexpectedly. "We had just started playing at The Trip in fall of '65 when a group of people approached the stage between songs and angrily said 'who are you guys? You're not the Grass Roots!' That's when we found out about the other group, which then changed its name to Love," Ellis recalled. "They hadn't secured legal rights to the Grass Roots name, and didn't fight for it. I remember Dave and I going to Bido Lito's backstage and talking to them about it."

Although time has faded and smeared memories of that hectic era like a tattered tie-dye, certain moments still stand out in sharp contrast for Ellis. "I remember sitting backstage at The Trip with my friend Leslie talking about Love with Marvin Gaye while his band warmed up the audience. Frank Zappa coming over to our house to talk about music, and then taking part in his *Freak Out* recording session. The Grateful Dead coming in to the Whisky to hear us play, and hanging out together while they were doing the L.A. Acid Test [LSD party]."

The Roots flew to New York to perform with Barry McGuire in an October 31 appearance on the *Ed Sullivan Show* – the premier prime-time talent showcase in that era. Back in the studio in December, the Grass Roots recorded a couple of more tracks, "Where Were You When I Needed You," with the flip side "(These Are) Bad Times." Both were written by Sloan and Barri. A song that epitomized the folk-rock genre, "Where Were You When I Needed You" was an assertive declaration by a once-despondent man who is now rejecting the girl who once left him. The baroque-flavored tune had an instrumental bridge sweetened by an instrument uncustomary in rock: a harpsichord. With those songs in the can, the Grass Roots and McGuire headed to New York City again in early January, this time for a two-week gig at the Phone Booth nightclub in the midst of a public transit strike that crippled the city and frayed the nerves of New Yorkers. Unlike the relaxed atmosphere of The Trip, the Phone Booth imposed a demanding schedule on the performers – particularly on the Grass Roots, who alternately performed 45-minute sets of their own, then remained on stage as the backup band for a 45-minute Barry McGuire set, a cycle that continued into the early hours of each morning. "A piss and a drink is all we had time for between sets," Stensen recalls.

While playing on a billing with McGuire at the hungry i nightclub in San Francisco, the Grass Roots met two people who were pivotal in the emerging San Francisco ballroom scene – John Carpenter, who briefly was Chet Helms' partner in Family Dog Productions, and Chris Brooks, who eventually did promotion work for Bill Graham Presents. "Chet and John invited us to play at the Fillmore Auditorium," recalled Stensen. The Grass Roots were vulnerable to that appeal because they had envied from afar the metamorphosis of the Bay Area music scene that had occurred during the time they were based in L.A. "We played our first San Francisco ballroom gig at the Fillmore Auditorium on February 26, 1966, the day after my 19th birthday," Stensen said. The concert billing consisted of the Great Society with Grace Slick, the Grass Roots, Big Brother and the Holding Company, and Quicksilver Messenger Service.

Back in L.A. in the spring of 1966, the Grass Roots performed numerous dates at the Whisky on the Sunset Strip, including some double bills with the Beau Brummels, with whom they had hung out on the San Francisco Peninsula. Dunhill released "Where Were You When I Needed You" as a single (Dunhill 4029) in the spring of '66. It hit the national charts in mid-June and rose to No. 28 nationwide on the *Billboard* Hot 100. The Grass Roots had germinated.

But the band members were becoming restless. They wanted to compose their own songs on future recordings – not only for the creative gratification, but also for the enduring financial rewards of songwriting

The Grass Roots in 1967: (L-R), Rob Grill, Rick Coonce (standing), Creed Bratton (with chin resting on hand) and Warren Entner (photo by Guy Webster, courtesy of Creed Bratton)

royalties. Musicians are paid only for the time they're working. Lyricists and composers, in contrast, earn income even when other people record their songs. "A band can play club dates only so long until it becomes stale," Ellis observed. Seeking to establish longevity in the recording business, Denny, Bill, and Dave decided to return to the Bay Area in the summer of 1966 to concentrate on developing their own Grass Roots material to record for Dunhill. They rented a house in an industrial part of San Bruno so they could practice at any hour without disturbing anyone. Joel, however, chose to remain in L.A.

In San Bruno, Stensen, Fulton, and Ellis reunited with Larson's predecessor in the Bedouins, drummer Bill Schoppe, and began booking gigs in the Bay Area. They appeared as the Grass Roots on one more TV show. "We filmed a lip-synced version of 'Where Were You…' for *Where the Action Is* at Nepenthe in Big Sur. We could barely scrape together enough money for gas and a motel room," Ellis recalled. "That performance can be seen now on YouTube with a fresh overdub. We look so young, and we had all that hair! We also appeared on several iconic rock posters from the early San Francisco days."

Dunhill wanted the band members to complete the debut Grass Roots album for which they already had recorded several tracks, but the band members expressed dissatisfaction with the song list that Adler presented. Fulton and his band mates wanted to take a greater part in the creative process. "We were already a band, and we had dreams and visions of what we thought it was going to be like, and we had a certain type of material we liked to play," Ellis said. "It was also the '60s, and a lot was happening among other musicians. People were singing songs of social relevance or trying experimental styles. We all wanted to be a part of that, but we were being asked to play songs like 'Lollipop Train,' which is geared toward a 13-year-old audience. It was disillusioning."

Adler declined the band's request to develop material of their choosing because that would have conflicted with his strategy to retain the publishing royalties from the compositions of his staff writers Sloan and Barry. The discussion ended with a stalemate. Using "cover songs" the band already had recorded for television appearances, including Clyde Otis and Ivory Joe Hunter's "Ain't That Loving You, Baby" and Mick Jagger and Keith Richard's "Tell Me," Dunhill cobbled together an album, titled *Where Were You When I Needed You,* and released it in October 1966. The album cover depicted a weathered antique chair tipped against a rickety farm gate choked by tall dried grass, but the album jacket contained no mention or photos of the members of the Grass Roots. Stensen, Fulton, and Ellis meanwhile performed numerous gigs reveling in psychedelic jams at the Fillmore, the Avalon Ballroom, and other Bay Area venues – until Dunhill's lawyer sent them a letter warning of potential legal action for unauthorized use of the Grass Roots name. Unwilling to engage in a legal dispute or return to L.A. and conform to what the record company wanted, Fulton, Stensen, and Ellis regrouped as the Unquenchable Thirst – and as soon as they had done so, their bookings dried up because of the lack of drawing power.

The Grass Roots in 1968 – rear: Rob Grill and Rick Coonce; front: Warren Entner and Creed Bratton (photo courtesy of Creed Bratton)

Back in L.A., Larson began working with former Byrds guitarist Gene Clark's new band, joined Emitt Rhodes' group the Merry-Go-Round, and became a session musician. Lou Adler had begun a search for another Grass Roots band when he received an audition tape in late 1966 from a Los Angeles bar band called the Thirteenth Floor. Adler offered the band a tantalizing choice: sign with Dunhill as the Thirteenth Floor, taking a long-shot bet that they could score a hit record as unknowns – or assume a new identity that already had name recognition: the Grass Roots. Just as the Thirteenth Floor members decided to accept the proposal to become the Grass Roots, the band's rhythm guitarist-keyboard player Warren Entner, lead guitarist Creed Bratton, and drummer Rick Coonce faced a crisis: their bass player, Kenny Fukumoto – who was also their vocalist – had just received his notice to report for military duty. Through an ad that Entner posted at the local musicians' union office, they quickly found an able replacement in Rob Grill, who not only played bass but had a powerful singing voice that electrified Barri, Sloan, and Adler. "When we heard Rob's voice, we felt he really had the sound that we were looking for as a vehicle for our song writing. Selfishly, we were looking for an outlet for our songs," Barri told us.

The new quartet recorded as the Grass Roots for the first time in early 1967, cutting another Sloan-Barri tune called "Tip of My Tongue" that barely dented the regional charts on the West Coast. Then Sloan and Barri got wind of "Piangi Con Me" (Cry With Me), a pop hit in Italy performed in Italian by an English group called the Rokes. The song, written by David Shapiro, Ivan Mogull, and Michael Julian, was translated to "Let's Live for Today" in English. "We started messing around with an arrangement. I remember that we recorded a track on a Monday morning, and when everyone went to lunch, I wrote a 'B' side [called "Depressed Feeling"] that we cut in about two hours," Entner recalled. He and Bratton played acoustic guitars on "Let's Live for Today," accompanying Sloan, who played lead guitar. "We finished the vocals and mixed it on Tuesday. By Friday it was on about 180 radio stations." Released in April with Rob Grill and Warren Enter sharing lead vocal segments, "Let's Live for Today" hit the national top 10 and gave rise to an album of the same name. The *Let's Live for Today* album yielded another single hit, "Things I Should Have Said." Sloan and Barri wrote six of the album's 12 songs, but Bratton, Entner, and Grill wrote four others. Coinciding with the release, the band boarded a plane to Alaska, embarking upon a dizzying schedule of touring, sharing stage billing with an eclectic list of performers ranging from Every Mother's Son, Creedence Clearwater Revival, and Steppenwolf, to the Chambers Brothers, Frijid Pink, and Cream.

"Everything happened so quickly, I hadn't even checked out of college – I just left. I was barely 19," Rick Coonce said. "It was just a roller coaster ride from then on." In addition to nonstop concert touring, the Grass Roots also made numerous television appearances, including variety shows mixing traditional Hollywood fare with an occasional act for young people. When they appeared on the *Hollywood Palace* variety show in December 1967, guest host Jimmy Durante, a comic New York showman dating to the vaudeville era, introduced the band by saying, "Here's da Grass Roots – dey don't need a manager, dey need a gardener!" Although they were high on the charts, Entner, Bratton, Coonce, and Grill lived modestly. The Grass Roots set themselves up as a corporation, and the band members each drew a monthly stipend. As Adler became involved as one of the creators of the landmark Monterey International Pop Festival, he sold Dunhill to ABC Records.

From left, Rick Coonce, Rob Grill, Warren Entner and Creed Bratton in early 1969 (photo courtesy of Barbara Smith)

The third Grass Roots album, *Feelings,* recorded in the autumn of '67 for ABC-Dunhill and also produced by Sloan and Barri, achieved the dream that the Bedouins had sought. The album contained a predominant number of songs written by band members – including the title track, penned by Coonce and Entner with Kenny Fukumoto. The album, which included the Sloan-Barri composition "Melody for You" and Sloan's "The Sins of a Family Fall on the Daughter," further established the Grass Roots as a folk-rock mainstay.

Unknown to the public, the future of the Grass Roots appeared in doubt in the spring of 1968. While Barri loved writing and producing pop hits, Sloan was developing increasingly polarized political views and came to view music not strictly as an entertainment medium but rather as a forum for political expression. Their differences of opinion about the role of pop music led to the dissolution of the Sloan and Barri writing-producing partnership. Deciding to concentrate on a career as a serious solo folk singer-guitarist, Sloan packed up and headed for New York. But Barri chose to remain with ABC-Dunhill, and agreed to take on the full responsibilities of producing Grass Roots recordings. His first recording project as a solo producer with the group yielded a masterful work: composer Lou Josie's mesmerizing "Midnight Confessions," articulating the plaintive cry of a man who witnessed his true, secret love marrying another guy. He had confessed his love for her only to himself, at midnight in his lonely room. Punctuated by horns, the song marked the band's gravitation from folk-rock to pop. "Midnight Confessions" struck a resonant chord with fans, who sent it to No. 5 on the national charts and bought enough copies to qualify it for Recording Industry Association of America (RIAA) gold record certification, recognizing sale of 500,000 copies. "Midnight Confessions" and the band's next hit, "Bella Linda," were included in a 1968 compilation album, *Golden Grass.* "Midnight Confessions," the band's biggest hit, rose to No. 5 on the *Billboard* Hot 100, and the RIAA decreed it a gold record on December 3, 1968. The *Golden Grass* album earned RIAA gold certification on July 14, 1970.

Barri decided to withdraw from songwriting to concentrate on his role as vice president of A&R (artists and repertoire), in charge of developing new talent for Dunhill and ABC Records. In that role, he signed Three Dog Night, Steppenwolf, and Steely Dan to contracts, even more firmly establishing Dunhill as one of the nation's hottest record companies. "We had an incredibly large artist roster, and I felt it would be real awkward to pitch somebody on a song and say, 'by the way, I'm the writer on this one.' So I decided to stop writing. It's one thing when you sign an act that you're involved with producing, with the

The Grass Roots in late 1971, shortly before the departure of Rick
Coonce, seated on the wall. Standing (L-R) are Virgil Weber,
Rob Grill, Reed Kailing and Warren Entner, in front of Warren's house.
Joel Larson rejoined the band a couple of weeks after this photo was
taken (photo courtesy of Barbara Smith)

understanding that you're going to be the creative force behind them. It's another thing when you're supposed to be looking for songs for 20 or 30 different artists," explained Barri, who went on to executive A&R positions with Warner Bros. Records, Motown Records, and JVC Records before becoming director of A&R and president of Samson Records in 1998.

In early 1969 the Grass Roots completed recording another ABC-Dunhill album, *Lovin' Things,* which in addition to the title track included "The River Is Wide." That was the last Grass Roots album on which Creed Bratton performed. A dispute among the band members prompted his departure in April 1969. His replacement was keyboard player Dennis Provisor of the Blue Rose Band – giving the band a new organ lead sound. Provisor's appreciation of rhythm and blues music brought the band a more soulful edge. The Grass Roots later added lead guitarist Terry Furlong, becoming a quintet. *Leavin' It All Behind,* the first album by the new lineup, yielded two hit singles: "I'd Wait a Million Years" and "Heaven Knows." The band's momentum increased as they worked with arranger Jimmy Haskell and producer Steve Barri. The Roots hit their top stride in 1971, that year alone chalking up three uptempo top-20 hits: "Temptation Eyes," Sooner or Later," and "Two Divided by Love. During 1971 ABC-Dunhill released a more expansive compilation album, *The Grass Roots – Their 16 Greatest Hits,* which RIAA certified gold on August 9, 1972.

More personnel changes had taken place at the end of 1971, when Coonce left and was replaced briefly by Joe Pollard, until the other members persuaded Joel Larson – of the first generation of the Grass Roots – to return in early 1972. Dennis Provisor departed as the Roots re-signed with Dunhill in 1972, and the band brought in some new faces – guitarist Reed Kailing and keyboard player Virgil Weber. Between 1967 and 1972, the Grass Roots had remained on the national charts for 307 consecutive weeks, setting a record. But by the end of that extraordinary run, the greatest successes of the Grass Roots were behind them. The band did achieve some chart hits during 1972, but by 1973 radio programmers had lost interest. The band's final Dunhill album, *Alotta' Mileage,* which Grill, Entner, and Barri artfully co-produced, was released in 1973. The album cover pictured five pairs of well-worn boots and shoes. It yielded one chart single, "Love Is What You Make It," which hit No. 55 on the *Billboard* Hot 100.

Warren Entner, who after seven years with the Grass Roots decided that he had put in enough mileage on the road, departed the band in February 1974. Kailing left also. The Grass Roots regrouped, and with various configurations of performers – including Rob Grill, Joel

Larson, Dennis Provisor, and guitarist Reggie Knighton – continued doing concerts and club dates for a while. After Dunhill released the Grass Roots from their contract in 1975, the production duo of Dennis Lambert and Brian Potter – who had written the Grass Roots' 1971 hit song "Two Divided by Love" – persuaded the band to sign with their own label, Haven Records. Haven had scored success with the Righteous Brothers' song "Rock and Roll Heaven." Lambert and Potter produced an album called simply *Grass Roots* in collaboration with arranger Michael Omartian – who was instrumental in creating the melodic pop hits of Christopher Cross. The tracks ran the gamut of composers and styles, from Motown ("Something About You" by Holland-Dozier-Holland) to Gerry Goffin and Carole King ("Up on the Roof") to Randy Newman ("Naked Man") to Barry Mann and Cynthia Weil ("Nothing Good Comes Easy"). The album yielded one modest hit, "Mamacita," in the summer of '75. The Roots cut sides for four more singles, but as regular members of the group left one after the other, Rob Grill was the only one remaining. He kept the Grass Roots on the circuit by hiring musicians for gigs and continued touring until 1977, when he decided to come off the road and retire the group.

The Grass Roots remained dormant for only a few years. Grill, who had worked to establish himself as a soloist in 1979 with an album called *Uprooted* on which Mick Fleetwood and Lindsey Buckingham played, re-formed the band in 1980 under the banner of Rob Grill and the Grass Roots, which cultivated a welcome response on the "oldies" circuit. Although the band underwent recurrent personnel changes, Grill's Grass Roots continued to flourish into the new millennium. (Thirteenth Floor bass player and vocalist Kenny Fukumoto, who would have become a member of the Grass Roots if he had not been drafted into military service, today owns the Flying Fish Grill restaurant in Carmel, California, with his wife, Tina.)

Fans recognized just how much of their lives were intertwined with Grass Roots music. The record charts belie just how popular the Grass Roots really were. Although none of the band's singles hit No. 1, their records had longevity. "Temptation Eyes," for example, attained no higher than the 15th spot on the charts, but it remained on the charts for 18 weeks – more than four months. In the fickle world of pop singles, that represents remarkable staying power. Also contributing to the illusion was the fact that many Grass Roots records "broke" and achieved success in different parts of the country on somewhat differing schedules, weakening their apparent uniform national strength. The band's signature song, "Midnight Confessions," went gold, but notched no higher than

No. 5 on the national charts. "When oldies radio stations feature the best groups that never had a No. 1 record, you can count on two groups being named – Creedence Clearwater Revival and the Grass Roots," Grill told us. "But many of our records certainly sold enough to be No. 1."

Visit **www.the-grassroots.com** for more information.

The Grass Roots in 2003; from left, lead guitarist Chris Merrell, keyboard player Larry Nelson, bass guitarist and lead singer Rob Grill, drummer Joe Dougherty (photo courtesy of Rob Grill)

GRASS ROOTS U.S. HIT SINGLES
ON THE NATIONAL CHARTS

Debut	Peak	Gold	Title	Label
6/66	28		Where Were You When I Needed You	Dunhill
9/66	96		Only When You're Lonely	Dunhill
5/67	8		Let's Live for Today	Dunhill
8/67	23		Things I Should Have Said	Dunhill
10/67	68		Wake Up, Wake Up	Dunhill
8/68	5	Δ	Midnight Confessions	Dunhill
11/68	28		Bella Linda	Dunhill
2/69	49		Lovin' Things	Dunhill
4/69	31		The River Is Wide	Dunhill
7/69	15		I'd Wait a Million Years	Dunhill
11/69	24		Heaven Knows	Dunhill
2/70	44		Walking Through the Country	Dunhill
5/70	35		Baby, Hold On	Dunhill
9/70	61		Come On and Say It	Dunhill
12/70	15		Temptation Eyes	Dunhill
6/71	9		Sooner or Later	Dunhill
10/71	16		Two Divided By Love	Dunhill
2/72	34		Glory Bound	Dunhill
6/72	39		The Runaway	Dunhill
1/73	55		Love Is What You Make It	Dunhill
8/75	71		Mamacita	Haven

Δ symbol: RIAA certified gold record (Recording Industry Association of America)

Billboard's pop singles chart data is courtesy of Joel Whitburn's Record Research Inc. (www.recordresearch.com), Menomonee Falls, Wisconsin.

192

Epilogue: Joel Larson

Drummer and singer

Although one group of Grass Roots replaced another, and 16 musicians performed as members of the band at various times throughout its 10-year hit recording career, the Roots did have one thread of continuity that transcended the years, by virtue of Joel Larson. A member of the 1965–66 assemblage of Grass Roots, Larson subsequently became a part of the Merry-Go-Round with Emitt Rhodes, and recorded and performed with rock organist Lee Michaels, who recorded the mega-hit "Do Ya Know What I Mean?" But he rejoined the Grass Roots in 1972, touring and recording with the band on several of its latter albums, and continuing to play after others had departed. He eventually went on to become the Grass Roots member of longest standing.

Even so, Larson hasn't let rock and roll dictate who he is. As a pre-med student in college, he was torn between a career in medicine and an overriding interest in mechanical engineering, but in his youth he abandoned both pursuits in favor of music. As a musician trying to per-

Joel Larson at a motorcycling event in September 2012 (photo by Madona Larson)

suade nightclub managers to book his band, Larson turned the tables and became a club manager himself for five years until he "timed out" when he'd had enough. And without missing a beat, he went into rental property management in 1995 upon the urging of a friend who told him, "Here's the deal. I'm making $2,000 a month and I haven't paid rent in 10 years." And when he was in his mid-50s, he began a new career in transportation services in the Hollywood TV and film industry.

Larson and his wife, Madona, are managers of

an upscale 90-unit luxury apartment building in the posh western Los Angeles community of Brentwood, around the corner from the site of the Rockingham Drive residence in which O.J. Simpson had lived. The apartment building is a couple of miles from UCLA, which many of Larson's well-to-do tenants attend. Larson, who has managed apartment complexes with as many as 300 units, prefers large buildings to small ones. "In big units like this, you pretty much just do sales. If there's a plumbing problem I just call the plumber and hand him the apartment keys when he comes. In a smaller apartment building, the manager ends up plunging the toilets and doing that kind of shit, and I ain't there! Out of 90 units, we have only one vacancy, so the owners are happy with us and we pretty much just sit here." But even though Larson left the Grass Roots, he hasn't abandoned music. His drum kit is still set up in his living room, and he periodically beats out a cadence for pleasure and when practicing for periodic gigs. What about neighboring tenants who complain they're hearing pounding from somewhere? "Well, I'm the manager," Larson chuckles. "I say, 'I'll check on it and get back to you.' It's good to drive the train, ya know?"

Joel Larson is, by his own description, possessive and overbearing. "I do tend to get stuff I want," he declares. "And if I want something bad enough, you'd better hope you're not the guy who gets in my way." Particularly when he's roaring down the road in his vibrant blue Dodge Viper or on his Aprilia Tuono Factory model motorcycle, equipped with a 150-horsepower power plant capable of speeds to 200 mph. Just as he wanted that Aprilia bike, one of the first possessions he ever earned was another two-wheeled vehicle – a Vespa motor scooter that he bought as a teenager with the earnings from his job at a Danish bakery in South San Francisco.

Joel Scott Larson was born in San Francisco on April 29, 1947. His parents, Pete and Vernesse, had moved there in 1946 from Magna, Utah, where they were both involved in manufacturing bullets during World War II. Pete worked in Kennecott Utah Copper Company's monstrous open-pit mine, driving a train that transported ore to the smelter for use in manufacturing bullets. Vernesse worked at Hercules Powder Co., which made 50-caliber machine-gun rounds. When they moved to San Francisco at the close of the war, Pete went to work for the U.S. Navy at Hunters Point Naval Shipyard. On the side, the family operated a small egg wholesaling business from their home. Every week they'd drive 40 miles north to poultry ranches in Petaluma to buy 40 to 50 cases of eggs, which Joel and his older brother, Gene, helped to grade. "I probably handled more eggs as a teenager than you've ever seen in your life," Joel recalled. "We had candling lights that we used to look through the eggs to check for double yolks, and then we'd weigh them on a scale to sort them by size." The family bought a small truck and delivered chickens and butter as well as eggs to residential customers. Although Joel did help with the family business, neither he nor his parents ever considered that for a career for him. Rather, they encouraged his pursuit of music. "My dad was musical," explained Joel. "He could put a whole harmonica in his mouth and play a song on the guitar and stomp his foot. It was fairly entertaining."

At the age of 9, when Joel and his family lived on 27th Avenue near the Presidio and he attended Alamo Elementary School, he began taking lessons from a piano teacher. He quickly found an emotional connection to music through the *William Tell Overture*. "After we got past the initial scales, we played the overture, which was the theme from *The Lone Ranger* on TV. It was very rhythmic and percussive as well as being melodic. I knew what it sounded like and I was able to learn that by ear. I knew the chords, I knew where the fingers were supposed to go and I wasn't reading it off the page. I was playing it by heart." Joel's parents took his playing seriously. "My mother would whack me with a ruler if I wasn't doing it right," he laughed. After two years of piano lessons, he became interested in the drums. But the school band at Southwood Junior High, in the neighborhood where he and his family lived by then, had enough drummers. "So I got stuck on trombone for a couple of years. I think I got whacked for that, too. I would tend to look over and see where the other guy was putting his slide as opposed to learning the way I was supposed to learn."

He eventually was given a chance to play the drums, and quickly obtained a used high hat and a snare drum that an acquaintance wanted to discard. In 1961 Joel started a garage band called the Intruders Four, the members of which rehearsed in Joel's parents' garage. "Pretty soon we became the band of choice for all the little dances." They were hired for gigs at a South San Francisco Italian-American social club where dances and weddings were commonplace. They frequently played 45-minute sets at a German smorgasbord called the Starlite Hofbrau, where Joel began to develop style and endurance. "Playing five 45-minute sets in a night gives you blisters on your fingers and builds your stamina, allowing you to try different styles to see how the audience reacts. My fingers were actually bloody at the end of the night. I used to tape up, then I tried wearing gloves but I couldn't feel so I went back to playing barehanded, and I developed some serious big calluses on my fingers."

By the time Joel entered South San Francisco High in 1962, he heard about a surf band from the San Mateo area that was attracting attention. He drove down "the line" – the El Camino Real cruise strip – to see the band, called the Bedouins, a name referring to nomads. Its members were Dave Stensen, Denny Ellis, and Bill Fulton, along with drummer Bill Schoppe. "They were playing this good surf music that was tight, and I really liked it," said Joel. "So I started going to more of their gigs and started hanging out with them and playing music with them." He recalled the youthful prank that led to his becoming a member of the Bedouins. "They got a job at Frenchy's, a big nightclub in Oakland, but I called their drummer and told him it was cancelled. Then I took off for the club with my drums. I had heard him play and knew he wasn't as enthused about being in the band as he ought to be. I played that night with the band, and it worked out, because they were kind of enthused about me," said Larson, who soon joined the Bedouins. "We started rehearsing in my parents' garage, and by 1964 we were playing real jobs at dance clubs along the coast. We were all really tight. None of us were hitting on chicks. We were playing our asses off."

Joel, who was entertaining the idea of a career in mechanical engineering, normally got around on his Vespa motor scooter, but he got to rehearsals and gigs using another vehicle – his family's egg delivery van. "That ended up being the band vehicle," Larson chuckles.

When the band's audition for Dunhill Records owner Lou Adler at the Whisky à Go Go in San Francisco led to their transformation into the Grass Roots, the path also led to some independent session work for Larson. Just a few weeks after winning a battle of the bands at a Teenage Fair, he found himself in Studio 3 at Western Recorders in Hollywood playing drums on the session that produced Barry McGuire's stunning war-protest anthem, "Eve of Destruction." Larson began doing other session work as well, notably for the Byrds after the departure of Michael Clarke, and for the Mamas and Papas tracks after meeting the group's principal composer, John Phillips. "I was young and afraid to play fills," said Larson, referring to showy improvisational drumming. They said, 'Great,' because they didn't want some drummer that was splashing all over the place. So I started getting studio dates." Larson's reserved, controlled style modeled that of Hal Blaine, the most prolific and highly sought session drummer of the era. Joel performed on numerous recordings, including Turtles album tracks. And he found himself in some legendary company. "I'd be in a session at Western, and Hal would be across the hall recording with Paul Revere and the Raiders, and Brian Wilson would be down at the end of the hall in Studio 2 with the Beach Boys.

Next door was United Recorders, where a bunch of musicians would arrive, and it would be a Sinatra date," Larson reminisced. He watched from the United Recorders control room as the engineer did some run-throughs with Nelson Riddle's orchestra. "Then Sinatra went in and they recorded him with the background singers live as they were listening to him. There was no electronic syncing in those days. This was recorded on three-track equipment. The tunes weren't that hard, but Sinatra would hit 'em. It would be take two, and it's a keeper."

After the Grass Roots split, Larson, along with Monkees producer Chip Douglas and former Leaves bass player Bill Rinehart, joined the Gene Clark Group, a short-lived band that the former Byrds member founded. Larson's studio jobs subsequently led him to become a member of the Merry-Go-Round, a band that recorded two 1967 single hits "Live" and "You're a Very Lovely Woman." The Merry-Go-Round's leader, guitarist Emitt Rhodes, has a singing voice that is stunningly similar to that of Paul McCartney. Rhodes had first distinguished himself as the drummer for a band called the Palace Guard, which hit the Southern California charts with a song called "Falling Sugar." The Palace Guard had been the house band at the Hullabaloo, a large rock hall on Sunset near Vine in the building that in the 1950s had housed the elegant Moulin Rouge, which a decade previously was known as the Earl Carroll Theater. Rhodes formed the Merry-Go-Round with his school chum, lead guitarist Gary Kato. Because Rhodes had switched to rhythm guitar, he needed to find a drummer, as well as a bass player. Russ Shaw, an A&R guy for A&M Records who had discovered Emitt, thought of Joel Larson and bassist Bill Rinehart. "Russ took us in his car to El Segundo to Emitt's house and we heard him and Gary Kato play some songs in his garage. The four of us ended up being the band," said Larson. The Merry-Go-Round was signed by A&M Records and began rehearsing in an old television studio that the label had acquired. "We rehearsed on the old set of the *Perry Mason* TV show," says Larson. "Emitt would stand up where the judge was and I'd have the drums set up in the witness booth. A&M Records released their debut single, "Live," in late 1966. The Merry-Go-Round remained together until early 1969, when it dissolved amid contract disputes and legal tangles with A&M.

Larson then teamed with organist Lee Michaels, another A&M recording artist, and wound up playing on tracks of Michaels' *Barrel* album and other A&M studio recordings. He performed with Michaels on stage after colossal skin-pounder Bartholomew "Frosty" Smith-Frost and Michaels parted company. "On stage I set up my drums in front of those banks of amplifiers and speakers, and when he hit those bass chords, those speakers moved so much air that my pants legs would ripple," Larson recalled. Michaels subsequently gave up the keyboards for the kitchen, opening up what became a highly successful restaurant called Killer Shrimp in trendy Marina Del Rey. Frosty became a member of Sweathog in the mid-'70s.

Larson regards his return to the Grass Roots in early 1972 – and the subsequent three-year period during which he often was the only "real" Grass Roots member on tour – as validation of his status as the band's founding and most enduring member. In 1980, following the end of his second stint with the Grass Roots, he went into the nightclub business, managing the Whisky à Go Go and the Rainbow Bar & Grill in Los Angeles for Mario Maglieri and his old mentor, Lou Adler. It was a total break from band life. Then Joel became an entrepreneur. He and a partner, John Dunn, began presenting mobile parties that they called "Dance Craze Nights" by renting various nightclubs. They contracted with rock radio station KROQ to supply disc jockeys to spin dance music at the dance parties, and to promote the events on the air. "We didn't have live music. Instead, we let people dance on the stage to all that new wave stuff. So I was being subsidized by the radio station, and they loved it," Larson crowed. "It was all profit because it didn't cost anything to run except for paying the DJs and having my staff. I didn't have to pay a band or crews. I used the dressing room for my private area." The places were crowded with clientele who had money to burn – "all the little chicks from Beverly Hills. It was a really upscale group, with all the kid stars – Chynna Phillips used to come, and so did Pauly Shore when he was just a hang-out rug rat on the strip."

Larson and Dunn expanded their operation by shifting to larger venues – renting vacant warehouses or dormant ballrooms in hotels. "I'd bring everything in – sound, lights, a stage. I had my own security, my own crew, so I was running probably six nights a week and making serious money. It was really classy, drawing people dressed to the hilt, cute girls and people like [Warren] Beatty, [Jack] Nicholson, Heather Locklear, and Rob Lowe." Amid that venture Joel purchased the old La Cienega Lanes bowling alley at Santa Monica and La Cienega boulevards, and financed its conversion into a hot spot he called Flipper's. "You'll recognize it on old *Chips* [television show] episodes," Larson prompted. Larson fashioned Flipper's into an upscale roller rink at which skaters danced to music performed by live bands. Larson himself booked the talent, beginning with Prince to make a splash. "My heart was in music," he said, explaining his interest in working with performers. He found it exhilarating – and risky. "It was exciting to be in a position of trying to break new bands. But as I first began booking bands, I was wondering, 'Am I over my head? Am I going to make enough to pay the band?' But it was great! We built booths out of all the old bowling lanes. It was Quaaludes and alcohol, and people crashing all over the place. It was really popular. We had to make it a private membership club or we would have been swamped."

Larson kept that business running for several years, until it "timed out," as he says. That's when he turned to apartment complex management. "I got into some big buildings, like 300 units. I had management skills, and my wife was good at it, too," said Larson, who said that knowledge he acquired from the music business was applicable. "If you can take 15 rock and roll lunatics on the road and into the hotel

Joel Larson at work on the Warner Bros. studio lot in August 2012 (photo by Wes Adams)

and onto a bus and to the next gig, then managing 300 normal people is just a walk."

Larson's wife, Madona Vernick, whom he married in 1990, is a singer who during her career recorded backgrounds for Marvin Gaye, Bobby Womack, and Jackie Lomax. Madona has a grown daughter from a previous marriage. Larson also was previously married, to a woman named Lisa for five years. That was when he was on the road with the Grass Roots. That marriage produced no children. "I didn't have any when I was married, but who knows what happened on the road? I would expect by now that someone would have come knocking," Larson cracked.

Those days on the road wore heavily on Larson. "I was out there still keeping it alive when Rob wanted to fish and Warren wanted to do something else. I was tired and I didn't want to play 'Midnight Confessions' one more time," Larson acknowledges. "But I guess time makes the heart grow fonder, and now I want to do it again."

Joel still works in the entertainment industry, but behind the scenes. Since 2003, he has been a transportation staffer in the television and motion picture production business. The transportation department supplies cars, trucks, forklifts, carts, and other specialized vehicles for TV and film productions. Some are used to transport equipment, while others are "picture cars" – vehicles that appear in the film productions. Joel, a member of Local 399, the Motion Picture and Theatrical Trade Teamsters Union, works for Warner Bros. Studio Facilities in Burbank. Since his first assignment on the *Time Machine* documentary, he has worked on the set of the motion pictures *Sideways, The Longest Yard, Elizabethtown, Mission: Impossible III, The Bucket List, Iron Man, Get Smart,* and *I Love You, Man,* along with numerous made-for-TV movies. In 2012 he was assigned to work with Chuck Lorre Productions on three television series: *The Big Bang Theory, Mike and Molly,* and *Two and a Half Men.* "It's so much fun. I get cop cars for *Mike and Molly,* trailers for the talent to stay in – pretty much everything to do with transportation," Joel said. "If it has wheels and it's anything the actors drive on camera or sit in on stage, I arrange for that."

Joel got an unexpected reality check in the autumn of 2011, when a routine colonoscopy revealed cancerous growths that were removed in surgery. Shortly after that, he was diagnosed with Barrett's esophagus, a precancerous condition that developed as a result of chronic acid reflux that Joel had experienced since his 20s. He underwent successful surgery for that condition as well. "Both of those surgeries occurred when the shows were on hiatus. That's how I spent my vacation," joked Joel, who recuperated fully by the summer of 2012 and resumed performing weekend gigs.

He can't say for sure that he and Madona will always remain in apartment management. "I don't take it all that seriously. I'm not looking for the long term, because I don't know how old I'm going to be," he says wryly. "But if anyone's had a good time, I have up until now. I actually just live for today."

Just as the song says.

Visit **www.joel-larson.com** to learn more.

Epilogue: Bill Fulton

Guitarist and lead singer

The architects, home theater contractors, and consumers who buy custom-designed loudspeakers from a Portland, Oregon, manufacturer may recognize Willy, one of the store's technicians, as a meticulous perfectionist with a finely discriminating ear for music. Local audio enthusiasts know he's an expert on tube circuitry, and that they can count on him to restore and build tube amplifiers. Like them, Willy values the mellow, "full" sound of tube electronics rather than the clipped, artificial sound of solid-state, computerized stamped-circuit electronics that have dominated the consumer audio market since the late 1960s. Some of his customers also know that Willy's musical tastes encompass jazz, classical, and bluegrass music. But few are aware of his musical background and involvement in the music industry. Mutual friends in the music business brought about Willy's introduction to his wife, Susan, who had been

Bill "Willy" Fulton playing his guitar in March 2011 (photo by David Ramert)

Frank Zappa's executive assistant. Although he has played his guitar only among friends since the late 1980s, he had brought enjoyment to tens of thousands of fans, working with Doctor John, Barry McGuire, the Fifth Dimension, the Pointer Sisters, and for many years as part of Tower of Power. But Willy's first experience in the recording industry came as a member of the Grass Roots in 1966, back when he was known as Bill Fulton.

Retail experience is not new to Willy, who from the time he was old enough to hold a broom worked in Fulton's Stationery Store. That was the shop that his parents, Marjorie and William Fulton Sr., owned on San Bruno Avenue in downtown San Bruno, on the peninsula just south of San Francisco. Born William James Fulton Jr. in San Francisco on January 22, 1947, Willy swept floors, cleaned the bathrooms, stocked merchandise, and waited on customers. "I think my father wanted me to go into business with him, and to eventually take over the retail stationery store," Willy said. He was content with that vision through the late '50s and into the early '60s. Through his parents' encouragement, he had developed an interest in singing at family gatherings in which his mother played the piano and his sister, Joan, accompanied him, yet he had not considered music as a career path. "Singing came naturally to me and it was something I enjoyed doing," he explained. He found the private piano lessons that he began at age 11 uninteresting, however, because the training emphasized classical compositions. "I wasn't interested in classical music, and I really wanted to play rock and roll like I heard on the radio, but my teacher was a real rigid classical teacher and she didn't want to hear about it at all. It was all I could do to get her to let me play some sort of boogie-woogie piece once in a blue moon. But in hindsight I wish I had paid more attention because I studied a lot of theory but I forgot most of it, and didn't put as much effort into it as I could have," acknowledged Willy, who quit taking piano lessons within two years.

Although the lessons ended, Willy's interest in music did not, and he continued singing for his own enjoyment. As a 15-year-old sophomore in the spring of 1962 at Mills High School in Millbrae, he was singing along to the radio when a friend of his who played drums in a local surf-rock band called the Stringrays overheard him. Impressed by Willy's singing voice, the friend invited him to substitute for the band's regular singer, who was going on vacation with his family. "The band members were all a little older than me," Fulton recalled. "Their lead singer was Mario Torres, a real slick Latino guy who was 17 or 18. I was a young kid who had never been on stage before. I rehearsed with the band and did a couple of gigs, teen dances at the YMCA. I think the first song I did was

'Donna' by Ritchie Valens. I replaced Mario just until he got back from vacation, and then the job was over. But that was my first experience performing rock music." Fulton had not yet started playing guitar, but his new friendship with the Stingrays' lead guitarist, Larry Green, led him to learn the instrument. "When I started really getting into music the second time around, those piano lessons proved pretty helpful and started to come back to me in certain areas. So I hadn't completely forgotten all of it, after all," Fulton acknowledged.

During his junior and senior years, when he went by the name Bill, he played with several bands, but still didn't take music seriously. After graduating from high school in June 1964, he enrolled in the College of San Mateo with a commercial art career in mind. But few art courses were included among the first-year requirements for commercial art majors. "I was taking English, math, history – all the same crap I had taken in high school. I had really wanted to go to art school, but my parents didn't want to swing the money. To me it seemed that community college was like high school with ash trays," Fulton laughed. "So I was mostly cutting school and sitting around practicing guitar." That's when he heard from his musician friend Denny Ellis, who had seen Bill perform on stage numerous times. Denny, a guitarist, had begun talking about forming a band with some friends from other high schools, including bass player Dave Stensen, whom Fulton had known for some time. Fulton was interested. Along with drummer Bill Schoppe – who, like Dave, attended Capuchino High School in San Bruno – they formed the band that came to be known as the Bedouins. "Bill Schoppe had played drums for a long time, and was a really good technician. He had taken lessons for years, had played in marching bands. But he was real rigid and kind of a straight-laced guy, and his parents had placed a lot of restrictions on him. So we had problems getting him to do gigs and we kept running into a lot of walls playing with him," Fulton said. "In the meantime, we had met Joel Larson. We really liked his playing because although he was totally self-taught, he was real loose, and just a natural-feel player. He liked us and wanted to be in the band, so eventually he became our drummer."

The Bedouins were working regularly – which, for a high school band, meant dances on Friday and Saturday nights. "We were all still in school and living at home, and we were making pretty good bread working Friday and Saturday nights," Fulton recalled. "I was still working at my dad's store, and we used to practice there. It became quite a scene on Sunday mornings. The store was closed, and we used to set up right in front of the cashier counter because it was the biggest area of floor space.

Because the storefront was all glass, people could stand in front of the store and watch us play. We would get quite a gathering there on Sunday mornings. It was commercially zoned and everything was closed down, so it was a good place to rehearse, and it was free."

The journey from those storefront rehearsals to the Hollywood recording studio laying down vocal tracks for the Grass Roots is a dizzying blur for Fulton. Although he was disillusioned along with his other band mates about their paucity of participation in the recording process at Dunhill, he grew to understand the reason for the use of studio musicians in their place. "They were much better players than we were, and there was no reason not to use them," he now shrugs. Although the Bedouins had been formed as a cover band that played versions of the surf and "British invasion" hits of the day, and the Grass Roots were in the "folk-rock" vein, Fulton took intense interest in the series of Motown Records acts that were booked into The Trip, the Sunset Boulevard nightclub at which the Grass Roots were the house band. There the Grass Roots opened for numerous high-profile performers, including Smokey Robinson, the Four Tops, Marvin Gaye, Martha and the Vandellas, and the Temptations. "They were huge radio stars, but that was pretty much the first time that they had played on the West Coast. For me it was a dream come true because all these people were huge heroes of mine, and to get to sit there night after night in the front row and to watch them play live was amazing for me," said Fulton, who had long idolized the talents of Jimmy Reed, Freddy King, and other legendary blues guitarists, and had even infused his Grass Roots stage performances with some blues-influenced riffs. "At The Trip, I got to take some guitar lessons from Smokey Robinson's guitar player, who was a great player and a really nice guy. He must have been 45 or 50 years old at the time. I didn't know my ass from my elbow and he was kind enough to say, 'Sure.' I had led a pretty sheltered life in the Bay Area and hadn't had much of a chance to try new experiences, so it was a big thrill for me." That interaction also was instrumental in shaping the remainder of Fulton's musical career.

His decision to walk away from Dunhill in late 1966 and return to the Bay Area with Denny Ellis and Dave Stensen led to hard times, and their existence as the Unquenchable Thirst was short-lived. When that group broke up, he found himself scratching to make a living. He worked odd jobs and managed to find a gig here and there with an unorganized group of musicians in Marin County, north of the Golden Gate Bridge. To make matters worse, the military draft was breathing down his 19-year-old neck. He'd already taken and passed his pre-induction physical exam, and then received his draft notice to report for duty. In

throughout its stronghold areas – up and down the Pacific Coast and in the nation's urban areas, including Detroit, New York, Chicago, and Philadelphia. The band also toured Europe. Fulton and his wife had a son, Josh, but life on the road with Tower was hard, and it led to the breakup of their marriage in the early '80s. While on the road after that, he met a woman named Susan Adkins in Los Angeles through mutual friends. Susan, who then had just completed studies for her master of science degree in industrial psychology, had worked as executive assistant to

Willy Fulton in a 1985 Tower of Power performance (photo courtesy of Willy Fulton)

Frank Zappa, as well as for Sony's professional audio division. When Willy married Susan in 1986 after 15 years on the road, he reassessed his life.

"I was 40 years old. Other than becoming a millionaire, which was never my goal to start out with, I had done pretty much everything I had ever wanted to do in music, and then some. I had toured the world. I had met most of my idols and had a chance to play with them, made hit records, had a chance to be on TV. I had a pretty great run for a moderate amount of talent," Fulton said. "With the Tower we had to constantly be on the road to keep the band alive, and it kept getting tougher and tougher. I was lucky enough to eke out a living at it, to be able to survive and do what I love doing, which was all that I could ask for. But the fun factor got less and less, and the part about being a whole lot of hassle for very little reward got to be too much. I began to wonder if I really wanted to be slugging it out at a bar every night, five nights a week in the middle of nowhere. Do I want to wake up and look at myself at 60 years old and find this is what I'm going to do?" Willy Fulton's answer was "no."

While with Tower of Power, Fulton had done some product endorsements for Dean Markley Strings Inc., a manufacturer of guitar, banjo, and mandolin strings based in Santa Clara, California, near San Jose. When Dean Markley, the company's president, decided to begin manufacturing guitar amplifiers, he asked Willy to offer a musician's point of view about amplifier controls, sound quality, and other aspects of design. After impressing Markley with a design sketch, Willy was hired as a part-time design consultant for the project, on which he worked during the sporadic interludes between gigs. "I was lucky enough to work with Brent Butler, the designer, at the bench and essentially, I got a free education over the next couple of years in electronic products and circuit design."

By 1987, when Fulton decided to retire as a musician, Markley's amplifier manufacturing plans changed. Fulton thought about how to use the electronics knowledge he had gained. When a retail stereo equipment shop called Sound Goods in Mountain View had a sales opening, he applied and was hired. He remained there until the late 1980s, when Susan wanted to move to Los Angeles, where she was raised. Willy joined the sales staff of an audio shop in L.A., but had a tough time making ends meet in the face of a souring economy. "We were getting nowhere fast, renting and dumping money down the drain. We couldn't afford to buy a home." They decided to scout out Portland, Oregon, which they'd heard was affordable and attractive. They both liked Portland, and found a house they could afford. They packed up and moved there. Susan obtained an Oregon real estate sales license, and Willy quickly found work selling audio equipment in the electronics department at Smith's

Home Furnishings. After a short time there he joined the staff of Hawthorne Audio Exchange, a used audio equipment shop of which he soon became manager. That store eventually closed but its owner consolidated it into another nearby store, Fred's Sound of Music, where Fulton concentrated on work as a repair technician. "But I had spent enough time in retail, and wanted to move on," he explained. Fulton mentioned that to some friends of his who were working at Triad Speakers, a Portland custom-design manufacturer of speaker systems.

"A short time later David Bailey, who worked with me at the Audio Exchange, called and said a slot may be opening up at Triad, and said I should apply for it. I interviewed and got the job," said Fulton, who since 2004 has been a service technician at Triad and now goes by the name Willy. "It's a great place to work for me, because I get to be around music and work on audio gear all day. Quite a few other musicians work there as well, and after being hounded by a couple of them to start playing again, I did. So now we have a loose little trio to play at company picnics and such – just me on guitar and vocals, our international sales manager Mike Budd on bass, and sales rep Bill Rourke on drums. They are both very good players and make me work to keep up. So I'm back playing my Telecaster for fun, and really enjoying it," Fulton told us in July 2012.

Susan, meanwhile, joined the state of Oregon's Employment Department as a business and employment specialist. "She helped people find jobs, and she liked it a lot. She's a real public-service type of person," Willy says admiringly of Susan, who has retired. Willy and Susan live with their dogs and cats in northeast Portland. There, Willy also runs his own business on the side, designing, building, and restoring vacuum tube amplifiers for diehard enthusiasts. Fulton calls the business Valve Works. "Valve is the British word for tubes," he explained. "Working on vintage amplifiers is a good creative outlet for me and keeps my brain from freezing over." Some old tubes are difficult to find, but many tube numbers are still manufactured today in China, Russia, the Czech Republic, and other Eastern European nations. "The quality isn't like it used to be in the heyday of vacuum tubes, and they can be hellaciously expensive because they're manufactured in such small quantities." But for audio connoisseurs who crave the sound that only tube amplifiers can reproduce, Fulton is there to serve them. Not as Bill Fulton, the musician and pop star, but as Willy Fulton, the self-described "tube amp wizard" and part-time "Tele-twanger." He's perfectly content to have it that way.

Epilogue: Dave Stensen

Bassist and singer

Dave Stensen left the Grass Roots in late 1966, but he remains very involved with grass roots today. Not the band, but real grass roots. Since 1998, Dave has been a turf grass technician for the city of Portland, Oregon. He works for the city's turf grass maintenance department, and has responsibility for a softball complex as well as eight parks. Before that he spent more than a decade in superintendent positions at private and public golf courses. Pretty appropriate for a guy who was at the very roots of the band that would become the first group of Grass Roots.

Like many of the kids among his circle of friends at Capuchino High School in San Bruno, Dave played guitar. Back in junior high, several neighborhood kids including Dave had taken lessons from a local music teacher who taught them to play the lap steel guitar, so called because the musician must be seated to play it. Also known as the Hawaiian guitar, the twangy, florid-sounding instrument was popular among "western swing" country music performers of the 1940s and 1950s. "An enormous amount of kids took lessons from this instructor. He must have done very well," said Stensen. "We used to give recitals at one of the local

Dave Stensen in his studio in February 2006 (photo by Sarah La Du, courtesy of Dave Stensen)

middle schools, and the stage was filled with kids, all playing lap steels. It was probably one of the most horrible things you'd want to go hear," he laughs. When Dave was in seventh grade, his parents had bought him his own Fender lap steel and an amplifier, on which he'd pick out tunes by ear – Santo and Johnny's "Sleepwalk," Duane Eddy's "Because They're Young," the Ramrods' "(Ghost) Riders in the Sky," and other guitar instrumentals. He fooled around with the lap steel for a few years, and by his sophomore year in high school was able to switch to regular guitar to join some friends in pickup bands.

Dave credits his brother, Gary – eight years his senior – for first stirring his interest in music. Not only is Dave's musical talent homegrown; he is as well. David Alan Stensen was delivered on February 25, 1947, at his parents' home in San Bruno by his father, Paul, an accountant. "San Bruno didn't have a hospital and my mom couldn't make it to a distant hospital in time, so my dad delivered me right there at the house," he grinned. For Dave's 10th birthday, Gary bought him a Little Richard album and a Chuck Berry album. Gary also introduced Dave to the music of the Modern Jazz Quartet, saxophonist Gerry Mulligan, trumpeter Shorty Rogers, and other jazz artists.

Dave had played only in casual groups when an opening for a bass player developed in an established band of high-school juniors. He quickly learned to play bass and joined that group. Just after Dave began his junior year in the fall of 1963, he was asked to sit in for a weekend with Roy and the Starliners, a band composed of Capuchino High seniors. The band's manager was impressed by Dave's performance, and asked if he'd be interested in starting a band of his own, for the manager to handle. He first invited drummer Bill Schoppe, a classmate of his. One of the members of Roy and the Starliners had been giving rhythm guitar lessons at a local music store to a Burlingame High School kid named Denny Ellis and suggested him as a potential band member. And Dave thought of Mills High School student Bill Fulton, a singer-guitarist he knew. Together, Dave, Denny, and the two Bills formed the Bedouins, initially as a surf band that quickly filled its calendar with bookings. As the band members became more seasoned, they gravitated to the music of the "British invasion" bands, the Dylan-influenced Byrds, and the gritty blues of James Brown. Their friends included the members of the Beau Brummels, who were on the verge of achieving recording success. Dave credits drummer Joel Larson, who replaced Bedouins original drummer Bill Schoppe, for providing the "spark" that helped drive the band. "Joel is a real promoter. Denny, Bill, and I would stay up and try to write songs, and we just concentrated on learning what we could. But

Joel was a real showman type of guy, and we needed that. He gave us a spark of energy when we needed it," said Stensen. He credits his mother, Thelma, for helping make the Bedouins look sharp. "Mom was pretty cool. She used to make outfits for us when we were in the Bedouins," Dave said. "I used to make speaker cabinets because I couldn't afford Fender speakers. Mom helped me make fabric grilles for the speaker cabinets, and she made vests for us when we wanted to look more Stones-like."

After he graduated from high school as an industrial arts major in June 1965, Dave enrolled at the College of San Mateo, where he intended to learn the skills necessary to become a machinist. "My backup plan was to be a hairdresser," acknowledged Stensen. "My counselor at college looked at my grades and said, 'Do you really want to be here, or are you here just to get out of Vietnam?' I wasn't an outstanding student in high school because all I really wanted to do was to play guitar. I would come home, do my homework as fast as I could, and then I just played guitar and bass and listened to music until it was time to go to bed. The weekends were consumed with practicing and playing gigs." Dave had a part-time job cleaning, sweeping floors, and working in the stockroom at a furniture store, but even that had a music connection; the store's manager was a saxophone player. He and his musician friends would go to see Miles Davis, John Coltrane, and Tony Williams at the jazz clubs on Broadway in San Francisco. Virtually everything Dave did bore some relationship to music.

Dave's ties to Bay Area musicians exerted a powerfully magnetic force on him – to his detriment, he admits, when he was in the Grass Roots and he and his fellow performers rebelliously relocated the band there from Los Angeles, where Dunhill Records was based. While playing at The Trip in L.A., the Grass Roots had met the members of the Grateful Dead, Quicksilver Messenger Service, Big Brother and the Holding Company, and Jefferson Airplane, who were surprised to learn that the Grass Roots were from the Bay Area and not from L.A. "We wanted to come up to San Francisco and be a part of that scene, because it was so much more comfortable for us," Stensen explained. "But that really was not a good move for us. We played a couple of times up there with Joel, but he didn't want to move back home. He had become a Southern California guy. And we wanted to live where our friends lived." The Bay Area music scene did not fit the image that Dunhill's Lou Adler had created for the Grass Roots, nor did it fit the musical style in which Steve Barri and P.F. Sloan were writing material. "We told the label we wanted to record in San Francisco rather than in L.A.," Stensen said. The label adamantly opposed that idea.

Tensions erupted among Stensen, Denny Ellis, and Bill Fulton as they surrendered the Grass Roots name and struggled to eke out an existence as the Unquenchable Thirst. That band evaporated as Stensen and Ellis began working with another Bay Area band called the Serpent Power, led by guitarist David Meltzer – "kind of a beat generation poet," as Stensen recalled him. Stensen and Ellis recorded an album with the band, which Vanguard Records released in 1967. "That group didn't make enough money to sustain life. I ended up moving back down to the peninsula and marrying my high school sweetheart and starting a family," Stensen said. His high-school sweetheart was Melania Krumm. "Everybody calls her Melanie," Dave said. Together, they had a daughter, Amber, who was born in 1968. Dave decided to leave music behind. "I stopped playing because we got married, we had a daughter on the way, and it was time to start taking care of business," he said. He initially took a job with a food catering service, working on the tarmac at San Francisco International Airport delivering refreshments aboard passenger aircraft. While doing that he took a civil service exam and was hired as a mail carrier in Burlingame. "It was really a boring job, and I was young and still wanted to be a musician. Our marriage was kind of tipsy and I quit the Postal Service and started playing music again around 1969 with a group called the Backyard Mamas. We thought we could actually make it in the club scene." The brand of rhythm and blues music of that band – which despite its name consisted only of guys – didn't do well in the club scene after all.

Because of increasing crime in the Bay Area, including the once-mellow Haight-Ashbury district, Melania and Dave decided to investigate Oregon, where several of their mutual high school friends had moved. They, too, moved there – but not together. The couple divorced. Melania settled in Eugene, while Dave moved to Parkdale, near Hood River, in the Columbia Gorge area. There he worked for a time as a bus driver in the White Salmon School District, and then became an irrigation systems installer for a Hood River nursery. "I was designing and installing small irrigation systems for homeowners, and also built solid-set orchard irrigation systems," he said. While living in the Hood River area he formed a four-piece band called Foothill Diesel with John Johnson, an old friend from the Bay Area. Because Johnson played bass, Stensen played guitar. They performed in the Columbia Gorge area as well as around Portland. "We were able to make a pretty good living at it," said Stensen. While performing with Foothill Diesel, he met a woman named Penny Aronson, whom he subsequently married in 1973 and who gave birth later that year to a daughter, Autumn. Four years later they celebrated the birth of another daughter, Thea. Dave and Penny moved west to a town called Boring, in a raspberry- and apple-growing area at the eastern outskirts of Portland. There Dave held a number of jobs, including working as an equipment foreman for J. Frank Schmidt & Son. "That's one of the largest wholesale shade tree nurseries in the nation," Stensen notes. "During the summer I worked with crews doing pruning procedures and irrigation." But that was only his day job. He continued performing music, with a succession of groups – the Heavy Metal Thunder Band, the Street Corner Band, West Bound, Nasty Habits, and Streamliner – the members of which included guitarist Doug Fraser, who subsequently became a member of Quarterflash.

Dave's dual life – equipment foreman by day, musician by night – began to erode his marriage, and he and Penny separated briefly. But they got back together in 1983, just before their daughter Thea entered first grade, which was a sobering event in his life. Dave quit music once again, and this time he decided to carve out a career in the golf industry. He was hired as an assistant at a large resort. After three years in that position, he was promoted to golf superintendent, remaining in that position for eight years. Then in 1994 he moved to a similar opening at a public golf course. But he wasn't really done with music. While working at the golf courses, he continued performing music on the side in "week-end bands," playing gigs at clubs, parties, and wedding receptions. "I was actually making pretty good money doing that as a hobby, and I became content with that. I wasn't interested in cutting any records. I just wanted to play and enjoy myself," he explained.

Music was a safety valve through which Dave released the pressures associated with the responsibilities of his golf course job. "If things went haywire in the middle of the night, I got a phone call. If somebody doesn't come to work, I had to do their job. If at the end of the day there's more work than you can finish, you stay. I decided I really was more comfortable being a hippie, so my hair started getting longer, reaching the point where it was when I was playing music in the '70s – in the middle of my back. And I wanted to work at a less hectic job, so I decided to start looking around. The City of Portland had some job openings, so in 1998 I applied for and got a job as a turf grass technician for the Portland Bureau of Parks and Recreation, and that's what I do now. It's much more relaxing than being a golf course superintendent." The large commercial rotary mower he drives, with an enclosed cab, is capable of cutting a swath 16 feet wide. During the winter months, he services his department's landscaping equipment.

In the late 1990s, Dave established his own R&B-flavored group, called the Gunga-Dave Band. Stensen was dubbed "Gunga Dave" by his

Dave with bass in 2010 (photo by
Sara Stensen)

friend Lonesome Rags, a guitar player who has a group called Riff-Raff. "About 10 years ago I was telling Rags about my working at the golf course, then packing up equipment and driving to the coast to play a gig, and then driving back home and having to go to work the next morning, and then playing another gig that night. Rags said to me, 'you're a better man than I, Gunga Dave." It was a reference to a line from "Gunga Din," the poem by Rudyard Kipling. "I thought that was pretty funny, and he kept calling me Gunga. So when I started a band with Rags and Jim "Spanky" Stein, we decided to call it the Gunga Dave Band."

Following his divorce from Penny, Dave met and fell in love with Sara Louie, whom he married on April 1, 2000. Like Dave, Sara has three grown children from a previous marriage. In recent years, Dave developed a preference for working out songs alone in "Gunga's Garage" – his home recording studio. So when his old friends Doug Fraser and Pat O'Donnell from the Heavy Metal Thunder Band called in 2011 to say they were forming a band, Stensen was on board. Drummer Steve Shroy from the Foothill Diesel band joined them in the band, which they named Geezer. "Don't let the name fool you," Stensen says. "We're kickin' ass, playing rock." They perform at gigs from time to time – just for the fun of it. Dave Stensen may be a turf grass technician, but the roots of his soul remain embedded in music.

The passage of time has tempered Dave's perspective of his era in the Grass Roots. "Everybody kind of got what they wanted out of it in the long run. Joel got to be in the L.A. scene, Willy got to do his R&B thing with Tower [of Power], and Denny and I got to do our artsy thing with Serpent Power. I have no regrets. Anyhow, regrets and $2.50 will get you a cheap latte," Dave wryly observed. "The musicians I've played with here – some for 20 years, some for almost 40 years – are great buddies. I've had a wonderful life, and I've enjoyed everything that I've done."

Visit **www.gungadave.xbuild.com/** to learn more about Dave.

Epilogue: Denny Ellis
Rhythm guitarist and singer

The summer following graduation from high school is a period of transition for most young people. Many of them spend those three months preparing for entry into college and moving into a dormitory, or traveling abroad, or beginning their search for a full-time job. But imagine, if you can, the head-spinning changes that a 17-year-old boy would have experienced during a summer transformation that took him from the stage of his high school graduation ceremony to the stage of a ballyhooed nightclub as a member of a rock band with a hit record. Imagine him being swept from his parents' home in the safe suburbs of the San Francisco Bay Area to a crash pad just off the raucous, rebellious Sunset Strip, 370 miles away in West Hollywood. That was how Denny Ellis spent the summer of '65.

Denny Ellis with a Guild Starfire V guitar at his mother's house in Burlingame, California, in the spring of 1966, a few months before the Bedouins became the Grass Roots (photo by Irene Ellis)

During the ensuing three years, his pursuit of a musical career took him on a wild ride with emotional swings from exuberance to dejection. Denny ultimately traded Hollywood glitter for small-town sawdust, and while he prevented rock and roll from defining him, music remains an enjoyable part of his life. In the years since he stepped off the stage, he developed expertise in skiing and mountaineering equipment, became a skilled cabinet maker, launched a successful business in Eugene, Oregon, and raised a family – all of which have been far more fulfilling for him than his time as a rock musician. "The challenges of being self-employed and raising children proved to be a harder road than being a musician was, but I've found it more exciting because of all the things my family and I have done during the years. I was a baseball coach. I was a scout leader. My kids were all very active. My daughter, Ivy, was a cheerleader, a dancer, and participated in theater, and my son, Casey, sang in a community choir, played football and baseball, and was in scouting, so life has been pretty full," Denny said.

Denny Ellis in September 2010 (photo by Debra Hendsch)

Even when he was in high school, Denny didn't believe that he would remain a musician all of his life, but he did think he would remain involved in music. He had taken some business courses, imagining he might one day retire as a professional musician and then open a music store. Although it didn't work out that way, he has no regrets about the path he took. "Life is full of crossroads. You never know what would have happened if you had taken a different road, made a different turn," Denny observed in July 2012. "I might have ended up attending and graduating from college, I might have ended up being drafted and going to Vietnam. I could have ended up living in the Bay Area, rather than here in Eugene. In retrospect with regard to music, I think the Bedouins might have been better off waiting a couple of years, as we gained a little maturity and more skills as musicians. Then if we still wanted to be a band and perform, we could have called our own shots, or at least been the band we wanted to be, assuming that we got the opportunity. But San Francisco was a hotbed back then, and record companies were climbing over each other to find bands to sign. When we signed our deal with

Dunhill, I don't think we had a real good picture of what it was going to be like. We just went for it. We weren't saying 'no.'"

Dennis Ray Ellis, born September 7, 1947, came along nearly 20 years after the birth of his brother, Jack. Denny grew up in Burlingame, a suburban community on the peninsula south of San Francisco. He was a toddler when Jack joined the U.S. Air Force and left behind his collection of 78 rpm records. "When I was old enough to work the hi-fi, I started listening to his big band and jazz records," said Denny, whose preparation for performing began at 3½ years of age, when his mother, Irene, enrolled him in tap dancing lessons. He continued with lessons in tap and other styles of dance until he was a teenager, and additionally took up piano lessons, which he continued into high school. "My aunt and uncle, who were living in Berkeley at the time, gave me my first album of Dave Brubeck playing piano solos. And my piano teacher was a professional who played in a band at Bimbo's 365 Club in San Francisco," Denny recalled. When Denny began going to high school dances and noticed the bands performing there, he decided that he wanted to be a musician in a rock band. So he quit dance and piano lessons, and persuaded his parents to buy him a guitar and amplifier and enroll him in lessons with a private teacher.

When he was 16, he had become sufficiently proficient and his guitar teacher introduced him to Dave Stensen and Bill Fulton, who were forming a band – which, with Denny's addition as rhythm guitarist, became the Bedouins. "We wore madras shirts and sandals," Denny recalls. Neither of Denny's parents nor his brother, Jack, were musical. His father, Chester, was an electrical engineer and plant manager for a big electronics firm. "My parents didn't discourage my interest in music, but my father did not encourage it in any way that I can think of. He would have been happier if I had been involved with sports in high school and heading to college to be an engineer," Denny said. But during Denny's senior year in high school, his father suffered a heart attack and died at the age of 59. As Denny graduated from high school in June 1965, he enrolled for the fall 1965 semester at the College of San Mateo, hoping to major in sociology or psychology. But because classes in those subjects were in high demand, he had been placed instead in a business program.

The summer of '65 was a lightning streak of activity as the Bedouins became the Grass Roots, traveled to Los Angeles to record, then moved their belongings there on September 7, Denny's 18th birthday – the same day on which he and Dave Stensen withdrew from the College of San Mateo. "We started out living with a relative of Billy Fulton's in Inglewood. We all lived in a little travel trailer in the backyard for about a month or so before getting an apartment," he chuckled. "Yes, I was naive when it all got started, particularly about how the music business worked. But much of that changed in a hurry. Six weeks after we landed in L.A., I'd find myself at a bohemian artist's basement in Venice Beach with Dave and Bill listening to Ravi Shankar and John Coltrane's *Africa/Brass* album, and reading from D.T. Suzuki's *Studies in Zen* while beautiful geometrical forms floated before my eyes," Ellis said. "Suddenly, after taking LSD, everything was new and there was so much to experience in life. Away from home for the first time and with no restraints, we experienced all we could – maybe not focusing on our music as much as we should have, but having a great time."

After struggling to financially survive when the band members returned to San Francisco and became the Unquenchable Thirst, Ellis tagged along when Dave Stensen quit that band and moved into a flat in San Francisco. "Within just a few months, we went from living the high life in L.A. and being on the *Ed Sullivan Show* to being practically homeless in San Francisco," admits Ellis. He retreated to his family's home. "I think I was probably in shock from the whole experience. I had thought about being a professional entertainer for a long time. To have gone up so fast and come right back down to Earth was hard on my ego. I was pretty depressed when the whole thing was over, and it took me a lot of years to understand what had happened and why."

Even though the next band that Ellis and Stensen joined, the Serpent Power, didn't bring them financial success, they found the experience artistically and personally rewarding. They spent the first six months rehearsing songs written by the band's leader, David Meltzer. "We played only a couple of little gigs live, but I got to be much more creative than I had ever been with the Grass Roots, and really had a lot of fun. The music was unique stuff that was folk-based, but kind of offbeat rock and roll," Ellis said. "I can't compare it to another band. David Meltzer had quite a sense of humor, so a lot of the songs were parodies of rock and roll music. We would meet at his flat overlooking San Francisco Bay, and we would have these very nice vegetarian dinners with him and his wife, Tina, drink a little wine, and sit around the living room playing acoustically. And we did this night after night. Eventually we found a place where we could practice electrified. We learned enough material to do an album for Vanguard, and that was it," said Ellis, explaining that the album was under-promoted and did not sell adequately. "But being in that band really got my feet back on the ground again after the Grass Roots experience. David and Tina had three little children, a very beautiful, loving marriage, he worked at a bookstore, and they performed together as musicians. I saw a lifestyle there and I said, 'I can do this.' It really appealed to me. I kind of needed that after the craziness of being in the Grass Roots."

Denny came to the realization that he was consumed by music to his detriment, and for all the wrong reasons. "I recognized that I had become a musician as a means of getting attention and being famous," Denny said. "Being in performance was just something that I grew up with. I had been dancing and playing piano recitals when I was a kid. I liked the attention I got when I was on stage in front of people, but at a certain point that became less important to me as I recognized other more significant aspects of life."

Denny, who was paid union scale for the Serpent Power recording session, knew he needed to develop a more reliable means of income. Without a car, his options were limited, but he managed to land a job as a postal clerk during the summer of 1967 at the airmail facility at San Francisco International Airport. He sorted letters, and routed the bags that were loaded onto planes. His duties included handling military mail destined for Saigon, Bangkok, Luzon, and other areas where American forces were stationed during the Vietnam conflict. "I worked the graveyard shift with an assortment of characters – hippies, students, kids from the projects. It was a very diverse, very interesting crew," Denny said. Although he found the work interesting, he began to make new plans. "I had a pretty singular focus while I was in the Grass Roots. We lived music 24 hours a day. I realized there was a lot to learn in the world and a lot of things to see and experience beyond music. I thought about going to school and learning other things. Having a day job and having a little money allowed me to pursue a lot of other things."

He became interested in moving to Oregon. "A lot of people were evacuating the city at that time. There was a real back-to-the-country movement that a lot of people were involved in. It was like a virus. Before long many of us were thinking of it. We were all infected. David Stensen's first wife, Melania, said we should all move to Oregon," Ellis said. He realized that transfer as a postal employee to a preferred rural post office would require him to accumulate 20 years of seniority, and he was unwilling to wait that long. "And frankly, the Post Office job was kind of boring and not very challenging," Ellis added. "Friends advised me that I'd be better off learning a skill or craft where I could be a little more creative." So he quit the Post Office and answered an ad in the classifieds placed by a Burlingame ski equipment shop seeking someone to repair skis. "I had never skied before, but I went in and talked to a fellow who also had no ski experience. I was looking for something that I could

take to a rural area, like a ski resort. I got the job and trained as a certified ski technician, and I worked there for three and a half years repair-
ing and installing ski bindings and selling ski equipment during the
winter and backpacking and mountaineering gear during the summer."
When Denny was working at the ski gear shop, he considered resuming
the piano lessons he had discontinued when he was in high school. His
piano teacher declined to accept him as a student again, though. "The
piano teacher had been in the Marines during World War II, and he associated my long hair with the anti-Vietnam War movement – about which
he was correct," Denny said. "Our politics didn't mesh."

Denny made his first journey to Oregon while working for the ski
shop. In *Travels With Charley* fashion, he drove north in his old Chevy
panel truck, accompanied by his dog. "I discovered on that trip that the
Cascades were not nearly as developed as the Sierras were, and the ski
areas in Oregon were not surrounded by condominiums and retail businesses like they were in the Lake Tahoe area," Ellis said.

After he returned to work in the Bay Area, he made another important discovery one day in 1970. The little sister of a couple of old friends
of his had grown up. "I had actually met her a few years before, when
she was just the high school kid who babysat. She was really only about
three years younger than me, but at the time it seemed like a lot." The
age difference meant far less than it had back in 1963. "We ended up on
a double date by accident one night, and we played miniature golf. I was
23 and she was 20, and she was looking pretty good. Things continued
from there." Her name was Jennifer Allbaugh; before long she would
become Jennifer Ellis.

Although Denny wasn't making enough money at the ski shop to
finance a move to Oregon, opportunity presented itself one day in the
form of a young man who desperately wanted a job at the ski shop where
Denny worked. "He had an uncle who was a building contractor, and
we arranged a little trade. He got his uncle to get me into the carpenters'
union, and he got a job sweeping the floors at the sporting goods store.
So I became a union carpenter and went through an apprenticeship in
California prior to moving to Oregon," Denny grinned. Through the carpenters' union, he hooked up with a custom homebuilder who quickly
became his primary source of work. In addition to building homes in
Atherton and Menlo Park, the builder also had a contract for construction at Marine World-Africa U.S.A., the wild-animal amusement park
located at that time in Redwood City, so Denny worked on projects there.

By 1973 Denny and Jennifer married, bought a trailer, and moved
into a mobile home park in Redwood City in which their neighbors

ranged from Stanford University students to carnival workers. The apprenticeship gave Denny the credentials he needed. "I knew that the job market in Oregon was kind of tight, and that newcomers weren't necessarily going to be welcomed with open arms. But because I was a journeyman carpenter, the union in Oregon couldn't refuse me." Denny and Jennifer sold their fully paid-off trailer and used the proceeds to move to Eugene in 1975, when she was seven months pregnant with their first child, daughter Ivy. They selected Eugene because two longtime friends of Denny's were living there. Jennifer looked up Linda Dye, a high school classmate of hers who also lived in Eugene with her husband, Paul, a cabinetmaker. "Paul and I became close friends, and for many years attended every Grateful Dead concert tour that came through the state. We also became winemakers, and spent many hours gathering, fermenting, and enjoying our creations," Denny said.

In Eugene Denny was able to get work from numerous union contractors, for whom he worked primarily on framing and foundations for schools, office buildings, restaurants, and other commercial and public works construction projects. In 1978 he and Jennifer celebrated the birth of a son, Casey. When work slowed down, Denny would hang around Paul's cabinetry shop and observe him working. Denny suddenly had a lot more time on his hands to loiter at Paul's shop when a recession hit the Pacific Northwest in the 1980s, bringing union carpentry work nearly to a halt. "That was about the time Paul opened his first cabinet shop, and I helped him do some installations and developed cabinetmaking skills," said Denny. Cabinetry work was in sufficient demand for Denny to open his own shop in 1984. He subsequently became involved in a cooperative shop in downtown Eugene, with which he spent nearly four years doing primarily residential cabinetry. Then in 1990, Denny and Paul hatched the idea of starting what amounted to their own cooperative – operating their own independent cabinet shops under the same roof. There Denny Ellis Woodworking and Design opened for business. Denny and Paul shared some equipment, and often collaborated on jobs.

In 1999, in partnership with artisan furniture maker John Fisher, they established a new business partnership, Skyline Fine Cabinets and Furniture. The company crafts cabinetry primarily for residential building projects, for clients in locales as distant as Kauai and New York City. "We went through a three-year business development course at Lane Community College and formed an LLC, which has been very productive for us. We work with some very talented craftsmen, architects, and designers, and we've been fortunate to have some really great jobs," Denny said. Skyline contracts mostly for residential projects, including large and elaborate custom work involving veneers, intricate inlays, curved cabinetry, and other unusual specifications that require a high degree of skill and artistry. Their non-residential projects have included building custom display cases for a chain of cutlery stores. "Our work has been published in several books, and has been included in several American Institute of Architects exhibitions. I really enjoy what I do." A Facebook page at http://www.facebook.com/pages/Skyline-Fine-Cabinets-Furniture-LLC/107893118930 includes photos of some of Skyline's beautiful work.

When Denny and Jennifer first moved to Eugene, they paid $90 per month to rent a "funky" little farmhouse in a walnut orchard at the outskirts of town. Now they live in Eugene proper, which has a population of about 155,000. Jennifer, who has been a preschool teacher since the mid-1980s, works for EWEB Child Development Center, operated by employees of the Eugene Water & Electric Board. Denny and Jennifer's daughter, Ivy, is a hospice nurse in Eugene, and their son, Casey, is a bartender and restaurant manager at a sports bar in the Pearl District of Portland. Ivy and Casey each have two children of their own. Denny revels in the company of his four grandchildren, who in 2012 ranged in ages from 3 to 13. "And the three oldest, ages 10, 12, and 13, are all musical," Denny noted. "My 13-year-old granddaughter plays drums and trumpet, and sings in performance choirs. My oldest grandson plays saxophone and guitar, and my 10-year-old grandson plays piano. People say we should get a band together and go on the road and be like the Partridge Family," he joked.

He retains fond memories of his musical performance years. "Some memories are more vivid than others. A few years ago in the mail I got a videocassette of us doing a Grass Roots guest appearance on a TV show – *Shivaree*, I think – back in the '60s. Well, I had only a vague recollection of it. It was just a blur. Part of the reason may have been that we started in the morning with rehearsal with Glen Campbell. He came in with a six-pack of beer, and we all had a beer. Pretty soon the Mamas and the Papas showed up, and we went out behind the building with John Phillips and smoked a joint, and by the time it came around to filming, I didn't remember anything," he said, laughing. "My memories of a lot of the experiences down there in L.A. are clouded. But, of course, they happened 45 years ago."

After a long absence from music while training in cabinetry and establishing his business, Denny picked up guitar playing again for his own enjoyment as he reached his early 60s. "I bought a Guild Songbird acoustic electric guitar on eBay from Paul Sadler, who was Michael

Martin Murphey's lead guitar player. It's well-worn because he had performed with it on stage for many years, but it's a very nice guitar," Ellis told us in July 2012. Denny has no desire to perform publicly, however. "I break out the guitar and strum once in a while with some of my friends here in town who play music."

Ellis gained a new perspective about life after confronting two unexpected medical conditions. "I'm a prostate cancer survivor," said Denny, who in 2005 was diagnosed with the disease and underwent successful brachytherapy seed implant radiation treatment. Although the cancer treatment was fully effective, he began feeling tired much of the time by 2007. "I couldn't mow the lawn without having to stop and catch my breath. I couldn't keep up with my wife on hikes and other activities. My friends just said, 'Oh, you're just getting older. You can't expect to do as much as you used to do.'" Unconvinced, Denny consulted his doctor, who prescribed tests that revealed the presence of coronary artery disease. Two stent implants alleviated the blockages that had caused Denny's fatigue. He responded with firm dedication to physical fitness and dietary discipline. He joined a health club, and took up bicycle riding and jogging after reading an inspirational book while recuperating from his stent implant procedure in the hospital.

"I read *Bowerman and the Men of Oregon: The Story of Oregon's Legendary Coach and Nike's Cofounder.* It's about the beginning of Nike shoes, and the history of track and field at the University of Oregon here. I made up my mind that I was going to start jogging. And my physical rehab counselor was a runner, and we just started off nice and easy," Ellis said. Still at it, Denny jogs nearly every day, and additionally takes part in a few 5Ks or four-mile runs each year.

Fitness is among the pursuits that Denny came to realize are more important than music. Love of his family and pride in his craftsmanship take priority as well. As he observed, "life is full of crossroads." Contented as Denny Ellis is these days, he apparently made all the correct turns and jogged down all the right roads.

Epilogue: Rob Grill

Bassist and lead singer
November 30, 1943 – July 11, 2011

When Rob Grill was a student at Los Angeles City College, contemplating a career in law, he and a friend named Dennis Ryder formed a band with some other pals for the fun of it. With Rob singing and playing bass, they performed "cover" versions of popular tunes at bowling alleys, clubs, and charity events. But mostly they were hired for fraternity parties around the UCLA campus, where they developed proficiency not only in playing their instruments, but in dodging flying beer cans and dealing with drunk frat brothers who would wrestle away their sole microphone, snarling, "Gimme that! I know the *real* words to Louie, Louie!" The band performed under various names: the Changing Times, the Blessings, and Rob Grill's favorite, the Tap Roots. He was fond of that name because it was the closest he could come to calling it the Grass Roots, whose songs "Ballad of a Thin Man" and "Where Were You When I Needed You" he really liked. Unwilling to keep playing for rowdy crowds, he decided to see if he could land a spot with a more established band. Either that, or he was going to quit music entirely and concentrate on pursuit of a law career.

So Rob went to the musicians' union to look at the job board. There he found a card containing a notice: "Nationally known group with hit record looking for lead singer, bass player." Without knowing the identity of the band, Rob called the number listed on the card. The ad had been posted by Warren Entner. The band was the Thirteenth Floor – soon to become the Grass Roots. When Rob heard that, he just about leapt through the

Christian, Nancy, and Rob Grill backstage at the Greek Theatre in Los Angeles on September 17, 2006 (from the collection of Nancy Grill)

phone. "I'm your guy!" he proclaimed to Entner.

That was quite a transition for a young man who hadn't shown any interest in music all the way through high school other than singing along to the radio. Born November 30, 1943, in Hollywood, Robert Frank Grill grew up amid the entertainment industry but was never drawn to it. Unlike many of the other kids at Hollywood High School, he never had picked up an instrument. What he did pick up was a job selling subscriptions for *Look* magazine. After doing that for a few years, he began selling newspaper subscriptions for the old *Los Angeles Herald Express* after he enrolled in college in 1962. He was able to sell his subscriptions after his classes let out for the day. It paid him about $20 per night for three hours of work, which was more than adequate because he was still living at home with his parents, Louis and Anna Jo Grill, and he needed only spending money.

As Rob went house to house, he sang jubilantly along with songs on the radio. The other guys on the crew who heard his singing included Dennis Ryder, who called Rob after work one evening. Dennis explained that he had written some songs, and that he'd been invited to audition them for Lester Sill, president of Screen Gems-Columbia Music. Dennis asked if Rob would be willing to help him demonstrate the songs by singing along with him. Rob asked his mother what she thought. "You know, Lana Turner was discovered in a drug store," she reminded him. "If I were you, I'd go." So Rob went along to the audition and helped Dennis sing his songs. Sill rejected Dennis' songs, but instead offered to sign Rob to a recording contract. Rob was skeptical, particularly of Sill's advice to form a band, and he objected because he didn't play any instruments. A booking agent at the studio advised him to try bass guitar because it's relatively easy to learn. Rob bought a bass guitar and amplifier at a pawnshop and as he began hanging out with the musicians who were regulars at the recording studio, they taught him to play the instrument. The band he eventually formed was the Changing Times – alternatively the Tap Roots.

When he answered the ad posted at the musicians' union hall, he learned that he would audition to replace Thirteenth Floor bass player and vocalist Kenny Fukumoto, who had received his military draft notice. The remaining band members – rhythm guitarist Warren Entner, lead guitarist Creed Bratton and drummer Rick Coonce – needed to find a replacement quickly because of the contract offer they'd received from Dunhill Records to become the Grass Roots. Grill initially auditioned for Entner, Bratton, and Coonce, and once they accepted him they brought him to Dunhill Records to meet songwriter-producer Steve Barri. "Steve brought out an acoustic guitar and said, 'sing something for me.' So we sang some stuff and he told me, 'I like your voice.' It reminded him of P.F. Sloan," Grill explained. "So they told us we could be the Grass Roots, that the label would own the name, and that after we live out our five-year contract we would own the name. We thought it was a great name and because the album that came out had no names or pictures of band members, we said it wouldn't be a big deal. I've had to answer questions about that, but I'm not ashamed. I think we would have gotten the string of hits if we had called ourselves the Fried Frogs."

Grill held great admiration for Steve Barri. "We would mix the singles for AM radio using little tiny car speakers on the console. Steve Barri was a big part of the Grass Roots and that was one of his things. Thank God for Steve Barri," Grill declared. Grill remained with the Roots when they renewed their recording contract with Dunhill in 1972, and said he tried to discourage keyboard player Dennis Provisor from leaving. "Clive Davis at Columbia wanted Dennis for a solo act, so he left and he left behind his royalties, his percentage of the band – everything. Although Terry Furlong came along about the same time that Dennis joined the band, Terry was just an employee, but Dennis was a member of the band and owned a percentage of it. Dennis was quite a songwriter, and his 'Walking Through the Country' was a hit for the Grass Roots. He's a friend of mine and I told him, 'Don't leave. At least get the money.' When he left, there were three of us left who owned stock in the corporation, but they didn't want to tour. I don't blame them, but through some maneuvering I got them to go away," he laughed mischievously.

Rob kept the Grass Roots before the public by hiring musicians, including first-generation Grass Roots member Joel Larson on drums, to perform with him on club dates. But by early 1977, Rob tired of the succession of smoky, boozy clubs that he was playing. Deciding to leave that behind, he mothballed the Grass Roots, rented an office in the historic Taft Building at the corner of Hollywood and Vine, and set up shop as Hollywood Talent, a talent agency specializing in oldies bands. During the two years he ran the agency, he befriended bass player John McVie – soon to become world-renowned with Fleetwood Mac. McVie urged Grill to resume his performing career, and persuaded him to cut a demo record. They selected a tune called "Rock Sugar," which Dennis Provisor had written. Provisor and McVie agreed to perform on the demo, along with two of McVie's friends – drummer Mick Fleetwood and guitarist Lindsey Buckingham of Fleetwood Mac. The demo managed to grab the attention of executives at Mercury Phonogram. That label signed Grill to a record deal, with John McVie as producer. That partnership yielded an album, *Rob Grill Uprooted*, which thrilled diehard Grass Roots fans when it was released in 1979. "The record company hated the title.

They didn't want anything to do with the Grass Roots," Grill explained. "But I went with Fleetwood Mac on their *Tusk* tour. When I went to radio stations to promote the album, the radio programmers would say, 'Yeah, OK, that's great. But why don't you put the Grass Roots back together?' So that's what I did."

Grill hired lead guitarist Terry Oubre, keyboard player Charles Judge, and drummer Ralph Gilmore as members of the new Grass Roots. Rob began knocking on doors, and landed a record deal in 1982 with MCA, which had just acquired ABC-Dunhill and with it the entire Grass Roots catalog of former hit albums. MCA thought a new Grass Roots recording would help rekindle interest in the band's catalog. Grill, who by then had bought out Entner's and Coonce's shares and was the sole owner of the Grass Roots name and trademark, agreed. The new Grass Roots recorded an album called *Powers of the Night,* which yielded a single called "She Don't Know Me," written by Mark Avsec of the band Wild Cherry. Grill so firmly believed in the hit potential of the song that he mortgaged his house to invest in promotion. "The independent promotion guys I hired got it on about 270 stations, but I needed the record company to help me because I just didn't have the funds to keep the promotion going on my own," Grill said. "We actually got it to top 10 in some markets. The record company was working on the Oak Ridge Boys and Olivia Newton-John at the time and said they couldn't help. So the song got dropped. Then this unknown group named Bon Jovi recorded it, and it became their first hit. We had given it a shot, and ours was really good." Grill was feeling defeated by 1984, but a phone call brought new opportunity.

The growing popularity of oldies radio programming led entertainment agent and tour producer David Fishof to assemble an entourage he called the Happy Together Tour, featuring the Turtles, along with Gary Lewis and the Playboys, the Buckinghams, and Tommy James and the Shondells. The Grass Roots signed on with the tour, which went from city to city for more than six profitable months during 1985. The band by then consisted of Rob along with lead guitarist Dusty Hanvey, keyboard player Larry Nelson, and drummer Joe Dougherty. The following year, the Grass Roots joined Fishof's next road show, headlined by the Monkees. And in 1987, the Grass Roots were part of Fishof's show called the Classic Superfest, which included Paul Revere and the Raiders, Herman's Hermits, Bachman-Turner Overdrive, Dr. Hook, and the Byrds featuring Gene Clark. "By that time we were building a following again, the oldies stations were cooking, and the Grass Roots were back on the air again," grinned Grill. Those shows gave the Grass Roots new momentum that continued to propel the band – much to Grill's surprise. Paradise

Artists booking agent Howie Silverman, whom Rob regarded as a close friend and confidant, was influential in Rob's decision to continue performing. "I'm pinching myself. We're going 80 to 95 nights a year all over the United States," Rob told us in January 2000. Along with Grill on bass, the early-2000s Grass Roots consisted of keyboardist Larry Nelson, drummer Joe Dougherty, and either of two guitarists – Chris Merrell or Dusty Hanvey, who also performed regularly with the Righteous Brothers.

Around the time Grill signed the Grass Roots to join the Happy Together Tour, he sold his condo in Culver City. After living all of his life in L.A., he was ready for a change of scenery. Focusing on two of his interests, golf and catch-and-release freshwater bass fishing, he selected a little town in central Florida, 30 miles northwest of Orlando. He bought a home in a pristine wooded area on the shore of a lake. The town is small enough that just about everyone knows everyone else. And Rob liked that just fine. His fishing buddies included fellow Dunhill Records recording artist Cory Wells of Three Dog Night. Rob regularly played golf in a recreation-oriented community known as The Villages outside the neighboring town of Lady Lake.

Grill's introduction to central Florida occurred three years before he moved there. A local radio personality named Nancy Pilski was in charge of finding talent for the grand opening of the Lamp Post nightclub in Mount Dora, Florida. She was hoping to book a nationally known act, and when she heard that the Grass Roots would be playing at Disney World the day after the event, she scheduled them because "I'd Wait a Million Years" was one of her favorite songs. Although Rob was divorced by then, Nancy was dating someone. But they stayed in touch for professional reasons, and over time their friendship grew. "We became such good friends that we fell in love," Rob smiled.

"When we met, we hit it off right away," Nancy told us in September 2012. "It was love at first sight to me, and Rob said it was for him also. Even though we were both adults, Rob asked for my father's permission to marry his daughter." Rob and Nancy married in November 1986 in the Catholic church her family attended in her hometown, Greenbelt, Maryland, where her father had been mayor.

Rob's first wife, Arie, had given birth to a son – Rob's only child, Christian Leigh Grill, who was born October 6, 1970. Christian served as best man in Rob and Nancy's wedding ceremony. As a teenager, Christian lived with Rob and Nancy until he decided to return to Southern California to follow in his father's footsteps and pursue a music career as a drummer.

Nancy retired in 2000 after a career as a well-respected and popular high school teacher with the Lake County School System, at schools in

Umatilla and then in Tavares. "She had to come home and take care of the old guy," Grill laughed. Although Rob had begun to develop health problems as a result of avascular necrosis, a degenerative bone disease, he continued to take delight in the persistent popularity of the band. He told us in 2000 that he had no plans of his own to retire. "We always used to think that our newest hit would be our last one," he recalled. "We thought there's no way we could ever get another one. No way that I can keep doing this when I'm 30. No way can I keep doing this when I'm 40, or 50. Now I know I'm going to be working well into my 60s."

As he reached his early 60s, however, his health deteriorated into an agonizing nightmare that he endured with pain-dulling medication. He underwent multiple hip replacement surgeries and two shoulder replacements. Despite his own ailments, Rob performed a benefit concert in May 2007 for Grass Roots guitarist Chriss Merrell, who was diagnosed with metastatic prostate cancer. Merrell died from his illness in March 2010. Meanwhile, Rob's son, Christian, had been diagnosed with melanoma in 2008. Christian underwent treatments, including advanced care in Houston after the disease metastasized. He initially responded so well that he and his longtime girlfriend, Carla, married in June 2010. The remission was brief, however, and a few weeks later the aggressive disease claimed Christian, who died at age 39 on August 11, 2010.

"Christian was a wonderful human being, and I really adored him," Nancy said. "He was an excellent drummer. He sat in with the Grass Roots on numerous concerts. He would have been the drummer of the Grass Roots if Joe Dougherty had moved on. Rob was honorable – he refused to fire someone in order to hire his son. But Rob loved having Christian around. When Christian died, Rob's decline went steeper."

At the time of Christian's death, Rob was undergoing another medical crisis. A pre-surgical examination preparatory for a knee replacement revealed a potentially life-threatening deep-vein thrombosis – a blood clot in Rob's leg. Surgeons treated the condition by inserting a mesh stent into the vein, but while Rob was hospitalized he contracted pneumonia, which led to collapse of one of his lungs and an extended hospital stay. Because Rob had committed the Grass Roots to another Happy Together Tour, Nancy hired a replacement for Rob – singer and bass player Mark Dawson, who previously had performed with Rob on several gigs. "Rob hand-picked Mark for his replacement. He had told Mark, 'You're going to be the guy if I ever have to retire.'"

By sheer determination and with Nancy's loving support, Rob resumed touring in late 2010, relying upon a brace or a cane during his performances. On stage he told his audience, "As long as you and other fans continue coming to see me, I'm going to be here." He spent much of the spring of 2011 in and out of hospitals, though. Then at his home in mid-June 2011, he felt ill while watching a golf tournament on television. When Rob stood up, he tripped over his feet and fell. "Rob loved to entertain and make people laugh, and I thought at first he was joking around," Nancy said. As soon as she realized that Rob wasn't joking, she called for an ambulance. Rob had fallen because he had suffered a stroke, and was rushed to a hospital in Orlando. While in the hospital, he experienced additional hemorrhagic and ischemic strokes. The damage was devastating and irreversible. Rob's doctors recommended transferring him to Cornerstone Hospice and Palliative Care in Tavares, near Rob's home, for end-of-life care.

It was shortly before noon on July 11, 2011. Although Rob had difficulty communicating, Nancy could tell by his expression that something was bothering him. She realized what it was. "A country music song was playing, and the face he was making showed that he didn't like it. So I put a Grass Roots CD into the player, and the first song that came on was 'I'd Wait a Million Years.' I crawled in bed with him and held him, reassured him, told him I would always be there for him," Nancy said. "He was looking intently at a corner of the room, seeing a vision no one else but he could see. I was sobbing a little bit, but tried to keep from showing that. Then "Let's Live for Today" came on, and he gave me a contented look with his beautiful eyes. Then on the last beat of the song, he kissed me, the music went silent, and he was gone. It was surreal. A nurse came in, and that was it." Rob was 67 years old. "My whole life changed at the last beat of that song. He died peacefully, but he lives on in his music, and he'll be in my heart for a million years."

When Rob was still touring with his beloved Grass Roots, he had told us, "The audiences really want to hear our music, and the band is better than ever. And I'm really loving it. I drive down to the airport in my new Escalade and fly first class where we're going. I get picked up in limos and get to play a concert. I consider myself one of the luckiest guys in the world." Rob took particular satisfaction in the newfound respect that the Grass Roots were accorded in the new millennium. "When we go to an FM station now, the disc jockeys tell us, 'Man, you guys were like *there*. Your music is part of what got it all going.' I play golf with friends of mine who own companies and they're really wealthy. They tell me, 'Don't you ever complain. Look what you do for a living. It's fabulous.' And I have to remind myself sometimes just how lucky I am," Rob reflected.

Under Nancy's direction, Rob's Grass Roots band continues touring with its current members: guitarist and singer Dusty Hanvey, bass player and singer Mark Dawson, keyboard player Larry Nelson, and drummer Joe Dougherty.

Epilogue: Creed Bratton
Lead guitarist and singer

In the middle of a restless night in early 1964, Creed Bratton bolted upright from his bed in Sacramento, California, awakened by a nightmare that he believed was a vision of his own future. "I saw nylons hanging from the shower rod and I saw diapers, and I woke up in a cold sweat," Bratton recalled. That vision was frightening enough to him that he called a friend and in a panic declared, "I don't want to do this. I'm not ready to settle down." He needed to get away – to anyplace else. Lacking cash to travel, Bratton sold his Austin Healy, and then he and a friend, Mickey Miguel, stuck out their thumbs and began hitchhiking. The first ride took them to the Mojave Desert town of Needles, California. From there they snagged a ride in a car headed for New Orleans, where they managed to get passage aboard a freighter bound for Venice, Italy. So relieved was Bratton to step on land after a 28-day voyage at sea that he began celebrating with wine in a bar, where he borrowed someone's guitar, sang well into the night, and drank himself into a stupor before passing out in Piazza

Creed Bratton with his Guild guitar in March 2010 (photo by Andrew Hreha, courtesy of Creed Bratton)

San Marco (St. Mark's Square). "When I woke up the next morning, I thought I had measles or something. Pigeon shit was all over my body," Bratton laughed. That was the beginning of a wild, unpredictable two-year adventure on which he would stow away aboard a train through Germany, perform with a folk group in subterranean bunkers beneath the sands of the Sahara Desert and in a brothel in Beirut, live on a kibbutz in Israel, land a part as an extra in a motion picture with John Wayne and Frank Sinatra, and invent a new name for himself – after learning his own real name.

Bratton, born William Charles Schneider in the Los Angeles community of Inglewood on February 8, 1943, was known as Charles throughout his youth. He is the son of Frank Schneider, who had a German-English background, and Cozette Fanshier, of French ancestry. The couple had met in Coarsegold, a mountain town in the Sierra range near Yosemite National Park, where Frank was a ranger. The couple had moved to Inglewood after Frank entered military service. Inglewood had been a primarily agricultural area until the outbreak of World War II, when aerospace and other defense-related industries took hold. Frank, who was a military pilot, died in an aviation accident in Hawaii when Charles was only 2 years old.

After Frank's death, Charles and his mother moved to Coarsegold, a Madera County village on California Highway 41 northeast of Fresno with just 300 residents. There, Charles' mother eventually met and married Sam Ertmoed, a highway maintenance worker. After completing elementary school, young Charles Ertmoed – as Creed was known then – traveled narrow, twisting mountain highways in a treacherous two-hour bus journey each way to Sierra Joint Union High School, in the Fresno County town of Tollhouse. He was one of only 80 students in his grade in school, which had dormitory rooms for students who traveled even farther than Charles to school. Those students would stay in the dorms on weekdays and travel home only on weekends. "My mom worked for the Post Office," said Bratton, explaining that employment choices in Coarsegold were limited. As Bratton spoke, his deep affection and respect for his mother were clearly evident. "Even in her 80s, she was still a beautiful woman," he said reverently.

Bratton believes his interest in music developed naturally, as a result of the strong musical influences within his family. His grandfather Gustav Adolph Schneider danced and "played bones" with a troupe called the Bulldog Minstrels aboard the battleship Oregon on which he served in the Asiatic Station in the Pacific during World War I. "My aunt said he could play any instrument that he picked up," Creed proudly declared.

Following military duty, Gustav became a motion picture studio art director in Hollywood, with prestigious credits that included work on the 1924 version of *The Thief of Bagdad* starring Douglas Fairbanks Sr. "My grandfather invented that old corny-looking moveable scenery that moves behind actors." Creed's maternal grandparents, Charles and Dot Fanshier, had a Los Angeles-area band called the Happy Timers, a semi-professional country and western group in which Charles played guitar and Dot played drums. And Creed's father played the banjo.

Creed's first instrument was the trumpet, which he initially picked up when he was in grammar school and continued playing all the way through high school. But at 13, he also started playing electric guitar on the Silvertone model that he had ordered from what he called the "wish book" – the Sears Roebuck catalog. The guitar case contained a built-in amplifier and speaker. "So I could take the Silvertone out, plug it into the case and play," explained Bratton. He'd often go to a roadhouse called The Falls at the nearby settlement of Bass Lake, where local bands played. "It was a real hub of social activity in the mountains in the late '50s." There, he'd study the musicians' techniques, and then practice on his own. By age 17, Bratton was good enough to join a local pop group called the Torquays, which had a female vocalist. Bratton performed with them in 1960 and 1961.

When Bratton enrolled at the College of the Sequoias in Visalia in the fall of 1961, he joined a group called the Leanders. After two years he transferred to Sacramento State College (now California State University, Sacramento), where he continued playing with other local bands but concentrated on acting because he was majoring in drama. He was contemplating a career in acting when his vivid nightmare about domestic life awakened him that 1964 night. Not until he applied for a passport to travel to Europe did he learn that his name was not really Charles Ertmoed, as he had assumed. He applied for the passport under that name, but when the document arrived it showed his name as "William Charles Schneider" – his birth name. He realized at that moment that his stepfather had never adopted him, as he had believed.

After brushing off the bird droppings when he awoke in Venice that day in 1964, Bratton and his traveling companion stowed away on a train that brought them to Munich, Germany. On the way, Bratton's friend yearned for his girlfriend, and he boarded a plane for the United States to be with her. Bratton, who was determined to remain in Europe, managed to get a job as an assembly line worker at an electronics factory in Munich, and enrolled in classes at Goethe Institute to learn to speak German. At the American Express office one day about four months after his arrival in Munich, he was struck by the appearance of two long-haired guys wearing bizarre outfits fashioned from animal skins and furs. They were Americans, Greg Fitzpatrick and Lee Zimmerman, who introduced themselves as folk singers from California. When they learned that Creed also was a musician, they invited him to join them. "So I withdrew all my money from the bank and I bought a guitar, hiking boots, a big anorak jacket with a fur collar, and other clothes, and a rucksack, and met them at noon in front of the American Express and we took off together as a group," said Bratton. For the next two and a half years, the itinerant trio traveled through Europe. They bought matching outfits, wore clean-cut hair styles, and performed uptempo folk songs in the mode of the Kingston Trio – particularly enjoyable for Bratton because he was influenced by the Kingston Trio and the Modern Folk Quartet. Calling themselves the Young Californians, Bratton and his companions played in clubs throughout Europe, and when they couldn't land a club gig, they'd perform in train stations or other public places for donations. "We sang outside the entrance to the Swiss Expo, and we made so much money there!"

After performing for the British military at Gibraltar, the three folk-singers made their way to North Africa, landing a gig in the Al Waddan Hotel in Tripoli, Libya. There a bush pilot working for Mobil Oil caught their act on the last scheduled day of their gig and told them he could line up some additional jobs for them. They agreed and with him boarded a pre-1942 Douglas DC-3 propeller airliner. "It landed somewhere out on the Sahara Desert, and then we got on a little Piper Cub that flew out to the middle of the desert. The pilot had a bottle of whisky between his legs and he was drinking the whole time he was flying the plane, and we were scared to death," Bratton acknowledged. "We were trying to make jokes but I thought we were going to die out there." But the pilot landed, guided by flags posted in the dunes. At one spot he began kicking the sand aside and revealed a hatch cover that opened into a tunnel. He led the trio down below into a complex of large corrugated cylinders that formed the living quarters for oil crews working out in the desert. Still grasping his bottle in his hand, the pilot led the way to the bunkhouse where all the workers were sleeping. "In a drunken stupor he kicked all the beds, yelling, 'Hey, wake up!' The oil workers gathered in the commissary and he made them pay us $500 to perform," Bratton chuckled. For most of a month, the pilot escorted the singers from one oil workers' camp to another, where they picked up additional cash for performing. When they had completed the Mobil Oil circuit of camps, the pilot dropped off the trio in Algeria, where they picked up a ride to Egypt.

There they landed some gigs in bars, and managed to get themselves a couple of appearances on Egyptian television.

They booked passage aboard a passenger boat to Beirut, Lebanon, where they earned a singing engagement at the Kit Kat Club, a brothel where patrons could choose from liquor or hashish. "At that time Beirut was like Paris on the Mediterranean. I was about 22 years old, working in a brothel, getting laid, smoking hashish, and playing every night for Rolls Royce-rich Arab oil sheiks," exulted Bratton. "It was unbelievable!" From there the Young Californians traveled to Syria and then on through the Mandelbaum Gate from Jordan into Israel, where they were able to find work performing in *kibbutz* collective settlements. They arrived in time to perform at a folk festival. Those in the audience included Warren Entner, a UCLA student who had taken a break from studies to travel. After the show, Entner approached Bratton, complimenting him on his guitar playing. Entner said he wanted to put a group together and asked if Bratton would be interested in joining him when he returned to California. Bratton obligingly wrote down Warren's number, but didn't think much more about it at the time.

Since leaving college, Bratton hadn't given much thought to acting, but unexpectedly was handed an opportunity to try his craft when the film crew for the motion picture *Cast a Giant Shadow* was doing some location shooting there in Israel. Bratton was hired to play a role as a British soldier in the film about the life of Col. David "Mickey" Marcus, an American Army officer who helped shape Israeli volunteers into a potent, disciplined armed force in the newly established nation of Israel in 1949. On the set Bratton met the picture's stars: John Wayne, Frank Sinatra, Kirk Douglas, and Michael Douglas – whom he first encountered body surfing on an Israeli beach. Bratton also met Lynne Shavelson, the daughter of the film's director, Mel Shavelson. Creed and Lynne became romantically involved and traveled together through the Greek Islands before he went on alone through Yugoslavia, Czechoslovakia, and Poland, along the way booking himself for gigs as a soloist, performing folk tunes and some old rock and roll.

At the Oktoberfest in Munich in 1965, Bratton spotted Greg Fitzpatrick and Lee Zimmerman. They reunited and performed during a two-week engagement as the Young Californians. The trio traveled to London with plans to record. Their concept was offbeat: performing rock music on a banjo and two acoustic guitars. When it became apparent that the recording process was not going well, Greg took off to Sweden, Lee returned to the United States, and Creed remained in England, uncertain of what to do or where to go next. "Without the band, I was doomed," he realized. But the departure of his musical partners paved the way for a new partnership.

At a butcher shop in London, Creed had met Greg Fitzpatrick's sister, Jo Anne. Greg and Jo Anne had an entertainment-business father: James A. Fitzpatrick, the "voice of the globe" who narrated numerous MGM travelogues ("…as the sun slowly sinks in the West, we reluctantly bid farewell to Bali…"). In the brief time Creed and Jo Anne were together in London, they developed a friendship that was interrupted when she returned to her hometown of Los Angeles and Creed decided to travel to Athens. There in a saloon, as he was becoming drunk on ouzo, he met a couple from Oregon who were on their way to Crete to teach English. They asked Bratton what his plans were, and he told them he planned to return to America to become a rock and roll star. "I could see this. I had a mental image in my mind. I saw myself becoming very success-ful," he said. They asked his name. "Chuck Ertmoed," he replied. The couple asked, "Are you still going to be Chuck Ertmoed?" The question caught Bratton by surprise. "Oh. That's right," he acknowledged. "That's not a very good rock and roll name. So let's think about this." As all three downed ouzo, they began concocting potential names, which they wrote on the tablecloth. Then they began a process of elimination, crossing out names that they discarded. The next morning, when Bratton woke up at the *pensione* bed and breakfast inn, the tablecloth was hanging on his rucksack. All but one of the names that had been suggested the night before were crossed out. The only remaining name was Creed Bratton. He stuffed the tablecloth into his rucksack.

Shortly after that, in mid-1966, Chuck Ertmoed took a flight to New York and hitchhiked to L.A. There, he contacted two people he had met while in Europe – Jo Anne Fitzpatrick and Warren Entner – and took part in the formation of the Thirteenth Floor, for which Creed became lead guitarist. Then, as the band was invited to sign with Dunhill Records as the Grass Roots, he entered his name on the contract as "Creed Brat-ton" – to Entner's surprise. "Hey Chuck," Entner asked, "what's this Creed Bratton?" Chuck Ertmoed explained that he was not going to be Chuck, he was going to be Creed Bratton. He remembers that Ricky Coonce and Warren Entner looked at him as if he were crazy. "It was just one of those things. I couldn't stand the name Ertmoed. You've got to understand, if you're a kid, a sensitive artistic kind of kid, and you've got a name like Ertmoed, you're walking around and other kids are saying, 'Hey, Ertmoed' with their finger in their throat making a gagging sound. I couldn't be cool with that name." Ertmoed doesn't know who on that ouzo-fogged night suggested the name Creed Bratton, or what inspired it. "Maybe this book will reach that couple from Oregon, and they can tell me how we came up with those names," laughed Bratton, who legally adopted that name.

When he married Jo Anne in 1968 at the Self-Realization Fellowship on Sunset Boulevard in Hollywood, Bratton was decked out in a Nehru suit and beads – reflective of his growing interest in other cultures and spirituality. Toward the end of his tenure with the Grass Roots, in the spring of 1969, Creed began some personal experimentation that puzzled the others. "I had a phase of spirituality at the time and I think I made everyone nervous. I was heavily into yoga and I was fasting. They'd walk into the room and I'd be standing on my head. One time Warren walked in and I had gauze over my nose and on my mouth as the Indian guys do. I was out there, and it wasn't drugs because I was never into heavy drugs," asserted Bratton. But the differences that set him apart from the others involved more than just his spiritual explorations. "I was drifting away and I wasn't seeing eye-to-eye with everyone. One night after a gig in New York we were in the limo going back to the Plaza Hotel. I had been listening to Robbie Robertson's group, the Band, and I told the guys that if we didn't start writing some stuff and taking control of our destiny, and stop being a cookie cutter pop factory, we were going to lose. At that time we didn't have much credibility with the rock and roll public because we were good-looking guys in *16 Magazine*. People didn't take us seriously, and I was frustrated. I told them I was having trouble going out and acting like I'm having a good time, when I wasn't. They said they were having trouble playing with me. We were such close friends in the beginning. We were like brothers, but toward the end there was this bitterness."

Although Bratton's decision in April 1969 to leave the group was prompted in part because of friction that had developed between him and the other band members, he was motivated primarily by his desire to spend more time with his daughter, Amie (pronounced AH-me), who was by then 1½ years old. Bratton regretted being on the road with the band much of the time after her birth. The other Grass Roots bought out Bratton's portion of the band's corporation, paying him a financial settlement of $20,000. Creed, Jo Anne, and Amie traveled to Europe, bought a Morris Minor roadster and drove to Morocco, on the northwestern coast of Africa. "I saw people I had met before, and I played at many of those clubs where I had played before. And I had improved," he declared. "The new and improved Chuck Ertmoed."

After a year in Europe, Bratton and his family returned to Southern California, choosing a home in Ramirez Canyon, adjacent to Barbra

Streisand's residence, in Malibu. Creed decided to pursue the acting career he had envisioned as a college student. After taking additional acting lessons from private instructors in Hollywood and signing with a talent agent, he landed roles in numerous 1970s television shows, including *Quincy* starring Jack Klugman, *Kolchak: The Night Stalker* and *Eight Is Enough*.

Unfortunately, his marriage to Jo Anne ended in divorce in 1975, when Bratton again resumed his musical career. While performing as a soloist at a club in Visalia, he became acquainted with Henry Lewy, engineer for many of the recordings of Joni Mitchell, Crosby, Stills and Nash, and Neil Young. Lewy introduced Bratton to Peter White, who played with Al Stewart. White, another musician named Dave Camp and Bratton formed a group called Lucy Goosie. In the midst of that project, Bratton met and married Claudia Anderson in 1977. The couple had a son, Beau Bratton, in 1978. In the early 1980s Bratton formed the Creed Bratton Band, which performed a diet of what Bratton terms "aggressive, nasty, hard-driven heavy metal." But he acknowledges that style of music was out of character for him. "That was totally unlike me, but necessity is the mother of invention," he observed.

Focusing once again on acting during that time, he made brief appearances in episodes of TV series in the mid '70s, worked on the 1982 film *The Kid From Nowhere* with Beau Bridges, and on a 1982 made-for-TV film called *Dangerous Company,* with Bridges and Alan Autry. Bratton had a small speaking role in the 1985 movie *Mask,* starring Cher, Sam Elliott, and Eric Stoltz. In that film, Bratton played a carney worker at a bumper car ride. As Elliott and the grotesquely disfigured character played by Stoltz prepare to enter the ride, Bratton's character sneers to Elliott, "Well *you* can ride, but I won't be responsible for the retard here." Bratton's daughter Amie Ertmoed and her husband (at the time her boyfriend) watched the movie together in New York. "What an asshole," he said during that scene, without realizing the carney worker was played by Creed. "Amie called me and said, 'Dad, I was so proud of your acting,' because I'm not that way at all." He was a stand-in for Beau Bridges in the 1989 movie *The Fabulous Baker Boys*. The same year he played a role as a corrupted cop in a scene with Patrick Swayze in the film *Roadhouse,* but the scene didn't make it past the rough cuts when the film editor noticed that Bratton's character had somehow avoided being beaten to a pulp by the combative, righteously indignant Swayze character.

Divorced from Claudia in 1984, Bratton has been single since then. He has no special companion in his life now, and he understands why.

"Women don't appreciate you saying, 'I gotta write for a few days.' Or, 'I'm going fishing.' I like to go elk hunting or fishing, then I want her to be there when I get back." If he were advertising for a companion, he might be tempted to write: "Wanted – self-contained woman. Likes artists. Doesn't mind if they don't have to be around all the time." He says solemnly, "It's not fair to lie to someone." Defining the essence of Creed Bratton is difficult – even for him. "You've got to think about February 8 people. They're Aquarians. It's a tough date. It's James Dean, it's Nick Nolte, it's volatile, high-strung individuals who appear detached on the surface. A lot of people think I'm very cold and detached, like that guy in the movie *Mask*. I'm not at all, but I come across that way sometimes," he allows. "I'm an artist, so sometimes the muse hits and I go inside. I think people find that hard to deal with. In conversations, I'll just drift off, pick up a piece of paper and start writing. If somebody did that to me, I'd think it's very rude, but I just don't think about it when I'm doing it. So that woman would have to be very thick-skinned."

Bratton scored the music for a couple of motion pictures, which he found to be a learning experience. "They gave me the rough and I played along with them, watching the motion, and putting music to it. I came up with some pretty cool stuff," said Bratton. "I was so naive, though, that I spent way too much money in the studio getting the sound to be perfect. When they finally backed it to the film or tape, some of the segments were played at such low volume that I could have recorded it on a cassette at home, because it wouldn't have mattered. But that's how you learn. I thought if they did play it loud, I wanted it to be great. If I have the opportunity to do it again, I'll ask how it will be played."

Throughout his 40-year acting career, Bratton has appeared not only in motion pictures and television dramas and comedies, but also in commercials, including a Folgers coffee commercial in which he acted, sang, and played his guitar. "I've done anything that's come along. I worked part-time for a catering company – setting tables and serving when things got tough, you know. It was feast or famine. I'd get checks in the mail, and months could go by before something else comes in for a movie or TV show. So you do what you have to," Bratton shrugged. "I began working for a company called Lori's Kitchen, the best caterers for the movie industry." While he was serving food at one event, he spotted an old friend: Ray Manzarek from the Doors. Bratton and Manzarek got together with Doors member John Densmore and on a lark put together a group called Rich and Randy. "We did a gig in Palm Springs, which turned out to be a real fiasco. The name was a joke," said Bratton. It was intended to allude to "wealthy and horny," but not enough people understood the tongue-in-cheek meaning. Creed continued to act in television and motion pictures, persisted in writing songs, performed with a musical group called Many Names, and worked on catering assignments from Lori's Kitchen, which is based in the San Fernando Valley community of Van Nuys. He quickly pointed out that he served meals to guests at events, but he had no kitchen duties. "I could burn a salad! When I say I don't cook, the flies in my neighborhood chipped in and bought me a screen door," Bratton joked.

Music composition and singing captivated his interest again in the early 2000s, when he recorded and released three solo albums: *Chasin' the Ball, The 80s* and *Coarsegold.* He wrote or co-wrote all songs on those three CDs. By 2006 he was back on TV, this time in guest appearances on the *Bernie Mac Show* and, since then, as a member of the cast of *The Office* comedy series – playing a character named "Creed," a jaundiced, eccentric, unpredictable former rocker.

Music and acting remain intertwined in Bratton's life. In 2008 Kindred Records released a folk-rock and blues-flavored solo album titled *Creed Bratton,* produced by Jon Tiven. The following year Creed appeared in the comedy film *Labor Pains,* starring Lindsay Lohan. In 2010 he completed and released another music CD titled *Bounce Back,* with moods ranging from jubilant pop-rock to earthy ballads, and in 2011 he issued *Demo,* a compilation album of tunes culled from his previous solo CDs. Bratton shared top billing with Jacob Wysocki and John C. Reilly in the critically acclaimed 2011 comedic drama motion picture *Terri,* which was an official selection that year at the prestigious Sundance Film Festival. He played prominent roles in the 2011 comedy movie *I Am Ben,* produced and directed by Mathew Brady and Gaelan Connell; in the 2012 fantasy comedy film *The Ghastly Love of Johnny X,* in which he also performs two songs; and in the 2012 motion picture *Saving Lincoln,* a Civil War-era drama in which he plays a U.S. senator.

Bratton thinks of his two children, Amie and Beau, as the greatest achievement of his personal life. "I'm so proud of them. They're so beautiful and so open, and they're such a contribution to society. I'm just so lucky," he said. Bratton performs on stage periodically with Many Names, an acoustic group that also includes Paul Downey and Don Frankel, who in the early 1980s played in the Creed Bratton Band. The group's name is somewhat of an inside joke, a reference to the various names by which Bratton has been known. "Don's a high harmony, I sing the low fifth, Paul sings in the middle and sometimes we all switch off. We sing three-part harmony on new songs and new versions of Grass Roots hits. I was sick of singing those songs toward the end of my time with the Grass Roots, but in Many Names we sing them with a little different arrangement to make them more contemporary," he declared.

Although he acknowledges that he's growing older, he jokingly says he doesn't think fans can yet accuse him of being on a "rockers with walkers" tour. "The point is, I still love to play. We've got great harmony, and we sound really good." He extends a nod to the Grass Roots' producers for encouraging his musical development. "I want to thank Steve Barri and P.F. Sloan, right here on the record, who were very gracious to allow me to experiment in the studio. They let me play my sitar and my mandolin. On 'Let's Live for Today,' I played acoustic guitar and sang harmony." Through his music production company Alien Chicken, Bratton completed a 2012 album titled *Move To Win,* produced by Dave Way. Bratton describes it as an autobiographical "concept psychedelic album," the participants in which include two of his friends: *The Office* co-star Rainn Wilson and P.F. Sloan.

Bratton's home in the Hollywood Hills in which he's lived since 1990 is not far from the Beverly Glen pad where he lived during his days with the Grass Roots. He has a studio in which he writes music and studies his acting lines. He enjoys playing the Grass Roots music once again in part because he's more at ease with himself than he was when he was younger. His views of spirituality still remain somewhat unconventional, as he prefers to subscribe to his own vision than to that of any organized institution. "Spirituality is God's laws, religion is Man's laws. I think there's probably been more harm done in the name of religion than anything else," Bratton declared. "I get up, I meditate, I do my yoga, I exercise and stay in really good shape, and I don't judge anybody else. I work on me. All these preachers and most people would want you to be like them. I think people should show by example and just shut up. If I were to have a religion it would probably be something like Buddhism because it doesn't seem to judge. I think people think too much. I know when I meditate I realize that my problems have been caused because I get in my own way. If I just stop that little inner dialog, and get out of my way, boom! All of a sudden there's some music. The meditation seems to eliminate anger."

And just to remind himself of who he is and where he comes from, he still has a precious memento: the tablecloth from that ouzo-drenched night in the Greek restaurant bearing many names, all crossed out except one – Creed Bratton.

Visit **www.creedbratton.com** for more information.

Epilogue: Warren Entner
Guitarist, keyboard player and singer

Pop music fans would be challenged to find any common strands of influence between the folk-pop-oriented Grass Roots and hard-driving, heavy-metal bands such as Quiet Riot or Faith No More. Yet they do, indeed, share a linking bond: Warren Entner. Guitarist for the Grass Roots for six years at the height of the band's popularity, Entner is the founder and principal owner of Warren Entner Management Inc., a personal management company that has guided the careers of Quiet Riot, Faith No More, Rage Against the Machine, and numerous other successful bands.

At the agency's peak, Entner had a staff of four associates to assist musician clients in negotiations for recording contracts and concert tours, and handle news media relations and promotional arrangements. The firm, which Enter founded in 1982, has avoided pop-music acts, instead concentrating on performers that Entner considers at the cutting edge of musical evolution. Entner is so confident in his firm's reputation

Warren Entner in the control room at Pulse Recording in Los Angeles in September 2012 (photo by Neil Anderson)

and his own abilities that Warren Entner Management does not have a Web site, and he does not carry a business card. He bases that confidence not on an inflated ego, but on his own pragmatic analysis of his talents and skills, which brought him to a critical decision as he approached age 30 in 1973, when he decided he would remain with the Grass Roots for only one more year.

"I don't think any one of us in the Grass Roots felt that we accomplished what we wanted to do musically. We performed pretty well-crafted pop stuff, and even though I enjoyed touring a lot, I felt at a certain point that there was more to life that just doing that. I didn't feel that the band had the originality or magical talent that some people are gifted with – like Neil Young and other special artists with a calling that drives them," Entner said. "And I didn't think I was really qualified to do that for another five, 10, or 15 years. Once I recognized that the band wasn't going to grow, I put a time limit on my involvement. I wanted to try other things."

Although the "other things" that Entner tried after departing the Grass Roots involved various elements of talent management, he had been interested as a young man in a career as a motion picture director. But no matter where he turned, he was drawn toward music – even while he was a film student at the University of California, Los Angeles, where his fellow students included eventual Doors members Ray Manzarek and Jim Morrison. Entner was influenced as well by other friends forming bands and by the evolving music scene on the Sunset Strip, within view of his family's Hollywood Hills home. He was further persuaded by an unexpected phone call from Creed Bratton, whom he had first encountered in a chance meeting while traveling in Israel. Back in California, Creed called to ask if Warren would like to form a band. That phone call set both of them on a course toward pop music fame.

As a teenager in Los Angeles, Warren had attended Fairfax High School, where Steve Barri, P.F. Sloan, Herb Alpert, and legendary producer Phil Spector also had gone. And he grew up in a household of pianists: his older sister Elaine and their parents, Lou and Mildred "Millie" Entner, all were accomplished musicians. As a young woman, Millie Entner had worked for the Boston Metropolitan Opera.

Warren was born in Boston on July 7, 1943, but because Lou was a rising department store manager the family moved – first to the Jackson Heights section of Queens, New York, then to the Midwest, and then on to Los Angeles in 1952 when Lou became a group manager for Lerner Stores. Warren, then 9 years of age, was drawn to the music that Elaine, then 17, tuned in on her radio – rhythm and blues and early doo-wop tunes by the Crows, the Spaniels, Big Joe Turner, the Penguins, Ruth Brown, the Clovers and other performers. Not long after Warren entered junior high school, he began playing drums on his own. By 1958, he was in a small combo called the Checkers, which performed cover versions of popular tunes of the day. In Fairfax High, Warren took up the guitar, and along with a fellow classmate, Russ Titelman (later producer for Paul Simon, Eric Clapton, Steve Winwood, George Harrison, Gordon Lightfoot, Randy Newman, and Chaka Khan), began harmonizing, specializing in Everly Brothers tunes. Phil Spector asked Entner, Titelman, and Titelman's girlfriend, Annette Merar, to be part of a vocal group he called the Spectors Three. (Annette later became Spector's first wife). Spector hoped the trio would build upon the success that his Teddy Bears had begun to achieve. The Spectors Three didn't fully materialize, so when Titelman went to New York to write with Spector and launch his eventual career as a Grammy-winning recording producer, Entner enrolled as a film production major at UCLA in the fall of 1961.

After completing three years of study at UCLA, Entner and an artist friend decided to take a break before completing the requirements for a degree. "I took a year off school and bummed around Europe with a guitar on my back. My friend did pen and ink drawings, and I played music on the street [for donations]," Entner told us. He was at a folk music festival in Israel when he met fellow Californian Creed Bratton, and the two struck up a friendship when they signed on as extras for a motion picture being filmed there. As Entner prepared to move on, Bratton told Entner he'd call him when he returned to Los Angeles. Not really expecting to hear from Bratton, Entner returned to Los Angeles and resumed his studies at UCLA.

But Bratton did, indeed, call, asking if Entner would be interested in forming a group with him. Thinking that might be a fun way to pick up a few bucks, Entner agreed, and together they brought on a couple of other guys, drummer Rick Coonce and bass player Kenny Fukumoto. They called themselves the Thirteenth Floor. Between the four of them, they knew 30 songs they could play, and that was enough to land them a gig at a strip joint in the San Fernando Valley. "They had a girl on a swing, and when we were on stage we had to make sure we were out of the way or we'd get hit by the swing," Entner laughed. Also performing at that club was a band that came to be known as the Fraternity of Man, which recorded "Don't Bogart Me." At another club the Thirteenth Floor took to the stage following a band that included Bobby Hart, who co-wrote numerous Monkees songs, beginning with "Last Train To Clarksville." There were more gigs in more clubs, including one on the Sunset Strip. It wasn't as much fun as Entner had thought it would be. "It was horrible," Entner acknowledges. "We were playing five sets a night in some places, and I had classes in the morning. And we were drinking up our profits. It was killing me." Entner, who had gained some experience about the music business through his involvement in the Spectors Three, knew even then he was unwilling to play clubs for the rest of his life. He took a leadership role and urged the band members to make some recording demos. "Warren was the brains behind that effort," Rick Coonce declared admiringly. "He already had been learning about the music business. He's pretty brainy." The band did make a couple of demos, and in late 1966 Entner managed to generate some interest at Warner Bros. as well as at Dunhill Records – with which the group ultimately signed as the Grass Roots after Fukumoto's replacement by Rob Grill.

Despite the late-night gigs and the determination of the band members to step smoothly into the shoes of the Grass Roots, Warren managed not only to complete his undergraduate studies and obtain his bachelor's degree from UCLA, but also to gain acceptance in graduate school, which he entered in the spring of 1967. But when he realized that the band had an earnest opportunity to achieve success, he dropped out of grad school. And he surprised himself at the ease with which he made the transition from ordinary college kid to trend-setter. Although he did continue to buy some of his clothes in conventional stores, he enjoyed finding and bravely wearing unusual apparel. "In England, for example, I picked up all sorts of clothing items that weren't in the States yet, and that was fun."

Entner's appreciation of the British was not limited to attire. In Los Angeles in 1968, he met and befriended Welsh-born Rosemarie Frankland, who as Miss United Kingdom in 1961 had been crowned Miss World at age 18. Warren and Rosemarie married in 1970 and reveled in the celebrity circles in which their lives revolved. "The cross section of people who visited us at our home and the parties we attended were a lot of fun. Without anyone getting hurt, we were living in the fast lane," Entner smiled.

When Entner left the Grass Roots in February 1974, he went to work for an English management production company called the Gem Toby Organisation Ltd., with which he connected through mutual friends in England. The London firm, which was planning to open an American division, was involved in projects with David Bowie, Mott the Hoople, the New Seekers, the Sweet, Gary Glitter, and other performers. Entner launched a joint venture with Gem Toby to develop new talent in America. His job was to find diamond-in-the-rough talent and polish it. To do that, he prowled nightclubs in search of young musicians with potential to develop careers as stage performers and recording artists, and to scout out labels and negotiate contracts on their behalf. In that role, Entner worked with a heavy-metal band called Angel, which landed a contract with Casablanca Records, and singer-songwriter Tom Jans, who had written "Loving Arms" for Dobie Gray.

In 1977 Warren and Rosemarie celebrated the birth of a daughter, Jessica. But by 1979, their nine-year marriage had come to an end. Entner also became involved in another business venture, becoming part owner and managing director of the former ABC-Dunhill recording studio at 8255 Beverly Boulevard in Los Angeles where the Grass Roots and Steely Dan had regularly recorded. Renamed Concorde Recording Center in September 1980 under Entner's co-ownership, the studio became popular among a list of distinguished artists that included Kenny Rogers and Lionel Richie. When Kenny Rogers expressed interest in buying the recording studio, Entner said, "Fine. Here are the keys." Seeking a temporary change of scenery, Entner journeyed to Australia and before long lined up assignments developing soundtracks for motion pictures. But that was a momentary diversion, and his attention quickly snapped back to recording artists. "I saw a great deal of talent emerging from Australia at the time," Entner explained. "Besides the Little River Band, there were the Divinyls and Men at Work." On his flight back to the United States, Entner thought about establishing a talent management agency in Australia. But before he had the chance to give that notion more serious thought, he received a phone call in the fall of 1982 from one of the members of Quiet Riot, a band that had worked with Gem Toby. It was the first debut album by a heavy-metal band to reach No. 1 on the chart, and it sold more than 7 million copies. The band members asked Entner to manage them once again. He agreed, and helped them secure a contract with Pasha Records, which had a distribution contract with Columbia Records. The band subsequently scored back-to-back hits, the boisterous "Cum On Feel the Noize" and "Bang Your Head (Metal Health)."

On the strength of that success, Entner decided to launch Warren Entner Management, which has boasted a roster of prominent bands, including Faith No More, the Deftones, Rage Against the Machine, L7, and Faster Pussycat. All of those bands achieved either gold or platinum record sales status. Early in the growth of the company, John Vassiliou joined the staff, playing a key role in the development of careers with Entner for more than 22 years. "The bands we handled were more cutting-edge, harder, more concert-driven than the Grass Roots. I felt that if I handled pop artists, I'd be dependent upon record-to-record, rather than building a career that can survive the whims and tastes of radio," Entner told us in April 2000. "If you can develop a band that's fantastic live and can generate strong word-of-mouth appeal, you can build a career around that. We usually have anywhere from five to eight acts in different stages of development."

One of the firm's staff members was in charge of press and retail coordination, and another coordinated touring and relations with agents, promoters, and road crews, and monitored associated costs. Entner dealt with record labels and marketing. "It's funny because some of the guys who I used to smoke joints with, who were assistant managers at some record store, are now presidents of record companies," Entner laughed. "I have dealt with record labels, managers, attorneys, and band members on a daily basis. No two days are the same, and I've seen more of the world as a manager than I ever saw as a Grass Root because we never left the United States, which is a shame. Today, music is a worldwide market."

Even though four decades have passed since Entner left the Grass Roots, he offers effective guidance to musicians by helping them focus their vision rather than heavy-handedly trying to impose his preferences upon them. "If I as a manger were going to dictate the direction, style, and mode of presentation to a band, then I might as well get into the pop business and start something like the Backstreet Boys," said Entner with a toss of his hand. "That's fine, but that isn't what I do best. I try to find artists who on their own have a strong sense of who they are, where they want to go, and who their audience is. That way I don't have to shape that sense, but I can hone it, and present opportunities to them. I won't be arrogant enough to say, 'Do this song instead of that song.' I *will*, if I can, suggest that their set could be arranged in a different way, but I try to embellish what they do rather than to formulate what they do. And we've had great success with bands that have a good sense of who they are. Faith No More and Rage Against the Machine were cutting-edge bands of very talented guys who needed doors to open for them to be exposed. They were so dynamic on their own. I become interested when I see a spark, and enthusiastic audience reaction, which reaffirms my belief that this band really has something to offer. I study marketplace, the style of music and what the competition is doing, and then evaluate whether or not this is something worthy."

Despite Entner's best efforts to set aside his personal predispositions, his inner voice sometimes speaks louder than some bands can play. "In one band we handled, not one of the members had graduated from high school. Working with them was like banging our heads against the wall," gasped Entner. "The band was booked to play in Alaska, and after we got off the plane there, one kid said, 'They speak good English up here.' I thought, 'Good English up here? Where do you think we are?' So we've had a range of bands, some with guys who couldn't tie their shoes, to a band like Faith No More, in which three members were literature majors at the University of California. Even though they looked like black sheep of their families, they were very bright and came from families of attorneys and doctors. They weren't interested at first in the commercialization of their music. But when we opened up some doors for them, and success arrived, they wanted and learned how to read the P&L statements. And they ended up with the greatest little pension plans you can imagine. They were smart, and they're set, and we helped to take them to that place. Part of what we do is teaching them the industry and surrounding them with the best agents, best accountants, best lawyers, and I think that's part of our responsibility." As much as he'd like his young protégés to benefit from his experience, Entner exercises restraint. He does not, for example, coach musicians in stage presence. "There were times when I told someone, 'I can do this better than you. Move over.' But I've learned that if they don't have it within them, you can't teach it," said Entner. "They must have some natural abilities within, or their discomfort becomes very transparent."

Although managers have been known to snare as much as 50 percent of the recording, touring, and merchandising proceeds of musical groups that they assemble and manage, Entner's talent management firm takes a commission of 15 to 20 percent of their clients' gross record sales and concert appearances, and helps them carefully manage and minimize the remainder of their expenses. Believing that his years as a performer accord him credibility with his clients, Entner avoids preaching to them. But he'll speak up when he has to. "We spend band members' money more frugally than they will. When a musician on tour says, 'This is really hard,' I say, 'Hey, don't even start with me. You've got seats in your van. We didn't even have seats. We just laid down on the floor with Army cots.' One band we handled said they wouldn't go to Europe again unless they get to fly first class. I told them it was a waste of money. 'Take a melatonin and sit back, because I'm going to be sitting next to you in coach.' I can also get up way earlier than they can in the morning, ready to do a day's work. I think they respect the fact that we put in a hard 80 hours a week looking out for their best interests. I've been fortunate not to have had too many 3 a.m. phone calls from musician clients. I tell them, 'Call me if you're in jail, in the hospital, or the promoter hasn't paid you. Then you can wake me up – those are the three criteria.'"

Coinciding with the establishment of Warren Entner Management, a new phase in Warren's personal life began in 1982 when he met Stacey Babbitt, who became his second wife. They had a daughter, Lauren, in 1988, but by 1990 the marriage was on course for eventual divorce. "Stacey is a lovely lady, and we're still the best of friends. I'll tell you, one of the things that ruins these relationships is that I travel a lot." But despite the destructive effects of his career upon his two marriages, Warren always remained a dedicated family man. "My kids have always come first, that's not even a question," he declared. "I was away a lot, but I'd come home off the road just to be with my family on the weekends. I raised my older daughter from the age of 15 to 22. My younger daughter was with me regularly, and she didn't live too far from my office, so I picked her up a couple of times during the week. I get along with Stacey great, so it still feels like a family. But it's hard for a woman to be married to someone like me when I've got six bands – about 24 people – and I have to remind them that I'm not their father. Maybe I should have been better at delegating time in different ways, but unfortunately it didn't happen like that."

Sadly, Entner's first wife, Rosemarie, who battled depression, was found dead at the age of 57 in December 2000, in her home in the Marina del Rey section of Los Angeles. Warren and Rosemarie's daughter, Jessica, works in the creative and business aspects of an international company that develops and makes music for commercials. She also composes songs, and sings in a style reminiscent of jazz crooner Sade. His younger daughter, Lauren, continued to live in San Francisco after her graduation from college, and is working for the social network gaming company Zynga. "Both of my daughters continue to expose me to all kinds of music and performers," he acknowledges.

When Entner turned 67 years of age, he thought he was ready for retirement, and stepped away from the business in 2010. His retirement lasted barely two years. In the spring of 2012 he learned of a Scottish band named Biffy Clyro, which is hugely popular in the U.K. and is now building a strong following in North America and around the world. Watching the band perform re-energized Warren, who now is co-managing the band.

Entner, who is most proud of his two daughters, expresses personal satisfaction in the camaraderie he's developed with people in the industry. His professional sphere of influence extends beyond his firm's clients. He is held in high regard across the spectrum of the music business, and is a recurrent speaker at industry conventions as well as career seminars at academic institutions – including the place where he began his music career, his alma mater, UCLA.

Epilogue: Rick Coonce

Drummer and singer
August 1, 1946 – February 25, 2011

Of all the members of the Grass Roots, drummer Rick Coonce was decidedly the most modest and self-effacing, despite a proud record of achievement. Coonce remained convinced that the success of the Grass Roots was attributable to practically everyone else but him, declaring, "The other guys were very, very talented and they had good production with Steve Barri, and they had very good engineers and good studios. We had people picking just killer material for us. All I had to do was to count to four and not fall over." Despite his earnest self-critical assessment, Coonce had much in which he could take great pride: five years as the percussive foundation of the Grass Roots, and the knowledge that during more than a quarter of a century as a career social worker before retiring in 2002, he helped countless numbers of troubled children and teenagers to correct their misguided courses and lead productive, fulfilling lives.

He was able to do so because of a profound life change he made when he left the Grass Roots. Physically and emotionally burned out after nearly continual concert touring and recording, Coonce took advantage of a rare break in the fall of 1971, as the band completed a tour swing

Rick Coonce at his retirement party in 2002 (photo courtesy of Barbara Smith)

through Canada. "We had just played Toronto, then the next night Regina, followed by Calgary, then Edmonton, and the last night of the tour in Victoria on Vancouver Island. Then we were going to take 30 days off because we had never had a holiday since 1967. We flew back to L.A., and from there I took the Amtrak up to Seattle, I rented a car and came across to Vancouver Island on the ferry. I went all the way to the north of the island, to Beaver Cove and Port Hardy and logging roads just as far north as you could go on the island, and I went as far west as Long Beach and Tofino, and it was a dirt road across the mountains at that time," Rick said. "When I was driving

251

back, I came to a place called Coombs about a third the way up Vancouver Island. I saw a three-acre farm with a small house for sale there, I
pulled over and looked at it, and I bought it."

He returned to Los Angeles, but played only briefly with the Grass
Roots until leaving the band and selling his home there – which coin-
cidentally was on a street called Koontz Way, off Topanga Canyon Boulevard in the Santa Monica Mountains south of Woodland Hills. Until
picking up roots and moving to Canada, he had lived all of his life in Los
Angeles, where he was born Erick Michael Coonce in the old Queen of
Angels Hospital in Echo Park on August 1, 1946. Rick's paternal grandparents, who had come from Germany, had changed the spelling of the
family name from Kuntz to Coonce to avoid persecution after World War
I. As a 5-year old child in the San Fernando Valley community of Pacoi-
ma, Rick took tap dancing and ballet lessons upon the recommendation
of his family doctor as a means to correct his congenital knock-kneed
condition. He soon became a fairly accomplished tap dancer, and in the
process straightened his knees. A couple of years later, after his family
moved to Granada Hills, Rick became interested in taking up a musical
instrument, as his older brother Gary had. But because Gary played guitar, his mother wanted Rick to play another instrument – choosing accordion for him. He reluctantly tried it for a while, but then quit.

When Rick turned 12 in 1958, he told his mother that he had
become interested in music again – and he wanted to play the drums.
"She didn't say much about that, but that Christmas I got a snare drum
and a high-hat. Then I started playing and she got me a drum teacher,
Sandy Robertson. He taught me a lot, and I was quick to pick it up,"
said Rick. He progressed quickly because he already was familiar with
drumming terms and could perform many drumming patterns – with his
feet. "Once I started playing drums, it came across me like a freight train.
The rudiments from tap dancing are the same rudiments that drummers
use. I already knew what flamadiddles are, I knew what paradiddles are.
They're among 26 American standard rudiments and rolls that you can
do with your feet, and it's all tied together. And the teacher thought I was
a genius!" Rick dropped tap dancing, because it was no more cool than
accordion playing, and instead concentrated on developing his drumming skills. He enrolled in the band at his junior high school and joined
a four-piece Dixieland combo there called Tony and the Five Tones.

After Rick's family moved once more and he began attending brand-
new Simi Valley High School, he joined Freddie Trujillo, Ruben Ariso,
Mike Vasquez, and John Sepulveda in a band called the Beethovens,
which began playing "cover" versions of rock and roll hits of the day,

but switched to Beatles songs when the "British invasion" began in early 1964. "The Beatles were so fresh, and unlike anything I ever heard before," Coonce told us in March 2000. "I remember where I was and what I was doing the first time I heard a Beatles song. I was driving over the pass from the Simi Valley to the San Fernando Valley to play a gig, and I heard 'From Me to You' on the radio, and it just blew my socks off." One of their gigs was a dance packaged by Casey Kasem – at that time a disc jockey on Pasadena radio station KRLA – held at the Sunkist citrus fruit packing plant in Simi Valley. "It was a big, cavernous place with a stage at one end, and also appearing on that show was a singing duo called Caesar and Cleo, who later became Sonny and Cher. They didn't have a band then, so they mimed to recorded songs," recalled Rick. The Beethovens became good enough that they entered a "battle of the bands" contest at the Teenage Fair at the Hollywood Palladium and placed second among stiff Southern California competition. But when the band that placed first was later disqualified, the title was awarded to the Beethovens. "Rob Grill is going to kill me for saying this, but the band members had to all be amateurs, and they were disqualified because one of their players belonged to the musicians' union. The member of that other band who caused the disqualification was Rob Grill," Rick chuckled.

When the contest was decided, Rick returned to Simi Valley, unaware that his performance had caught the attention of a talent manager, Tom Pritchard. When Creed Bratton and Warren Entner decided to form a group in Los Angeles after their return from bumming around in Europe, they had contacted Tom about the possibility of being their manager. Pritchard suggested the addition of Coonce, who he tracked down at the Simi Valley music store where he had become a drumming instructor. With the addition of bass player Kenny Fukumoto, the new quartet – the Thirteenth Floor – began rehearsing at Rick's home – using some amplifiers and other equipment that Rick was able to borrow from the music store. Despite working in the music store, Rick hadn't considered a career in music. Although an aptitude test he had taken in high school prophetically indicated that his abilities were most applicable to the arts or social work, he followed his high school graduation in 1964 by enrolling in Ventura College to study pre-law. He was considering becoming either a law enforcement officer or a lawyer. His involvement in the Thirteenth Floor was just for fun and a few extra bucks.

"The Thirteenth Floor was just a beer band, working in the San Fernando Valley and L.A. We played some really shit gigs," Coonce acknowledged. "I was under age for many of those places, so I had to hold a bass drum over my head when we walked in to keep from being questioned. We played some rough places that were so much out of our element, places where fights broke out. I remember coming outside after a gig one night and walking with my drums right through a big fight that broke out in the parking lot. I had a Volkswagen Beetle and I could get my drums and Kenny's amp in the back, and Kenny would sit next to me and hold his bass between his legs." But the band put their earnings to good use. "We paid for the demos that we recorded out of a week's worth of beer bar wages. Warren shopped those tapes and brought them to Dunhill."

Rick had some fond recollections of his years with the Grass Roots. "We had some hoots that were just unbelievable," said Coonce, whose speech developed a distinct Canadian lilt. "One time we were guests along with Steppenwolf on Hugh Hefner's *Playboy After Hours* TV show. If you did his show, you were a guest at his mansion in Chicago, where we spent the night," Coonce explained. "It had endless hardwood floors, and a pool downstairs, and it was just deluxe. If you had a cigarette and flicked an ash, before it hit the floor there was a butler with an ash tray underneath it. And ever since I had seen the Beatles on the *Ed Sullivan Show*, I wanted to be on the *Ed Sullivan Show,* so when we were, it just blew my socks off. We spent three days there for seven minutes on the air. First we showed up and their set designers, makeup artists, and other people had a look at us. They asked what we were going to wear that night, and we showed them. Then we went back to our hotel. The next day we show up and there was more planning and then we went back to the hotel. Then on Sunday, the day of the broadcast, we showed up and we went into the green room, and they had everything in the world for us. There was a bar and catered food. We put on our clothes and had our makeup done and did a dress rehearsal on the stage. Then we went back to the green room and nobody was allowed to leave. We did another dress rehearsal at 6 o'clock with an audience and then went back to the green room again, until the show started at 8 o'clock, and we were locked in there until a stage assistant knocked on the door and told us it was our time to go on. Ed Sullivan was in control, and we knew he could cut your act at any time."

To his surprise, Coonce found that his musical background eased his immigration into Canada. The couple who owned the house across the road from the property he'd purchased in Coombs, B.C., were struggling to qualify for immigration under the point system that the Canadian government established. "You get so many points if you could speak French, so many points for your occupation, and so many points for this and that," Coonce explained. "My neighbor was a psychologist and his wife was a special education teacher, but those were low on the priority list because Canada had plenty of those at the time. But I got the full 20 points because Canada needed musicians," he grinned. But rather than entertaining or recording, Coonce just hung around his farm for the better part of two years. When a 21-acre tract of woods and pasture near his three-acre farm became available, he bought the land, graded a road and built a new house in the middle of the property. He built a new life for himself, marrying a young woman named Candace Cox, whom he'd met in Los Angeles shortly after he left the Grass Roots.

Deciding it was time to do something, Rick applied for a job as a child care worker at the Brannen Lake Juvenile Centre in Coombs, operated by the British Columbia provincial government. He was hired after a grueling three-hour interview. For eight hours a day, Rick and a coworker were responsible for a cottage of 12 adolescents who were serious offenders – arsonists and murderers. "They weren't locked in, because of Canadian law for juveniles. They were only locked out of places, and that was accomplished by us and the other people who looked after them from day to day." Despite working closely with violent juveniles, Rick was injured only once, sustaining a broken finger when one of the inmates attempted to take him hostage in a foiled escape attempt. "A girl came up behind me in a school room and held an X-Acto knife up to my throat. She told two kids sitting next to me at a table, 'We're going to get out of here.' I twisted her arm and got the X-Acto knife away from her, and I pulled her outside into the hallway. A fellow outside the room took her to security. Here's the irony," said Rick. "After the whole thing was over a social worker asked the girl, 'Why would you do that to Rick? He's the nicest guy around here and he's always been real good to you.' And she told him she did that because she knew I wouldn't hurt her." The attack did not alter Rick's helpful, compassionate demeanor. "They're just kids," he shrugged.

When the Brannen Lake Juvenile Centre was closed, Rick was reassigned as a case worker in the Ministry of Children and Families, counseling troubled adolescents in Port Alberni, about 40 kilometers (25 miles) from his farm. He also was assigned child protection social work duties on island Indian reserves, to which he commuted by seaplane. Although he initially had no formal training in that discipline, Rick enrolled in numerous continuing education programs that gave him expertise in family, crisis, substance-abuse, and career counseling.

Together, Rick and Candace had two children: Trevor, who was born in 1975, and Emily, born two years later. When their four-year marriage ended in 1978, Rick retained custody of the two children – evidence of his devotion to young people, with whom he worked tirelessly, one-on-one. "Kids are survivors and they're resilient," he declared. "I took care of kids who were 'permanent wards,' which means they're not adopted and they're going to be in the government care until they're 19 years old. My job was to work with these kids in the context of a foster home, and guide them through life. Some had contact with their parents and extended family, and some didn't. After they turned 19, a program I also ran gave them funding and direction for two years of education after that. So I was responsible for their lives from the time they got on my case load until they turned 19, and then I was able to help them with schooling and vocational training."

In 1980, Rick met Barbara Smith, a lawyer who was born and raised in Victoria, B.C. The couple married in 1984. "She never set out to have kids – she just married into it," Rick chuckled. Barbara was in private practice in Port Alberni, which is situated on the shore of a long, crooked finger of an inlet from the Pacific Ocean. On their farm, they produced about 18 tons of hay each year, and they raised pigs and cows. After Barbara retired from her law practice in 2008, she concentrated on horses. "She has taken over the barns with horses. I've got horses coming out of my butt," Rick said, in feigned grouchiness. "She rides every day, all she can. We sell some hay, but keep enough to feed our animals. Warren flew up to visit one year during haying time, and he was out driving the tractor. Goddamn it, he looked happy!"

Rick had been working in the community long enough that he began counseling the children of "alumni" that he guided years before. "People who I counseled as kids at Brannen Lake way back when are adults now," Rick told us in March 2000. "One of them who lives in Port Alberni brought his nephew to me and told him, 'You listen to Rick. He turned me around.' The kid had been in trouble and in foster homes, and was a runaway. The uncle harbored his nephew for two or three weeks, and he listened to his stories and then he brought the kid to me. And that just made my black heart come glad." Throughout his career, Rick never had any intentions of becoming a supervisor, choosing instead to work directly with kids, counseling a caseload of about 35 wards ranging from infancy to age 19. "I just was not a supervisor. I'm a hands-on, person-to-person type."

Following retirement in 2002, Rick contentedly tended to his farm. "I barely leave the island, other than to go to another island. I go to Vancouver [on the mainland] maybe once a year for something or other," he said. He rarely ventured into the United States, preferring the rural charm of Coombs, where the biggest tourist attraction is the Old Country Market – which has a sod roof on which goats graze. Rick enjoyed spending as much time as possible with his grandchildren Chloe, Aidan, and Alina. Emily and her family live in Victoria, and Rick's son, Trevor, also lives on Vancouver Island working as a logger with a helicopter crew. "They fly him by sea plane to a float camp, which is towed around into different inlets. He is what they call a choker and chaser. He weighs the log and then 'chokes' it – he puts the cable around the log on the ground and give the 'high sign' to the helicopter. He's in camp for seven days , then out of camp for seven days, and he never knows where he's going when he flies out." Rick's younger brother Phil also lives on Vancouver Island. His older brother Gary stayed in Los Angeles, employed as a bus driver, and their sister Joan is a school principal in Missouri.

Rick remained engaged in music, but strictly as a private pursuit, to help alleviate the tensions and frustrations incumbent with his counseling career. He converted a shed on the farm into a music studio, where he recorded alone and with friends. He was thrilled to learn that Vancouver Island has a vibrant music and arts community. "If I need a horn or string section or female vocalist, I can quickly pull one together from friends I know within 20 miles," said Rick, who in early 2000 completed *Lackadaisical Day,* a CD of his new music, on which he played guitar, dobro, percussion, drums, and sang. He wrote eight of the album's 11 songs. "I started off with the basic tracks and I called friends to do certain parts. And when they have something they want to record, I reciprocate. But it's for my own amusement. I have no aspirations to become famous. I don't think I ever want to perform in person again. I'm just old and cranky, I guess. But I love to record." Rick's health slowly diminished, however, and he unexpectedly collapsed due to heart failure. When he died at Nanaimo General Hospital on February 25, 2011, he was only 64 years of age.

While engaged in social work, Rick went out of his way to avoid letting his background in music influence his interactions with his wards. "Some of the kids knew what I did, and they heard the Grass Roots' records on the radio. But I tried to downplay that. I didn't want to be a role model because kids have their own potential," Rick insisted. "I don't believe in holding up Wayne Gretzky or any other role model and saying, 'Be like them.' But some kids like to play music, and I channeled them into what they do best by working with their teachers and everyone else who is dealing with them." The advice that Rick Coonce dispensed to his young wards for more than 25 years is good advice for the rest of us as well. "I tried to build trust, and help them understand that the solution is within them, not me," Rick emphasized. "That's where the answer lies."

Epilogue: Dennis Provisor
Keyboard player

Keyboard player
Dennis Provisor
had no intention of
becoming a member
of the Grass Roots. He
was perfectly content
making 60 bucks a
week as a member
of the Blue Rose
Band with guitarist
Terry Furlong and
drummer Bill Lordan
(who would later play
with guitarist Robin
Trower). Provisor,
who long had a deep
affinity for rhythm

Dennis Provisor (rear, third from left) with his group the Persuaders in 1966 (photo courtesy of Dennis Provisor)

and blues, had joined the Blue Rose Band in 1968 and enjoyed the experience of playing nightclubs in the San Fernando Valley, sometimes headlining and other times opening for emerging recording artists, including Delaney and Bonnie Bramlett.

One night in the spring of 1969 when the Blue Rose Band was performing at a San Fernando Valley club called the Mirage on Van Nuys Boulevard in Sherman Oaks, in walked Warren Entner, Rob Grill, and Rick Coonce. Lead guitarist Creed Bratton had just left the Grass Roots, and they were looking for a guitar player to replace him. They had come in to see about persuading Terry Furlong to join the Grass Roots, and sat in the audience during the Blue Rose Band's last set. After the gig, the Grass Roots and the Blue Rose Band members all sat down to talk. As the conversation went on, the Grass Roots became more interested in Dennis than in Terry. Provisor's initial reaction about the Grass Roots' repertoire was disapproving: "That's not suited to my background." But his pragmatic side spoke louder. "There I was, going nowhere with the Blue Rose Band. And I thought – here are these guys, the Grass Roots, who are really popular. Maybe I should join up and make some money." He initially caught flak for making that choice. "All the musicians that I played with in the [San Fernando] Valley thought I was a big sellout for joining the Grass Roots."

But Provisor neither deserted his friends nor his musical roots. Not long after he joined the Grass Roots, he persuaded the other band members to bring Terry Furlong into the band as lead guitarist. And after establishing himself securely with the Grass Roots, Dennis eventually returned to the music he loves. "I know that's where my roots are – in the smoky clubs amid the booze and the soul and the sweat. And that's where I am now. I'm right back where I was," he told us in January 2002.

Dennis Provisor is often credited with moving the Grass Roots away from a purely pop sound and giving the band earthier, bluesier undertones. Driven by Provisor's lead organ, the Grass Roots made the transition from a '60s folk-rock band and ushered in an era as an iconic '70s rock band taken seriously by fans and critics alike. Starting with "Heaven Knows," followed by his composition "Walking Through the Country," Provisor made his imprint on a string of hits, including "Temptation Eyes," "Sooner or Later," and "Two Divided by Love." Joel Larson speaks glowingly of Provisor. "Dennis is an amazing talent – a songwriter and singer extraordinaire with a soulful voice," Larson said. "If you listen to 'Sooner or Later,' you'll hear that he just burns it. He is an excellent player."

Provisor followed his successful Grass Roots years with a ruinous attempt in 1974 to establish a solo career with Columbia Records. "Producers there had told me they were going to make me a big star," he said, rolling his eyes. The album that he recorded remained in Columbia's vaults. Instead of becoming a star, Provisor dropped out of sight for a couple of years. "I can't describe those years, but I can tell you that a lot of drugs were involved, and that's pretty much where those years went." But Dennis managed to right himself,

Dennis Provisor relaxing at home in September 2012, wearing a shirt that says "Provisor Greco-Roman Wrestling" (photo by Mike Preston)

remaining true to his musical pursuits as a result of something his father beseeched: "Whatever you do in life, do what makes you happy. That's the most important thing. It doesn't matter how much money you have – do what makes you happy." Dennis did follow his dreams, and he's a happy man today as a result.

Dennis's father, Ben, who owned the Sir Guy shirt manufacturing company, spoke with the wisdom acquired through disappointment. "My dad always told me that he always wanted to be an artist," said Dennis. "He was sorry all his life that he never became a commercial designer. That was what he really wanted to do." He compensated somewhat by designing many of the company's shirts. But he was more immersed in the details and headaches of business ownership than he was in textile design. Ben had inherited the business from his father, who had launched it in Toronto as a women's garment manufacturer after emigrating from Europe. When the company relocated to Los Angeles, it began manufacturing work uniforms for gas station operators, then shifted its product line to men's casual and dress shirts. Sir Guy developed a striking product line of brushed rayon shirts that became wildly popular among fashion-conscious young people and attracted the attention of celebrity clientele, including Elvis Presley and mobster Benjamin "Bugsy" Siegel, who had bankrolled construction of the pioneering Flamingo Hotel and Casinoin Las Vegas in 1946. "My dad went there the day the Flamingo opened," Dennis said.

Dennis Errol Provisor, who was born in Los Angeles on November 9, 1943, helped out at Sir Guy, but he was never expected to enter the business. Dennis took an early interest in music at age 7 after hearing his cousin Sheila Provisor, two years his elder, play piano. "I wanted to play, so I took lessons with her teacher over at her house. I would get a star every couple of weeks when I would finish something, and would get to pick out a new toy." Dennis continued with piano lessons for about two years, learning classical pieces as well as boogie-woogie tunes and pop ballads such as the then-popular melodious "Song From Moulin Rouge." By age 10 in school he joined the choir, and was captivated by the mesmerizing effect of well-blended voices. "I remember singing 'Hey There (You With the Stars in Your Eyes)' with the choir on stage, and it sounded just beautiful." He abandoned the piano and singing lessons in favor of typical boyhood pursuits – sandlot baseball, racing bicycles, and building model cars and airplanes. As he built his models, he listened to music on the radio, which struck a dormant chord. He began fooling around on the piano in his room, just to see if he could figure out the notes in songs that were playing on the radio. After he figured out the piano notes, he'd sing along. One of his early favorites was the Chords' 1954 rhythm and blues hit "Sh-boom."

Dennis's brother Joey was not born until 1955, but his sister Diane was much closer to his age. Together, they'd bike nine miles from their home in Cheviot Hills, at the northern edge of Culver City, across town to Wallichs Music City, a large record shop at the corner of Sunset and Vine in Hollywood. "We'd go into a sound booth and listen to 'In the Still of the Nite' by the Five Satins. I was turned on to all the black music. That was it for me." Dennis resumed piano playing in earnest, receiving encouragement from his father, who also played piano, and from his mother and uncle, both of whom had been professional dancers at one time. As a student at Alexander Hamilton High School in the late 1950s, he joined a band called the Hollywood Hurricanes, which played not only at high school dances but also at UCLA fraternity parties. Most instruments were not amplified in those days, but Dennis rigged up his father's Bogen 35-watt hi-fi amplifier with a microphone placed near his piano strings so it could be heard over the amplified guitar. In addition to playing guitar, he also began singing with the group – and on his own. When he was 17, he signed with Imperial Records as a solo artist, under the name Denny Paul. Attempting to groom him into a teen idol modeled after Fabian, Paul Anka, and Frankie Avalon, the label released a couple of singles, "Little Girl Lost" and "Mickey Mouse," and booked him for appearances on the *Lloyd Thaxton Record Shop* on Los Angeles TV station KCOP, channel 13, and on Dick Clark's *American Bandstand.* 'Mickey Mouse' had a soulful feel and got some airplay on R&B stations, including KGFJ in L.A. "But when the stations found out I was white, they dumped it," he smiled.

After graduating from high school in 1961, Dennis enrolled at nearby Santa Monica College – where he admittedly didn't do well. After completing the program there in 1963, he enlisted in the Navy-Air Force six-month reserves program. With that behind him, he began attending classes at Woodbury Business College in downtown Los Angeles. "I thought I'd try to become a businessman, but realized I couldn't do that," he said. Still living with his parents, Dennis continued playing with his buddies in the Hollywood Hurricanes quintet. Dennis and his band mates managed to get weekend bookings as far away as Winnemucca, Nevada – where in a scene akin to *The Blues Brothers* motion picture, they faced a hostile crowd that preferred country music rather than the surf music that they played.

Dennis subsequently joined an L.A. group called the Four Sounds, which included two soon-to-be important figures in music – Deke

Richards and Laurin Rinder. Richards, the band's guitar player, later joined Berry Gordy Jr., Alphonso "Fonce" Mizell, and Freddie Perren in forming the Motown songwriting-production cartel known as The Corporation, which wrote numerous hits, including the Jackson 5's "I Want You Back," "ABC," and "The Love You Save." Rinder, the band's drummer, came to be a producer and was considered one of the architects of disco. The Four Sounds played gigs in Southern California, in the San Francisco Bay Area, and in Hawaii. In 1965 Dennis joined a rhythm and blues group called Al and the Originals, all of whom were black except bass player Al, who was Latino. The band's repertoire consisted fundamentally of tunes popularized by James Brown, Chuck Berry, the Impressions, and Motown recording artists. "They taught me a lot about what soul was," acknowledges Dennis, who by then was playing a Vox organ like that used by the Animals and the Dave Clark Five. The experience of playing with Al and the Originals inspired Dennis to help form another rhythm and blues group called the Persuaders. "There was a surf group called the Persuaders, but we were a white R&B group that played like we were black. We did Tina Turner songs, we did real heavy black soul, and I went on the road a lot with them, to Hawaii and even to Europe," said Provisor. After nearly two successful years, that band broke up in late 1967. Dennis then joined a psychedelic-flavored band called the Hook, consisting of guitarist Bobby Arlin (formerly of the Leaves), drummer Craig Boyd, bass player Lee "Buddy" Sklar (who went on to become a highly sought session musician in L.A.) and vocalist-drummer Dale Loyola (who had been with the Persuaders). In 1968 the Uni label released two Hook albums: *The Hook Will Grab You* and *Hooked.* By the end of the year, however, the band broke up.

For the first time in nine years, Dennis was not in a band – and he was out of work. "I bummed around for awhile, and lived at the beach," he shrugged. A girlfriend of Dennis's knew a guitarist who she thought might complement Provisor's keyboard playing. She called the guitarist and asked him to play a few riffs for Dennis over the phone. Dennis liked what he heard, and soon got together with the guitarist – Terry Furlong. The result was the formation of the Blue Rose Band – an affiliation that led to their eventual inclusion in the Grass Roots.

Provisor was a member of the Grass Roots from 1969 to 1972, and rejoined in 1975. It was during his second tenure with the Roots that Dennis first took notice of Wisconsin. "We did lots of dates in Wisconsin, and the group that opened for us, the Kansas Road Band, was so great that I wanted to join that group," said Dennis. Instead, the band's guitarist, Glen Shulfer, wound up playing with the Grass Roots on the road for a while. In 1980, after the Grass Roots dissolved, Provisor moved from Los Angeles to the central Wisconsin town of Stevens Point, about 150 miles northwest of Milwaukee. Stevens Point is along the Wisconsin River, which farther downstream flows into the Mississippi River. There he joined with Shulfer in a band called the Hits, with which he's remained since then. The Hits perform at shows, weddings, nightclubs, fairs, and corporate and private parties an average of three gigs per week. The group, which also includes drummer Cookee Coquoz, has worked steadily for three decades. The Hits play everything from contemporary hits, country, and oldies to waltzes, the "Beer Barrel Polka," and the "Chicken Dance" song. "Gloria," "Louie, Louie," and "YMCA" are all in the band's repertoire. Dennis' stage setup encompasses three vintage keyboard instruments: two Rolands – a JD-800 and an S-10, which he uses as a "left-hand bass" – and an Ensoniq Mirage "sampler" keyboard instrument to replicate horns, guitars, and other special-effects sounds. Dennis proudly says the Hits can perform everything from classical music to heavy metal. That reflects the scope of his personal musical preferences, which he said ranges from oldies to rap.

Dennis Provisor in his current band, the Hits (top to bottom) – Cookee Coquoz, Dennis, and Glen Shulfer (photo courtesy of Dennis Provisor)

When he's not performing locally or on the road with the Hits, Dennis drives a bus to make a few extra bucks. For several years, he drove a school bus route on which he logged 100 miles each day. If he had an evening gig with the Hits in Appleton or Green Bay, he would put 300 or 400 more miles behind the wheel – often over icy, snowy roads. Instead, he now drives motor coaches for Lamers Bus Lines, a charter bus company, with a more manageable schedule. He drives sports fans two hours from Stevens Point to Green Bay Packers games or three hours to Milwaukee Brewers games, takes groups of seniors to gambling casinos, church and civic groups to various events, and drives on other private charter trips. His gigs with the Hits have included periodically opening for the Grass Roots, who have toured through Wisconsin nearly every summer. For the fun of it, Provisor occasionally sits in with the Roots.

Dennis married in 1988, and he and his wife Tammy have a daughter, Kayla, who was born later that year, as well as a second daughter, Melissa. They also have a son, Ben, who was born in 1990 and was named in honor of Dennis' father. Tammy is the manager of a Culver's Restaurant in Stevens Point. Kayla, who has shown a strong interest in music, has a good singing voice. Ben, a competitive wrestler since he was 7 years old, was the 2012 U.S. Olympic Team Trials champion and competed in the London Olympics in the 74 kg (163-pound) class of Greco-Roman wrestling for Team U.S.A. Earlier in the year, he won the Curby Cup by defeating the 2008 Olympics gold medalist. In 2011, Ben captured first place in the U.S. Open, as well as a silver medal in the Pan American Games and a second-place showing in the World Team Trials. He may eventually pursue a career in coaching. Kayla, who graduated with a degree in theater and dance from the University of Wisconsin – Stevens Point, enjoys singing. "She has an amazingly big, strong voice. She performs with me on stage several times a month," Dennis told us in August 2012.

His personal values and approach to life mirror those of his father. "I believe in trying to do your honest best, and putting your heart into whatever you enjoy," Dennis explained. "It's a matter of believing in your dreams and your imagination and pursuing them. My kids are so talented. I think they'll be fine." Dennis enjoys Wisconsin's open roads and fishing. He is a catch-and-release fisherman. "After I catch fish, I throw them back in. Once they're dead, they're dead, and you can't catch them again," he says. Dennis, unassuming and thoughtful, makes a surprisingly modest assessment of his own abilities. "I'm pretty slow, not the brightest or sharpest knife in the drawer," he says. That's reflective of his easygoing nature rather than of his intellect. As a young man, he made the conscious decision to shun the corporate rat race – a choice that his talented parents understood. The resulting course has suited Dennis just fine.

Visit **www.dennisprovisor.com** for more information.

Index

Index

Index

About the Authors

Marti Smiley Childs and **Jeff March** are business partners in EditPros LLC, an editorial services firm in Davis, California. Their first book, *Echoes of the Sixties* (1999), included 12 chapters featuring the Fireballs, Gary "U.S." Bonds, the Tokens, the Angels, Peter and Gordon, Mike Pinder of the Moody Blues, Sam the Sham and the Pharaohs, the Lovin' Spoonful, Gary Pucket and the Union Gap, Country Joe and the Fish, and Iron Butterfly.

Where Have All the Pop Stars Gone? – Volume 2, is the second in a series of books of the same title that will feature "then and now" portraits of bands and artists whose music helped define the popular culture of their time. The authors' website – **www.editpros.com** – offers more information about Childs and March and their works. We invite you to "like" our Facebook page at **www.facebook.com/WHATPSG** for updates and conversation about these performers.

You'll also enjoy reading **Where Have All the Pop Stars Gone? – Volume 1** (2011), which contains authorized firsthand accounts of the adult lives of 26 singers and musicians who recorded top hit songs in the late 1950s and '60s.

This 320-page book, published by EditPros LLC (www.editpros.com), includes 58 then-and-now photos, 40 of which are rare or never previously published.

Volume 1 is available in print (ISBN 978-1-937317-00-3) and e-book (ISBN 978-1-937317-01-0) through Amazon, Barnes and Noble, and other online book sellers.

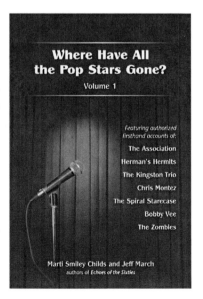

Where Have All the Pop Stars Gone?

Volume 1

Featuring authorized firsthand accounts of:

The Association

Herman's Hermits

The Kingston Trio

Chris Montez

The Spiral Starecase

Bobby Vee

The Zombies

Marti Smiley Childs and Jeff March

authors of *Echoes of the Sixties*

CPSIA information can be obtained at www.ICGtesting.com
Printed in the USA
BVOW020300141112

305483BV00006B/1/P